Conquest and resistance in West Africa

Manchester University Press

Studies in
Modern French and
Francophone History

Edited by
Julie Kalman, Jennifer Sessions and Jessica Wardhaugh

This series is published in collaboration with the Society for the Study of French History (UK) and the French Colonial Historical Society. It aims to showcase innovative monographs and edited collections on the history of France, its colonies and imperial undertakings, and the francophone world more generally since *c.* 1750. Authors demonstrate how sources and interpretations are being opened to historical investigation in new and interesting ways, and how unfamiliar subjects have the capacity to tell us more about France and the French colonial empire, their relationships in the world, and their legacies in the present. The series welcomes a wide variety of approaches, including, but not limited to local and regional case studies; microhistories; studies of specific individuals and families; and broader treatments of major themes or periods. It is particularly receptive to studies that break down traditional boundaries and conventional disciplinary divisions and that consider the French and Francophone worlds in imperial and global perspective.

To buy or to find out more about the books currently available in this series, please go to:
https://manchesteruniversitypress.co.uk/series/studies-in-modern-french-and-francophone-history/

The Society for the Study of French History

FCHS SHCF
FRENCH COLONIAL HISTORICAL SOCIETY
SOCIÉTÉ D'HISTOIRE COLONIALE FRANÇAISE

Conquest and resistance in West Africa

The Jeandet Affair and the illusion of colonial justice

Ruth Ginio

Manchester University Press

Published by Manchester University Press
Oxford Road, Manchester, M13 9PL

www.manchesteruniversitypress.co.uk

British Library Cataloguing-in-Publication Data
A catalogue record for this book is available from the British Library

ISBN 978 1 5261 8737 6 hardback

First published 2025

EU authorised representative for GPSR:
Easy Access System Europe, Mustamäe tee 50, 10621 Tallinn, Estonia
gpsr.requests@easproject.com

Typeset by Newgen Publishing UK

To Alisa with love

Contents

List of figures

List of maps

Acknowledgements

Writing this book was a journey, not only in the metaphorical sense of the word as is the case for most books. I have followed the Jeandet Affair from Verdun-sur-le-Doubs in Burgundy, to Mâcon, Lyon, Paris, Dakar, Saint Louis, and Podor and even reached the rare books library in Brandeis University in Boston, where a Koran offered to Jeandet by a local ruler had somehow landed. This journey began when I first heard about the Jeandet Affair in 2014. But back then I did not realize what I was hearing. I came to Dakar to give a lecture at the West African Research Center (WARC) about a book I was working on at the time on African soldiers serving in the French Army during the wars of decolonization. When I finished speaking, a man from the audience asked me some knowledgeable questions while noting that his father served in the French army during and after World War Two. I was intrigued and asked him if I could interview him. The man, Saddick Sall, kindly agreed and we met the next day in a café. His first sentence stunned me and I wrote it down, although it had no relevance to my research topic: 'My great grandfather,' he said, 'was a king in northern Senegal and was decapitated by the French in 1890.' No one can ignore such an opening sentence. The interview was fascinating and helped me rethink some of my basic assumptions about my research on African soldiers. I did not realize at the time how valuable Saddick would later prove to be for a project I had not yet begun.

Sometime later I came across the Jeandet Affair in the Senegalese archives. When for some reason I reread the transcript of my interview with Saddick, I suspected that his remarkable opening sentence was related to this story. The details were just too similar.

List of maps

Acknowledgements

Writing this book was a journey, not only in the metaphorical sense of the word as is the case for most books. I have followed the Jeandet Affair from Verdun-sur-le-Doubs in Burgundy, to Mâcon, Lyon, Paris, Dakar, Saint Louis, and Podor and even reached the rare books library in Brandeis University in Boston, where a Koran offered to Jeandet by a local ruler had somehow landed. This journey began when I first heard about the Jeandet Affair in 2014. But back then I did not realize what I was hearing. I came to Dakar to give a lecture at the West African Research Center (WARC) about a book I was working on at the time on African soldiers serving in the French Army during the wars of decolonization. When I finished speaking, a man from the audience asked me some knowledgeable questions while noting that his father served in the French army during and after World War Two. I was intrigued and asked him if I could interview him. The man, Saddick Sall, kindly agreed and we met the next day in a café. His first sentence stunned me and I wrote it down, although it had no relevance to my research topic: 'My great grandfather,' he said, 'was a king in northern Senegal and was decapitated by the French in 1890.' No one can ignore such an opening sentence. The interview was fascinating and helped me rethink some of my basic assumptions about my research on African soldiers. I did not realize at the time how valuable Saddick would later prove to be for a project I had not yet begun.

Sometime later I came across the Jeandet Affair in the Senegalese archives. When for some reason I reread the transcript of my interview with Saddick, I suspected that his remarkable opening sentence was related to this story. The details were just too similar.

Luckily, I had kept Saddick's number. I called him and asked what his great grandfather's name was. 'We have the same name,' he said, 'Saddick is just a version of the name Sidick. Like him, I am Sidick Sall.' The significance of this statement was that I found the best informant I could wish for without even looking for one. Saddick soon became much more than an informant. During the long years of researching the Jeandet Affair, he became a friend. He is a fountain of knowledge not only about the affair, but also about the fascinating history of Fouta Toro. Saddick is also a playwright, an author, and a scholar. A play he wrote about his great grandmother, whom he admires and who was the motor behind the affair, is cited in this book. He is now writing a book of his own about the affair, which I am sure will complete mine wonderfully. My book in its current form could not have been written without Saddick. He connected me with many other informants and clarified the complicated information I found in the archives, often correcting the mistakes and misperceptions of colonial administrators. He opened a door for me to the rich world of history and society of the Fulbe of Senegal, which I could never have entered without him. I am grateful to Saddick, his wife Aissata Ly, his sister Dieyneba Njerebi Sall, and his brother Tierno Sall for the warm welcome during my visits to Senegal, their assistance, and their kind hospitality.

Another significant person who accompanied this journey is David Robinson. His pioneering study on Fouta Toro served as a torch in the darkness. When I wrote to him to ask his advice about people I could interview in Podor about the affair, he did not merely settle for connecting me with the right person. He became incredibly interested in my research and offered much encouragement and good advice. During my stay in Michigan, I had the pleasure of meeting David in person. He directed me to the transcripts of his interviews in Fouta, conducted in the late 1960s, while I was only two years old. The combination of his massive knowledge about a place few know anything about, his good spirit, encouragement, and kindness made him a real asset for writing this book, and more than that I gained a wonderful friend.

Many other knowledgeable and kind people offered me valuable help during this journey. Mamadou Youri Sall from Gaston Berger University, Saint Louis, connected me with several crucial informants in Podor. In Podor I received assistance from Mamadou Diop from the Commerce Museum, his brother Seybato Diop, and the late Ibrahima Sy from the Podor fort, who also discussed the affair with me. Abdourahmane Niang was another fountain of knowledge, and my long interview with him helped me better understand the complexity of the affair's remembrance. To better acquaint myself with the region along the river, I took the *Bou el-Mogdad* boat trip from Saint Louis to Podor. During this journey I had the pleasure of discussing the affair with Ansoumana Badji, the tour guide who contributed from his knowledge of the route. The boat's captain, Mamadou Goudiaby, shared his knowledge about the steamboat and the way it used to be in the past.

During several different stays in Dakar, numerous people were willing to talk to me about their perception of the affair or offer their kind assistance. I am grateful to Xavier Ricou, Madeleine Devès Senghor, Alioune Deme, Niasse Hamedine Kane, Cheikh Baba Sall, Mamadou Sow, and Haruna Diop. Also in Dakar, I would like to note the wonderful hospitality of Ousmane Sene and Marianne Yade from the West African Research Center, who offered me their invaluable assistance, good advice, and a lovely space to work in, which became my academic home in Senegal. The numerous fieldtrips taken during this research project necessitated significant funding. I am grateful to the Israel Science Foundation (grant 148/19), which covered my travel as well as other vital expenditures.

As always, I relied on the intellectual generosity of my colleagues, who shared with me their deep knowledge on different aspects of my research: Hilary Jones, Elizabeth Foster, Emmanuelle Sibeud, Isabelle Surun, Eric Jennings, Denis Charbit, Lynn Schler, Eitan Bar-Yosef, Irit Bloch, Efrat Ben-Ze'ev, and Dior Konaté. Irit, Efrat, and Dior also read parts of the manuscript related to their areas of expertise. Sean Bebee told me about Jeandet's Koran, which he found in the library of rare manuscripts in Brandeis University after attending a lecture I gave. Joe Lauer from the special collections library of Michigan State University helped me to locate David Robinson's interviews, which are kept there.

The Jeandet Affair produced a large quantity of documents. A big part of these, especially Jeandet's letters, were handwritten. I am indebted to my research assistant Clément Hazan, who not only transcribed these documents, but also created an extremely efficient system of organizing them, adding charts of the main events, names, and dates mentioned in them. Clément's professional skills, his intellectual curiosity, and his deep interest in my research made him much more than a research assistant. His part in this research is invaluable and I am deeply grateful to him.

My Ph.D. student, Jean-Lémon Kone located documents for me in the Archives Nationales in Paris and looked up several important sources in the Bibliothèque nationale, which I needed towards the end of the writing process.

Writing in a foreign language is a challenge most non-native English speakers in the academic world need to tackle. Finding a good English editor is not easy. I was lucky enough to work with David Kahn, who skillfully managed to add elegance to the text while leaving my voice in it.

At Manchester University Press I am grateful to Alun Richards who began to work with me on this project, to Meredith Caroll who had later replaced him, to Humairaa Dudhwala, and Christian Lea, as well as to the two anonymous readers who made some wonderful suggestions that improved the manuscript. James Ryan, carefully and professionally copy-edited this manuscript. Gail Welsh, the project manager from Newgen Publishing UK, was professional and attentive throughout the final stages of copy editing and proofing.

Finally, I would like to thank the three most important people in my life: Eyal, Nitai, and Ophir. This is not the first research project my son Nitai and my daughter Ophir have accompanied. With two historians as parents, as well as one grandmother, history has been part of their life from early childhood. Nevertheless, this is the first book I have written in their adulthood. Their interest in my research and ideas about it (Nitai even offered some tips from a legal perspective) added much to the pleasure of working on this book. Eyal, as always, enthusiastically joined me in the journey of writing this book. As there is no corner of the earth that he does not find fascinating, a temperature of 40 degrees in the shade in a small town on a river separating Senegal from Mauritania seemed to him greatly alluring. He never tired of hearing about all the different characters in this saga, read the entire manuscript with the eyes of an eagle, and offered clever advice about different dilemmas in the process of writing. He also provided practical help by photographing sites along the way, as my own limited ability in this domain is a subject of frequent jokes in the family. Most of the photos in this book were taken by Eyal. I am grateful for having such a perfect partner in the journey of life.

This book is dedicated with love to Eyal's mother, Alisa Meyuhas Ginio, who, apart from elegantly disproving the common stereotypes about mothers-in-law, is a brilliant historian, a wonderful grandmother, and has been a constant source of support for my academic career over the years.

Note on transliteration

The Peul language was hardly used in written form during the period of this study and, if so, in Arabic letters. As a result, the only Latin version of names that existed then was the one appearing in French colonial documents. Therefore, I have chosen to write African names in the French form. Where there were several French versions for the same name, I have used the most frequent spelling. Nowadays, the local spelling of these names is slightly different in most cases. I used the local spelling while citing current Senegalese sources and noted the French version in brackets. For example, the name of the widow who sued the French administrators is spelled Diereby or Ndiereby in colonial documents and Njerebi in the play her great-grandson has written about her. I used the form Ndiereby and left 'Njerebi' while quoting the play, noting the French version in brackets.

The main characters in the Jeandet Affair

Africans involved in the affair

Boubakar Abdoul—Jeandet's personal interpreter before he was replaced by Abdoulye Kane. He was the one who brought Baidy Kaccé to Jeandet on the day of the murder and later allowed him to escape. He was suspected of being involved in the so-called conspiracy, but ultimately was not executed.

Sidi Abdoul—Boubakar Abdoul's brother and Lam Toro Sidick's cousin. He was appointed Lam Toro after Sidick's successor, Hamady Nogato, died in 1889 (the French suspected that Nogato was poisoned but had no proof).

Ndiereby Ba—Lam Toro Sidick's elder wife. She conducted a legal battle against the colonial administration after her husband's illegal execution.

Hamet Fall—An interpreter who was close to Jeandet and later served the administration and mediated Ba's interrogation in Saint Louis.

Samba Fall—An interpreter who was part of the Senegalese delegation to the Universal Exhibition of 1889 in Paris. He helped Ndiereby Ba to prepare for her lawsuit and served as her interpreter when she was interrogated by representatives of the colonial administration.

Baidy Kaccé—Jeandet's murderer. He served as a soldier in Jeandet's campaign against the ruler of Bossea. On 2 September 1890, after being punished by Jeandet for his rebellious behaviour, Kaccé shot Jeandet dead.

Abdoulaye Kane—Jeandet's personal interpreter and the one who conducted the dubious investigation following Jeandet's murder.

Bitti Lokho—A relative of Lam Toro Sidick from his mother's side. She was part of the Senegalese delegation to the Universal Exhibition in 1889, where she caused some problems. She helped convince Ndiereby Ba to submit the lawsuit and hosted her for a while in her house in Saint Louis.

Ahmet N'Diack—Lam Toro Sidick's uncle. In 1891 he was asked by the governor, de Lamothe, to convince Ndiereby Ba to drop her legal struggle and return to her village Guédé, but he failed in his attempts to do so.

Lam Toro Sidick—Ruler of Toro until his dismissal by Jeandet in 1887. He was suspected of conspiracy to kill Jeandet and was executed without trial on 15 September 1890.

Mamadou Yoro—Lam Toro Sidick's cousin, who was also suspected as an accomplice to the murder of Jeandet and was executed along with his cousin.

Supporters of Ndiereby Ba's legal struggle in Saint Louis and in Paris

André Chadelle—An attorney who worked closely with Gaspard Devès. There is no tangible evidence for his origin, so it is difficult to know whether he was métis, Antillean, or metropolitan French. He represented Ndiereby Ba in Saint Louis and protected her against the governor's constant harassment. At some point he agreed to let her live in his home.

Jean-Jacques Crespin—A métis attorney and politician. He was an ally of Gaspard Devès, despite some tension between them. He served as the mayor of Saint Louis for two short terms, in 1890 and in 1894. After his untimely death in 1895, rumours spread in town that Governor de Lamothe had poisoned him.

Félix Decori—One of the most celebrated French criminal attorneys in the late nineteenth century. He took part in several important trials, including as part of the defence team of the wrongly accused Jewish captain, Alfred Dreyfus. Decori served as Ndiereby Ba's attorney in Paris and represented her case before the court of first instance of the Seine.

Gaspard Devès—An influential métis politician and trader. He was considered an enemy of the colonial administration because of his fierce opposition to its policy of expansion into new territories. The illegal executions served him as another opportunity to obstruct this policy. He therefore initiated and supported Ndiereby Ba's struggle.

Paul Fawtier—The head of the division of interior affairs in Saint Louis and the only French administrator who supported Ndiereby Ba's struggle. At the time of the illegal executions, he served as an interim governor; there was no governor in Saint Louis as the previous one had already left the colony while his replacement had not yet arrived. Fawtier tried to stop the illegal executions when he heard they were about to happen by sending a telegram ordering the administrators on the ground to bring the suspects to trial in Saint Louis—but to no avail.

Alexandre Isaac—A representative of Guadeloupe in the French senate between 1885 and his death in 1899. In 1898 he took part in the establishment of the Ligue de droits des hommes. He was Devès's ally and helped Ndiereby Ba's cause in the senate and in parliament.

Henri Larrouy—An Antillean judge who replaced Ursleur as head of the judicial authority in Saint Louis, but who soon took Ndiereby Ba's side and insisted on opening an investigation against the administrators despite enormous pressure and threats by the governor and his supporters. He was eventually sent back to Paris.

Auguste Raymondon—An examining judge in Saint Louis who insisted on summoning the accused administrators following Ndiereby Ba's lawsuit and resisted the governor's pressure to drop the case.

Fréderic Conrad Ursleur—A judge from Guadeloupe who, in September 1890, immediately after hearing about the illegal executions, initiated an investigation against the administrators who had ordered it. He was consequently reassigned to New Caledonia.

Administrators hostile to Ndiereby Ba's struggle and their supporters

Aubry-Lecomte—One of the administrators who oversaw the illegal executions. He tried to escape to the Gambia in November 1890, when it seemed that he and the two other administrators who had worked with him on the executions, Edouard Martin and Riquetty, were going to be arrested.

Emile Chambaud—An Antillean judge who replaced Henri Larrouy in 1890 as head of the judiciary authority in Saint Louis. He encouraged de Lamothe to get rid of all the judges who supported Ndiereby Ba's lawsuit.

Léon Emile Clément Thomas—Governor of Senegal between 1888 and 1890. He left Saint Louis in September and was absent at the time of the illegal executions. He later insisted that he was the one who gave the order to carry them out, although no document could be produced attesting to that.

Jules Couchard—A shady character who arrived in Senegal from France under a cloud. He was part of the French settlers in Saint Louis called *Petits colons*. An attorney by profession, he replaced André Chadelle in February 1892 as Ndiereby Ba's lawyer, most likely against her will. He then made her drop her lawsuit and forego any recompense.

Louis Descemet—A métis politician and trader. He was a fierce rival of Gaspard Devès, and supported the administration's side in the affair. In 1892 he began to reconcile with Devès, as the two had shared political interests due to de Lamothe's attempts to limit métis power in the Grand Council, Saint Louis' most important representative institution.

Colonel Alfred Amédée Dodds—A métis who advanced well in the French army. He had supervised repressive colonial wars in various parts of the French empire. In Senegal, Dodds commanded the forces that defeated Lat Dior, the ruler of Cayor and took part in the final campaigns to suppress resistance in Fouta Toro. He supported de Lamothe's position in the affair and became Paul Fawtier's enemy because of the latter's support for Ndiereby Ba's struggle.

Eugène Etienne—The colonial under-secretary at the time of the affair. He was a leader of the colonial lobby in Paris and assisted de Lamothe in his attempts to end the affair. When the affair reached Paris, he managed to end it by writing a letter to court arguing that the accused governors could not be prosecuted.

Henri Félix de Lamothe—Governor of Senegal between 1890 and 1895. He replaced Clément Thomas and acted in dubious ways to end the affair.

Louis Rivet—The only notary in Saint Louis at the time of the affair. He refused to register Ndiereby Ba's complaint because of the use of the word 'murder' in it. He was consequently brought to trial by André Chadelle and lost. He was then forced to register the complaint.

Louis Tautin—The director of political affairs at the time of the affair. He was the person chiefly responsible for it. He instructed the administrators on the ground to find Sidick and Yoro guilty and execute them in a specified and brutal manner.

Admiral Aristide Vallon—A French deputy of Senegal in the National Assembly. In the initial stages of the affair, he worked closely with Alexandre Isaac because he did not believe the conspiracy asserted by the administration and thought that the administrators who ordered and supervised the executions should indeed be prosecuted. Later on, he changed his position, probably because of political pressure, and became a supporter of the administration's position. He helped Jeandet's mother in her efforts to commemorate her son in Senegal.

Introduction

It was pouring so heavily on the morning of 2 September 1890 that administrator Abel Jeandet was forced to take cover in his tent in the village of Aeré in northern Senegal. The recent weeks had been perhaps the most challenging for him during his four-year stay in the colony. He was just recovering from yet another illness, and was under immense pressure from his superiors to put an end to the turmoil in the region, which threatened to destabilize the already fragile French control there. The pouring rain thus provided him with a good opportunity to take a short rest in his hammock and smoke a cigarette before continuing his military campaign to wipe out all remaining resistance to French rule in the district. Suddenly an interpreter appeared, accompanied by one of Jeandet's African soldiers who was participating in the campaign. The interpreter told Jeandet that the soldier, Baidy Kaccé Pam,[1] had disobeyed his marching orders and had displayed a rebellious attitude. Jeandet ordered Kaccé to hand over his weapon and demoted him to porter duties for the day, as punishment for his defiant behaviour. He then returned to his rest. The soldier exited the cabin and picked up his gun and then returned inside. But instead of handing it to Jeandet, he shot him several times in the chest. Another soldier rushed into the tent and tried to shoot Kaccé, but the interpreter pushed his hand away, causing him to miss. This enabled Kaccé, the killer, to escape, though he was apprehended twenty-four hours later.

Under interrogation, Kaccé implicated two local African rulers, whom he alleged had instructed him to commit the murder. The administrators performing the interrogation were easily convinced that they were indeed dealing with a political conspiracy. They did not bother to investigate the allegations seriously, nor did they send the suspects for trial in the colony's capital, Saint Louis. They simply summarily executed Kaccé and, a few days later, also executed the two local dignitaries he had named—Lam Toro Sidick,[2] the ex-ruler of the chiefdom of Fouta Toro (with whom Jeandet had had a previous run-in three years earlier, ending in Sidick's demotion), and his cousin Mamadou Yoro. The men were decapitated, their severed heads were displayed on spikes, and their bodies thrown into the Senegal River to be devoured by crocodiles—all to inject fear into the hearts of the local population and to discourage any further insubordination.

Such brutality was not unusual for the French during their colonization of West Africa. Violence was the norm rather than the exception in the French African territories. French administrators and military officers had been ordered summarily to execute Africans who resisted French domination on other occasions, and had done so without any untoward criticism or legal consequences. Only five months before Jeandet's murder, the French had an Islamic reformer by the name of Samba Diadana Ndiatch decapitated in the vicinity of Saldé, on the banks of the Senegal River, with no repercussions whatsoever.[3] However, this time the situation was entirely different. Although the murder had taken place in the village of Aeré, a mere colonial protectorate, the men were executed in Podor, a commercial post on the river, where the full direct rule of French law applied. The reason they chose that location was that Podor had a much larger population to witness the executions. Legally, though, this was a mistake. In a legal sense, it were as if the French administrators had executed the men in Paris, thrown their bodies into the Seine and paraded their decapitated heads around the Palais-Royal. The three suspects were entitled to the protection of French law—the right to a fair trial under the laws of France.

Still, the fact that these executions were illegal was not bound to create a major scandal. After all, from the colonial administration's perspective, it was clearly a matter of gross insubordination, and a major threat to colonial rule, for an African soldier to murder an esteemed and influential French administrator during a crucial military campaign. It required a very forceful response. In any event, the chances of anyone mounting a protest were low. But again, specific local factors made a difference in this case. Gaspard Devès, a powerful métis[4] trader living in Saint Louis and deeply involved in trade on the Senegal River, had been a close ally of Lam Toro Sidick. He had also been a fierce rival of the murdered administrator, having objected vociferously to his policies. Responding to agitation by Devès, Conrad Frédéric Ursleur, an Antillean judge who served in Senegal, demanded a full investigation into the illegal executions. The French administration managed to stymie the investigation by insisting that only an injured party to the affair could file a lawsuit regarding it. They also removed Ursleur from his post as the head of the judiciary service in Senegal, and sent him to Paris to be reassigned elsewhere in the French empire, as far away as possible from Senegal. But Devès did not relent. He sent out his African allies to persuade Lam Toro Sidick's widow, a young woman named Ndiereby Ba,[5] to file suit against the French administrators who had executed her husband. Ba rose to the challenge. Bitti Lokho, a woman related to Sidick (who also had connections to Jean Jacques Créspin, a distinguished métis politician who later served as the mayor of Saint Louis and who was one of Devès's most important allies), welcomed the young widow in the colonial capital. Ba had arrived there from her village, Guédé, and remained there for 18 months despite incessant intimidation by the French administration designed to undermine her resolve and chase her back to her village. Again, the French succeeded in closing the case before it reached trial by declaring the tribunal of Saint Louis incompetent to judge a case involving political motives.[6]

Once more, the relentless Devès did not despair. He engaged the services of one of the best criminal lawyers in France, a man called Félix Decori, who would later serve as a member of the defence team in the famed Dreyfus trial, which started in 1894 and ended in 1906 with Dreyfus's final exoneration.[7] Decori represented Ba in the Tribunal de la Seine in Paris. The ensuing scandal became known as the Jeandet Affair or the Podor Affair, after the town where it began, and was vigorously debated in both the French press and the National Assembly.[8] This time, the lawsuit was not aimed at the administrators who had carried out the execution, but focused instead on Clément Thomas, the governor who had ordered it, and his successor, Henri Félix de Lamothe.

Devès was optimistic about the possibility of the suit's success because, just three years before, in 1888, the same court had convicted the then governor of Senegal, Jules Genouille, of forgetting to supply four African soldiers, whom he had posted to guard on a tiny island just off the West African coast, with water, causing them to suffer a prolonged and torturous death. The sentence, a fine of 600 francs, was not compatible with the offence, but still Devès could take encouragement from the fact that the court had found the governor guilty. However, it turned out that his optimism was misplaced. The court refused to allow the trial to begin, by means of an obscure legal article that protected public officials from prosecution while in office. With the case thus rejected in France, Decori could no longer represent Ba there. In the meantime, the French administration transferred Ba's attorney in Saint Louis, André Chadelle, to Vietnam, and appointed in his stead Jules Couchard, an enthusiastic supporter of the administration. In June 1892, the widow dropped her lawsuit, and the affair was over.

This brief narrative belies the complexity and nuance of the fascinating Jeandet Affair. The sequence of events I have described is partially based on colonial documents that may well have been biased, and many questions remain unanswered: Was the murder an act of an individual soldier wanting to avenge a humiliating punishment, or was it indeed the result of a political conspiracy? Was Kaccé a local hero resisting colonial domination, or an unstable man manipulated by others, or was he perhaps just a victim of his own impulse in a moment of uncontrollable rage? How did the interpreter, who had brought Kaccé to Jeandet in the first place, but who later saved his life and enabled him to escape, manage to avoid the fate meted out to the three other culprits, despite there having been grave suspicions against him? To what extent was Ndiereby Ba a free agent in this affair, and what made her abandon her struggle after it failed in Paris? Did she receive a payoff from the French, or was she intimidated by threats she could no longer withstand? These questions intrigued me throughout the process of my research, and I kept trying to answer them by delving into the written and oral sources. Each question yielded numerous alternative answers and, although there is much that may be learned from the different versions of events, we must accept that some of the mysteries imbedded in this affair will very likely never be solved.

The Jeandet Affair as a colonial micro-history

There are many similar accounts of the Jeandet Affair that appear in almost every study on the French colonization of Senegal at the end of the nineteenth century. Some are slightly more detailed than others, but none comprehend the full richness of the sources. Most scholars see the affair as a defining moment in the French colonial expansion into the hinterland of West Africa. Yet, to date, no one has delved deeply into it. Elizabeth Foster's book on the relations between missionaries and administrators in colonial Senegal, for example, points to the Jeandet Affair as the explanation for French policy of disannexation between 1890 and 1892. This policy meant to return territories that were already under direct French rule to the status of protectorates. This change of legal status solved the problem of colonial subjects using French law as a weapon against the administration. Foster discusses a court case that brought back recent memories of the Jeandet Affair to the French administration and reinforced its resolve to deannex the territory of the Petit-Côte to the south of Dakar in 1892. A Serer was accused of murdering a Wolof emissary of the French administration, and he duly pleaded self-defence. As the territory where the murder was committed was under direct French rule, the administration, remembering the Jeandet Affair, was deterred from imposing a summary punishment on their main suspect. Eventually, with the help of a priest's testimony, the accused was acquitted. The priest described the injustices and abuse that Wolof emissaries inflicted on the Serer with no French interference. This court decision enraged the governor, de Lamothe, who was also in office when the Jeandet Affair began, and he ordered the disannexation of the region to prevent any recurrence or similar acquittal.[9] As David Robinson notes, another advantage this change of legal status offered was the possibility to entertain relations with enslaving elites in these regions without the necessity to act against slavery according to French law.[10] Robinson briefly discusses the Jeandet Affair in an older book and in a more recent one, in the context of the intensification of colonial rule in Senegal and the French attempts to crush the remaining resistance in Fouta Toro.[11] In her study on the métis of Senegal, Hilary Jones mentions the Jeandet scandal as a point when the French administration became extremely concerned about the potential problems influential métis like Devès could cause.[12]

Three studies that discuss the Jeandet Affair in greater detail offer two different perspectives that allow us better understanding of its background. One is Cherif Daha Ba's study of the history of crime in the Senegal River valley from 1810 to 1970, and the second is François Manchuelle's article on the Devès family and its political activities from 1881 to 1897. Finally, Yamar Samp offers the most detailed description of the different stages in the affair from a judicial perspective. Ba's discussion of the affair sheds some light on the complex political struggles that erupted in the region of Fouta Toro between different ruling dynasties following the arrival of the French. He also examines the perspective of Kaccé, Jeandet's killer, relying on oral testimonies he had collected.[13] Manchuelle offers us a deeper understanding of Devès's involvement in the affair and the no less complex political struggles between the métis and the French settlers in Saint Louis.[14] Samp's article offers an interesting analysis of Algeria as a laboratory for the French legal system in Senegal.[15]

By employing the method of micro-history, I offer a detailed description of the Jeandet Affair, using it as a prism through which the process of empire-building may be understood as multi-layered, fragmented, and full of contradictions. The legal proceedings in the affair lasted less than two years, but I intend to focus on a far wider scope than this limited duration. Rather, my starting point is as early as Jeandet's decision to opt for a colonial career in 1886. His colonial policies and perspectives about the colonization of Senegal are vital to our understanding of the Jeandet Affair. While the affair officially ended in June 1892, its repercussions were felt much later, and its echoes have lasted until today. The story, therefore, will not be complete without a glimpse into current local traditions regarding the affair and their transformations, which can tell us a great deal about its significance in the region today.

The Jeandet Affair provides extensive information and fresh perspectives on three major themes pertinent to French colonization in West Africa at the end of the nineteenth century: colonial conquest, the intersection of law and empire, and the nuances of resistance. It also allows us a fascinating window into how the French conquest, and the resistance to it, were preserved in local memory, and how they became part of national memory through music, social media, and the project of rewriting Senegalese history.[16]

Colonial conquest

The unique circumstances arising from the French decision to expand their dominion along the Senegal River, subjugating local rulers, some of whom fiercely resisted the French presence, served as the backdrop for the unfolding affair. Several conditions contributing to this scandal emanated from the French expansionist agenda. Firstly, the French ambition to circumvent African intermediaries and establish direct control over new territories and river commerce raised concerns among métis merchants like Gaspard Devès. This elite class had much to lose with the change of colonial dynamics, and they viewed the illicit executions as an opportunity to impede French expansion into the territories of their African allies. Secondly, the affair stemmed from the division between areas under French rule and those designated as protectorates during the colonization process. Thirdly, French concern regarding potential resistance, whether real or perceived, influenced the administrators' decision to carry out the execution in a central location. It also solidified their objection to the notion of implementing French justice in newly conquered regions and extending its protection to the inhabitants. An analysis of Jeandet's policies, his interactions with African intermediaries and rulers, and his perception of the emerging French empire in West Africa, will thus shed light on the colonial conquest process in the late nineteenth century and its legal and political features.

Law and empire

One of the primary tools at the disposal of administrators like Jeandet as of 1887 was the *indigénat*, an administrative mechanism allowing officials to penalize colonial subjects in the newly colonized territories at their whim for a range of offences. Gregory Mann examines this system of sanctions, which endured until 1946, as the core of the French colonial presence in West Africa.

He argues that the term 'Empire of Law,' often employed by historians of French colonialism in Africa and Southeast Asia is misleading. According to Mann, French authority in West Africa did not primarily rely on the legal system, nor did it consider the legal system the central pillar of the colonial enterprise. Instead, he asserts that the *indigénat* and its central role in the administration of French West Africa underscored the primacy of violence, rather than the law, in the French colonial project. Focusing on law tended to downplay the significance of violence—whether enacted or potential—and emphasized legal institutions and procedures over the daily practices unrelated to the concept of law.[17] Mann also highlights the possibility of inflicting collective punishments on the indigenous population, which the *indigénat* allowed during conquest and even later, despite being illegal under French Law.[18] Violence pervades the narrative of the Jeandet Affair from its inception and throughout every phase. Jeandet's actions were inherently violent, despite his pretence of being an 'enlightened despot.' The executions themselves constituted pure and brutal violence serving as a horrifying spectacle that aimed to instill terror in the local population. A collective punishment was inflicted on the population immediately following the murder. Furthermore, even when the affair was debated in the legal arena of Saint Louis, a French territory since 1638 (except for a short British occupation between 1758 and 1779), the French administration resorted to violent measures against Ndiereby Ba to pressure her into dropping her lawsuit.

However, even though violence, rather than law, stood at the heart of French colonial rule, the legal arena in this early period of colonial expansion still bore some significance and could function as a space for contesting colonial authority. In her study spanning over 500 years, Lauren Benton discusses the relationship between law, geography, and sovereignty in colonial empires and, while her emphasis is on periods earlier than the one discussed here, some of her insights are relevant to the debate aroused by the Jeandet Affair. She argues that law represented a particularly important factor in the construction of empire and the division of different territories within it. Europeans travelling in new territories extended the reach of European law and variations of familiar legal practices. They defined the rights of subjects in different parts of the empire and the measure of their own law's authority. Benton observes that 'the problem of subjecthood corresponded in interesting ways to the imagined political significance of subjects moving through space.'[19] She also mentions the European perspective of distinguishing between European-controlled areas where a legal system prevailed and lawless extra-European territories.[20] The Jeandet Affair clearly intersected the realms of law, geography, and subjecthood. The issue of 'subjects moving through space' played a pivotal role in this legal scandal. One of the principal arguments put forth by the French in their efforts to quash the affair was the assertion that Ndiereby Ba, as a colonial subject residing beyond French direct rule, was not entitled to the protection of French law even when she relocated from her village, Guédé, in the protectorate, to Saint Louis, for over two centuries the colonial capital under French jurisdiction. Her subjecthood took precedence over the territory in which she filed her lawsuit just as her husband's subjecthood justified his extrajudicial killing. The relationship between geography and law is also prevalent in the affair. The scandal arose from the decision to conduct the executions in a different location from that of the murder. While the murder occurred in a geographical area beyond the reach of French law, the execution took place in a town subject to direct French law. The protectorates in West Africa, in a sense, represented lawless regions, but this lawlessness extended beyond what the French perceived as despotic rule devoid of any legal framework. It also encompassed the absence of French law. The designation of an area as a protectorate allowed the French to disregard their own legal system. After all, if the three suspects had been executed in Aeré, the location of the murder, there would have been no opportunity for legal contestation of the executions. Thus, the French had an interest in maintaining the 'lawlessness' of protectorates, in contrast to their professed mission of bringing 'civilization' and 'justice' to these regions.

Resistance

The story of French colonization of West Africa, and the violence inherent in it, is also the story of resistance. Killing a powerful colonial administrator amid his attempt to subdue rulers who were still fighting against the French was no doubt an act of resistance. The legal struggle that followed represented a different kind of resistance, one that did not resort to violence and relied on the French metropolitan legal principles. The special characteristics of this resistance challenged the colonial administration in ways that no assassination of an administrator could do.

The affair unfolded at a time when the legal status of the French expanding empire was still under debate thus allowing Ba and the métis individuals who supported her, to mount a prolonged and determined legal battle against the formidable colonial administration despite immense pressure. This achievement underscores the role of the legal arena as a space for resistance, one in which even non-citizen women could participate, offering a potentially more effective tool than bullets in the heart of a French administrator.

It is essential to bear in mind the fragility of French colonial rule at the time of the affair. In his study of a later stage of French colonialism in West Africa, Frederick Cooper cautions against viewing the decolonization period through a teleological lens, which focuses solely on the eventual outcome and neglects the alternative possibilities that existed at the time.[21] This perspective applies equally to the early stages of French colonial expansion in West Africa. The Jeandet Affair unfolded at a time in which alternatives to full colonization were still viable. This period cannot be examined solely through the prism of our knowledge of French colonial rule in subsequent decades. At the close of the nineteenth century, political leaders in Paris displayed hesitancy toward colonial expansion in West and Equatorial Africa, apprehensive of the associated costs and questioning its benefits. Within Senegal, fierce disputes emerged among various interest groups regarding the nature of the French presence in the colony and beyond. These struggles involved military officers, administrators, métis politicians and jurists, African rulers, and interpreters. Thus, the affair serves as an excellent lens through which to scrutinize these conflicts, offering insight not only into what transpired but also into what might have unfolded differently.

Sources and methodology

As with many other legal scandals, the Jeandet Affair produced a myriad of documents. For the period before the murder, I rely mainly on a file containing dozens of personal letters that Jeandet sent his parents during the four years prior to his murder. The first letter, written in 1886, announced to his father his decision to pursue a colonial career, and Jeandet wrote the last one a mere two days before his murder. It reached his devastated parents when he was already dead. These letters are a unique source. Jeandet was deeply attached to his parents. He admired his father and cherished his mother. He wrote to them frequently and in detail. Following his son's assassination, Jeandet's father deposited his letters in the archives of Mâcon, where he worked, after censoring some paragraphs in several of them. Jeandet's letters reveal his worldview on numerous subjects, his deepest thoughts, his grudges, and frustrations. While they are filled with attempts to make his parents proud, they also expose his fears and weaknesses. Jeandet described in them his daily routine, his food, his lodgings, his relations with local rulers, with other administrators, and with his interpreters. He recounted his views on local customs he encountered in Senegal, his love for hunting, and his participation in military campaigns. The letters thus expose almost every aspect of the colonial administrative experience. This unique source is very different from formal administrative correspondence. An administrator who wrote to his superiors usually attempted to impress, and often tried to present a picture of full control over certain situations, therefore mitigating problems and crises. Personal letters are different, as they are usually more candid and open. To some extent they allow us to enter the mind of the person who wrote them. For a historian, reading such letters is almost like talking to the person who wrote them, even if this pleasure is accompanied by a sense of voyeuristic embarrassment.[22]

Another source that complements Jeandet's letters is a book his mother commissioned after her husband had passed away. Flavie Jeandet sold her house and her entire possessions to cover the expenses of this memorial book for her son and to create a fund within the Academy of Mâcon that would award an annual prize for the best study related to the colonies, with emphasis on Senegal. She gave the author, Bernard-Henri Gausseron, what seems to be full access to all Jeandet's letters, as well as to those his parents had sent him. Gausseron quoted these letters extensively in his book, adding his own interpretations. His paraphrasing of some of the letters often seems to contradict Jeandet's perceptions as they are revealed by a reading of the full versions. For example, in one of his letters, Jeandet recounted an encounter with a Senegalese officer who spoke fluent French (like me and you, so he wrote to his parents). Jeandet was deeply impressed by this man and saw him as an example of the success of French colonialism.[23] While this description is obviously paternalistic, it is by no means racist or downgrading. Gausseron, on the other hand, quoted this encounter while describing the African officer as comical, a term Jeandet never used.[24]

Yet, despite such distortions, the book adds important sources, as it contains letters from Jeandet's parents to him that are absent from the archives, as well as memoirs written by Jeandet's mother. Published in 1913, Gausseron's book is also useful to understand the spirit his author represents, one that saw the colonial enterprise as vital to the nation's grandeur. Jeandet, as we shall see, shared Gausseron's values to some extent, but the actual colonial encounter shaped them somewhat differently. Several other memorial books and articles that were published after Jeandet's death will also serve as sources, considering that their main purpose was to glorify the administrator rather than to provide information. All these books are available in the Bibliotèque Nationale de France.[25]

My study also relies on colonial administrative reports and correspondence from the time of arrival of Jeandet in Senegal until the end of the affair in 1892 that are found in the Archives Nationales du Sénégal in Dakar, in the Centre des Archives d'Outre-mer in Aix-en-Provence and in the Archives Nationales in Paris. These include detailed interrogation transcripts of the main characters in the Jeandet Affair, as well as reports on the initial investigation of the murder. The Archives Nationales in Paris hold files on several of the main actors in the affair, namely, members of the judiciary in Senegal and several administrators.

The Centre de Recherche et de Documentation du Sénégal in Saint Louis, Senegal, provided me with access to memoirs written by people who spent some time in Saint Louis, or travelled along the Senegal River in the period just before Jeandet's murder. These lively descriptions of the scenery, colonial projects (such as the railway between Saint Louis and Dakar), and even the fauna and flora of the region, allowed me to draw a fuller picture of the events that unfolded during this period.

Literature also serves as a source that helps visualize much of the information other material reveals. Pierre Lotis's *Le roman d'un spahi* sheds light on the racist perceptions and fears that accompanied most Europeans in Senegal. The *Fortunes of Wangrin*, by Amadou Hampaté Ba helps us understand the mind and inner thoughts of interpreters, key figures in the affair, who acted under colonial rule.

The events in Paris relating to the affair are accessible using contemporary newspapers and transcripts of political debates that took place in the National Assembly in Paris. I will examine the affair in the wider context of the culture of scandals in France during the *belle époque* and, more specifically, the relationship between the Jeandet Affair and the Genouille Affair, both of which are widely covered in both types of sources.

Finally, the story will not be complete without considering the oral traditions that have survived in the region of Podor about the affair. It was relatively easy to locate people with some knowledge about the affair, as one informant led me to another. All the interviews, except one performed online, were conducted on the ground in Podor and in Dakar. The interviews helped me in two ways. First, they pointed to issues on which there was disagreement, either with the information contained in the colonial documents or with a certain view expressed by other informants. While the oral information did not always make sense, and the boundaries between fact and legend were often pretty blurred, it did help in offering in some cases interpretations alternative to those offered by French administrators. Second, the oral interviews contributed insights about the remembrance of the Jeandet Affair and its lingering significance in Senegal to this day. While I tried to listen to as many voices as possible, my attempts were doomed to fail, especially in relation to the voices of women. I managed to speak with only one woman, who could provide only a little information about her father and his approach to the affair. While women accompanied some of my informants during the interviews, they did not seem very interested in the topic, and did not wish to offer any additional information. Also, due to the way in which I reached my informants, through recommendations of people I had already spoken to, several of them belonged to the same family. It was difficult to venture beyond these circles. Nevertheless, these interviews enriched my perspectives about the affair, its transmission, and its significance in current-day Senegal.

When I left Podor, on my way back to Saint Louis, I asked the taxi driver to stop at the village of Giya, from which Baidy Kaccé had originated. He was surprised, and wondered why I wanted to stop there. When I explained, he seemed delighted. He knew the story well, and so did almost everyone I talked to in Podor. I interviewed several local people. All of them felt related in some way to the main protagonists in the affair. Some were their direct descendants, such as Saddick Sall, the great grandson of Lam Toro Sidick, and Ndiereby Ba, who helped much in adding some of the pieces missing from his great grandmother's biography. Another two informants were a griot, a person responsible for the transmission of traditions, and the daughter of a school principal who had written a play about the affair in 1975, who was a descendant of the Lam Toro and his second wife. This play was performed only once in Podor, as it created so much commotion that the municipality decided to forbid further performances. The reason for the commotion was an allegation made in the play regarding a certain family's collaboration with the French and their betrayal of Baidy Kaccé and the two dignitaries who were executed. Another, more recent, theatre play was written by Saddick Sall. Both plays are also useful sources for me. Such sources are vital for understanding the still lingering effects of the Jeandet Affair in Senegal. While, for outsiders, the affair may simply be an intriguing episode in the history of the French colonization of Senegal, for the people I interviewed it means much more. For them it is an ongoing struggle around how the past should be remembered, and which connects this remembrance to present-day politics.

The structure of this book

Writing a micro-history presents a unique challenge: the risk of crafting a narrative so laden with intriguing details that it captivates the author but bewilders the reader, obscuring the proverbial wood for the trees. Nevertheless, the narrative remains paramount, serving as the foundation for our analytical endeavours. Therefore, I have deliberately chosen a chronological and coherent storytelling approach. However, I have ventured beyond this straightforward narrative by crafting each chapter to revolve around one or more of the major themes related to the French colonization of West Africa, which I discussed above—conquest, law, and resistance. In essence, the structure of this book underscores the salient themes that the Jeandet Affair illuminates, and highlights its profound significance in the grand tapestry of colonial history.

Chapter 1 follows Jeandet's colonial career and his itinerary from his small Burgundy village, Verdun-sur-le-Doubs, to Dakar, Saint Louis, and into the West African hinterland, until his death in the village of Aeré, 80 kilometres south-east of Podor, where he had served as an administrator of the region. It exposes the character of an ambitious and promising administrator at a time when French rule in Senegal, limited until then to four strongholds on the coast (Dakar, Gorée, Rufisque, and Saint Louis) was expanding, aiming at establishing a vast empire. The chapter examines the system of alliances that Jeandet created to overcome the weaknesses of the colonial administration, his reliance on local intermediaries, and the political schemes aimed at enforcing French influence on Fouta Toro, which eventually led to his death.

Chapter 2 deals with Jeandet's murder, which delayed the eventual conquest of Fouta Toro by almost a year.[26] The murder was a severe blow to the colonial administration, as Jeandet was regarded as one of the most capable administrators, and the only one the governor could entrust with the delicate mission of controlling Fouta Toro. The chapter examines the murder and the dubious investigation that the local administrator conducted with the help of a French officer sent from Saint Louis and Jeandet's personal interpreter. It also discusses the decision to perform the illegal executions and its motives.

Chapter 3 examines the beginning of the scandal that followed the executions, when Ursleur, the Antillean judge from Saint Louis, opened an investigation against the administrators who had ordered and supervised the executions. The chapter also deals with the person who was the engine behind the affair, Gaspard Devès. After the governor had removed Ursleur from the colony in response to his legal actions, Devès managed to keep the scandal alive by using his allies in Fouta Toro, who helped him to locate a 'person of interest' to sue the administrators. Ba's legal struggle with Devès's support became an act of resistance even more effective than Jeandet's murder. Finally, the chapter introduces the legal arena in Saint Louis and describes in brief the various legal stages of the affair in this city.

Chapter 4 analyzes the struggle between two positions. The one was that justice in the colony was above all other considerations and that everyone, including Africans from protectorates, was entitled to its protection. The other was that security and public order were more important than justice, and that outsiders who did not appreciate its principles could not have expected to benefit from it. Although, in general, the judiciary supported the first view, while the administration the second, this chapter will show that, when we delve into the affair, we can find cases in which an administrator sided with the judicial authorities and vice versa. The chapter will explore the main two measures the governor employed in this struggle—manipulation of laws and removal of anyone who opposed his view from office.

Chapter 5 deals with a unique character in this saga—the Lam Toro's widow, Ndiereby Ba, without whom the affair would have never extended as far as it did. Despite the difficulty of reaching Ba's own voice, this chapter will try to reconstruct it by relying on different sources, such as her lawyer's letters and the transcript of her interrogation. The chapter will also consider the extent of Ba's agency in the affair.

Chapter 6 takes us to Paris to examine the final stage of the affair. The chapter discusses the metropolitan legal arena in an era of scandals, the failed attempt of Ba's French attorney to bring her case to court, and the positions of the French press and the National Assembly regarding the affair and its significance to the metropolitan justice system and the debate around the colonial idea and the concept of the civilizing mission.

Chapter 7 takes us many years forward and discusses the local interpretations of the affair in recent decades up until today, and how the affair is embedded in local memory. It discusses the transformations the affair went through over the years, its recent 'nationalization' process and its becoming part of the rewritten Senegalese history. It also discusses who was remembered and who was forgotten in this process. Finally, it brings our attention back to Jeandet's village, Verdun-sur-le-Doubs, where our story began, to examine to what extent the murdered administrator became part of local heritage.

The concluding chapter will return to the main themes dealt with in the book to see how the Jeandet Affair contributes to their understanding.

Notes

1 The French called him Baidy Kaccé without adding the name Pam, but in oral traditions this is his full name. I will later refer to him as Kaccé.
2 Lam was an honorary title of the paramount chiefs of Fouta. Most only ruled over a cluster of villages, but some, such as the Lam Toro, managed to gain some authority at the provincial level. See: David Robinson, *Chiefs and Clerics: Abdul Bokar Kan and Futa Toro, 1853–1891* (Oxford: Clarendon Press, 1975), 10.
3 Robinson, *Chiefs and Clerics*, 152–153.
4 The métis were the descendants of French men and African women, living mainly in Saint Louis and Gorée. They played a crucial part in the Jeandet Affair and dominated the politics of the colony until the early twentieth century.
5 The widow's name is spelled as Ndiereby Ba in the colonial documents, but it is also written in two additional forms in other written sources: Diereby or Njerebi Bah.
6 Centre des Archives d'outre-mer, Aix-en-Provence (CAOM), FR ANOM Sénégal IV, 66a, 29 November 1890.
7 The Dreyfus Affair began when a Jewish military officer was wrongly accused of espionage in 1894. It divided French society and created a political crisis and instability as well as a surge of antisemitism. See: Ruth Harris, *Dreyfus: Politics, Emotion, and the Scandal of the Century* (New York: Metropolitan Books, 2010).
8 Both names appear in the various documents and in the press. Occasionally the scandal is referred to also as 'the Senegal Affair.' I will use the terms 'Jeandet Affair' and 'Podor Affair' interchangeably.
9 Elizabeth Foster, *Faith in Empire: Religion Politics, and Colonial Rule in French Senegal* (Stanford: Stanford University Press, 2013), 43–47.
10 David Robinson, 'French "Islamic" Policy and Practice in Late Nineteenth-Century Senegal,' *The Journal of African History* 29, no. 3 (1988), 434.
11 David Robinson, *Paths of Accommodation: Muslim Societies and French Colonial Authorities in Senegal and Mauritania, 1880–1920* (Athens: Ohio University Press, 2000), 64–65.

12 Hilary Jones, *The Metis of Senegal: urban life and politics in French West Africa* (Bloomington: Indiana University Press, 2013), 163–164.
13 Daha Chérif Ba, *Crimes et délits dans la vallée du fleuve Sénégal de 1810 à 1970* (Dakar: Editions L'Harmattan-Sénégal, 2010), 229–241.
14 François Manchuelle, "Métis et colons: la famille Devès et L'émergence politique des africains au Sénégal, 1881–1897,' *Cahiers d'études africaines* (1984), 485–498.
15 Yamar Samp, 'Affaire Albert [Sic] Jeandet: la peine de mort sans procès,' *Revue malienne des sciences juridiques, politique et economiques de Bamako* 5 (2018), 221–264.
16 In recent years several colonial historians have been successfully using the method of micro-history and examined a scandal or a legal affair in depth to shed light on broader issues. See for example: Danna Agmon, *A Colonial Affair: Commerce, Conversion, and Scandal in French India* (Ithaca: Cornell University Press, 2017); Joshua Cole, *Lethal Provocation: The Constantine Murders and the Politics of French Algeria* (Ithaca: Cornell University Press, 2019); Bertrand Thaite, *The Killer Trail: A Colonial Scandal in the Heart of Africa* (Oxford: Oxford University Press, 2009).
17 Gregory Mann, 'What Was the Indigénat? The 'Empire of Law' in French West Africa,' *The Journal of African History* 50, no. 3 (2009), 331–333.
18 Mann, 'What Was the *Indigénat*?,' 343.
19 Lauren Benton, *A Search for Sovereignty: Law and Geography in European Empires, 1400–1900* (Cambridge: Cambridge University Press, 2009), 3.
20 Benton, *A Search for Sovereignty*, 30–32.
21 This idea appears in several publications by Cooper. See for example: Frederick Cooper, 'Alternatives to Nationalism in French Africa, 1945–60,' in *Elites and Decolonization in the Twentieth Century*, ed. Jost Dülffer and Marc Frey (London: Palgrave Macmillan, 2011), 110–137.
22 On the use of personal letters for writing colonial history, see: Julie d'Andrurain, 'La correspondance privée des coloniaux,' in *Gouverner par les lettres: de l'antiquité à l'époque contemporaine*, ed. Agnès et Olivier Dard Bérenger (Lorraine: Université de Lorraine, 2015).
23 Archives de Saône-et-Loire, François Joseph Etienne Abel Jeandet, F 1413, Saint Louis 15 April.
24 Henri Bernard Gausseron, *Un Français au Sénégal* (Paris: Librarie Ancienne Honore Champion Editeur Edouard Champion, 1913), 74.

25 Philibert A. Soupé, *Bio-Bibliographie François-Abel Jeandet* (Lyon: Imprimerie Waltener et Cie, 1891); F. Fertiault, *François-Abel Jeandet—Sonnets* (Lyon: Imprimerie A Waltener et Cie, 1891); Unknown, *Quelques documents relatifs à la mort fr F--J.-E. -Abel Jeandet* (Mâcon: Protat Frères, 1892); Unknown, *François-Abel Jeandet: Un Héro De Nos Colonies Africaines* (Dijon: Imprimerie Darantiere, 1892).

26 Jeandet was on his way to subdue Abdoul Bokar, the last local leader who still managed to resist the French. Bokar was eventually killed by a Moor leader who was his host in August 1891, and only then could the French control the entire area of Fouta Toro. See: Robinson, *Chiefs and Clerics*, 149–159.

1

From Verdun-sur-le-Doubs to Fouta Toro

The story of Ba's legal struggle began four years before the murder of an esteemed administrator led to the unlawful execution of her husband, Lam Toro Sidick. This was when that administrator, Abel Jeandet, abruptly decided to change the course of his career and exchange the possibility of a post as a prefect in the Pyrenees for the certainty of gaining one in the colonial administration of Senegal, a colony about which he knew nothing at all. This chapter lays the foundations of the legal scandal, first by introducing Jeandet's motives for leaving the comfort of his metropolitan career and venturing into the unknown in a remote colony in West Africa. The chapter then follows Jeandet's integration into the colonial system and the ways in which his encounter with Senegal, its local rulers, and various forms of Islam, shaped his perception of the empire as well as his already hostile views towards the Third Republic. The chapter's last section examines Jeandet's policy in Fouta Toro, a region that still resisted French presence and had yet to be subjugated. I will show how Jeandet's policy and arrogance led to the events of 2 September 1890. In addition to setting the stage for the subsequent dramatic events, this chapter sheds light on the character of the French colonial administrator during the period of colonization, and highlights his dependence on local intermediaries.

Verdun-sur-le-Doubs: The call of empire

Born in the village of Verdun-sur-le-Doubs in Burgundy in 1852, Abel Jeandet was a cherished only child to his parents. They adored him and nurtured great ambitions for their talented boy. Abel admired his father and worshipped his mother. It is thanks to these deep attachments, which sometimes seem more appropriate for a child than a man in his 30s, that we know so much about Jeandet's deepest thoughts and aspirations, which he revealed in his numerous letters to his parents.

In his memorial book, based to a large extent on these letters, albeit in a very selective way, as I mentioned in the introduction, Gausseron describes Jeandet's family as 'one of those who rose with modern France, without denying anything of the France of the past, and in whom the persistence of religious sentiment only gave more power to the love of the fatherland and to liberty.'[1] This rather pompous description is in fact quite accurate. The Jeandets were republicans, but they were also deeply religious and their attitude to the regime of the Third Republic was complex and ambivalent. Gausseron continues his description by telling his readers about the involvement of the Jeandets in military combat—Abel's grandfather was a military surgeon in Napoleon Bonaparte's army and was wounded at Wagram. His mother's great-uncle was a general, mortally wounded in the Battle of Waterloo. Two of her cousins perished in the Prussian invasion of 1870.[2]

Jeandet's father, Jean-Pierre-Abel, began his career as a politician in the short-lived Second Republic (1848–1852). He acted closely with his friend, Dr Bertillon, father of Alphonse, inventor of the anthropometric system.[3] He gradually abandoned the political arena and studied medicine, like his father before him. He later became the conservator of the archives of Lyon and, when this position was abolished in 1873, he became the archivist of the city of Mâcon. He retired in 1884, two years before his son decided to join the colonial service in Senegal.[4] Gausseron describes Jeandet's mother, Flavie, only in relation to her husband and son, as a devoted wife and a loving mother. From Jeandet's letters, we can learn about her deep religiosity. Before Jeandet first set out for Senegal, for example, she took him to the Basilica of Notre-Dame de Fourvière in Lyon so that he could be blessed.[5] While Jeandet obviously cherished his mother, he also condescended to her as if she were a helpless child in need of his guidance. Before Flavie's visit to the Universal Exhibition, which her son fully paid for, he made all the arrangements for his mother's stay in Paris, and he urged her not to go out after dark and to be careful of the crowds and chariots in the streets.[6] In fact, Flavie was far from helpless. She was much more active than Jeandet's father in trying to influence her son to opt for a less dangerous career. She did all she could to save him from a destiny she feared was inevitable. After the death of her husband in 1899, Flavie offered the Académie de Mâcon her entire possessions, including her house, in return for the publication of the memorial book and other commemoration initiatives, such as an annual prize for the best study on colonial Senegal offered in her perished son's name.[7]

Although Gausseron only hints that Jeandet's father had encountered some obstacles during his career, Jeandet's letters reveal his bitterness on the subject. Apparently, the Jeandets had lost the respect of their social milieu owing to the debts they had accumulated. Jeandet's wish to restore his parents' standing was a major motive behind his decision to pursue a colonial career. Jeandet seemed to have had a very sheltered childhood both because of his being an only child and because of the great expectations his parents had had for him. They had made sure he received the best education possible, even when their financial situation became difficult. In one of his letters, Jeandet mentions the sacrifices his parents made for him and, especially, his mother's willingness to take menial jobs such as cleaning to allow him to study in expensive private institutions.[8]

After finishing a Jesuit high school (collège) in Dôle, a town 50 kilometres from his village, Jeandet followed in his father's and grandfather's footsteps by studying medicine, first in Lyon and then in Paris. His mother was unhappy with this choice, as she worried that her son would have to work long hours without sufficient renumeration. She wished that he would pursue a career as a distinguished professor in the Humanities. Apparently, in the nineteenth century such a career was much more rewarding and dignified than that of medicine. But Jeandet did not fulfil his mother's dreams. In 1873 he joined the army, in which he served until 1877. Two years later he married Alice Van der Meere.[9]

Alice was the daughter of a Belgian general, August Louis Nicolas Van der Meere, count of Kruishoutem, who found refuge in France after he had participated in a failed attempt to re-establish the Dutch throne over Belgium in 1831.[10] The absolute silence about the circumstances of Alice's death is almost deafening. The local newspaper of Saône-et-Loire only mentions her demise briefly, without stating the cause of death. Jeandet, who otherwise wrote freely and in detail about many of his relatives and acquaintances, both dead and living, never mentioned his deceased wife in his letters. In one letter he confessed to his parents that they were the only human beings he loved.[11] One may surmise that the circumstances of Alice's death were too unpleasant to discuss, but this is of course mere speculation. In any event, although Jeandet had already been deliberating what to do with his future before his wife's untimely death, it nevertheless, presented him with an opportunity to change his life's course.

After Alice's death, Jeandet found himself at a crossroads. For several years he searched for a new direction for his life. He published articles in various newspapers and journals but then opted to begin an administrative career in the prefecture of the Pyrenees. Two years later, in 1886, after waiting in vain for a promised promotion, he asked a friend who worked in the prefecture of Saône-et-Loire, to which his native village belonged, to help him obtain a post in the colonies. Within a few days, he received an invitation to join the colonial service in Senegal.[12]

Jeandet's decision to join the colonial service came at a time when France was licking its wounds after its defeat by Prussia, and was gradually establishing its second empire in Asia and Africa, perhaps as some sort of recompense. The new wave of colonization started a few decades earlier with the loss of most of the older colonies in wars with Britain in the late 1700s and following Napoleon's defeat in 1815. Algeria was conquered in 1830. Tunisia came next when France turned it into a protectorate in 1881, with Morocco following in 1912. From the 1840s onwards the French also took hold of strategic islands from Mayotte in the Indian Ocean to Tahiti and New Caledonia in the Pacific. Its forces landed in Cochin China in the late 1850s and, by the 1880s, French Indochina already included Vietnam, Cambodia, and Laos. In West Africa, France expanded from the coast, where it held several posts, to the hinterland, and conquered large parts of West and Equatorial Africa, from Mauritania to Congo. In the east, its troops colonized Madagascar.[13]

It is not surprising that Jeandet could so easily obtain a position in the colonial service of the expanding French empire. The fact that he had agreed to serve in Senegal, a colony that was unattractive to most (if not all) other applicants at the time, certainly expedited his acceptance. With the gradual colonization of the West African hinterland, the French needed more qualified personnel to govern the newly conquered territories. In the early period preceding the establishment of the federation of French West Africa in 1895, African leaders had much more leverage than in the later years. Their relative power made the administrators' task much more complicated than it became later. Before 1887, at the time Jeandet was recruited, each governor handled the recruitment of administrators to his own colony, and only in 1887 did the French establish a single recruitment division for the various colonies. All the African colonies faced the same difficulty in attracting qualified men to distant and dangerous regions that had earned the reputation of being the 'white man's grave.'

Louis Faidherbe, the governor of Senegal between 1854 and 1861 and again between 1863 and 1865, complained about the poor quality of colonial officers who did not bother to study anything about the regions to which they had been sent and ultimately left just as ignorant as when they had arrived. In this period, those who were recruited were all sourced from the navy. When Bernard Jauréguiberry, the governor of Senegal from 1861 to 1863, suggested in 1869 to recruit civilians, the naval ministry rejected the idea asking:

> Who then is the intelligent man with good education and liberal ideas [...] who would consent to exile himself to Saldé or Matam [in the remotest parts of Senegal], with ten black soldiers under his orders and a village of a hundred huts to survey; and how will he find the occasion to apply his intelligence?[14]

When, in 1879, Jauréguiberry became the minister of the navy, he finally had the opportunity to implement his idea. In Senegal, on his insistence, governors appointed only civilians to the territorial administration and, by 1880, eight out of ten district commanders (commandants de cercles) in that colony were civilians. However, this decision did not improve the quality of the administrators. Most of the civilian administrators were just as brutal towards the local population and just as negligent of the orders of their superiors as their naval predecessors had been. The unhealthy and uncomfortable life offered by the colonies did not attract the best Europeans, no matter their nationality. The French candidates were often even worse than the British. Because there were so few French candidates, it was possible that no educational restrictions nor any character qualifications were applied.[15]

William Cohen's classic study of French colonial administrators demonstrates that, before World War One, most came from the lower social strata and were poorly educated. Some were criminals escaping punishment or debtors evading their debts. Among those who opted for an administrative career, few chose sub-Saharan Africa as their preferred destination. The best candidates were sent to Indochina or Algeria. Jeandet could not have been further from the profile Cohen presents. In this respect, Jeandet was what Edorardo Grendi termed the 'exceptional normal.' He was hardly representative of his peers but, as Grendi argued, this is not what the micro-historical methodology looks for. It is the micro-scale analysis of a specific individual, local setting, or situation, different from the average or the norm, that can teach us much about his or her more normative peers.[16] Jeandet indeed diverged from the typical colonial administrator of his time. As we shall see, his outstanding and rare qualifications made his superiors value him greatly, and his murder especially horrified them. Understanding his mindset, his policies, perceptions of colonialism and metropolitan France, can therefore shed light on the more general characteristics of the early colonial administrator in West Africa.

With his high qualifications, Jeandet could probably have asked to be sent to a more popular region in the empire rather than Senegal, with better conditions and a healthier climate. Five years before Jeandet decided to join the colonial service in Senegal, Pierre Loti published *Le Roman d'un Spahi*, which is set in Saint Louis, Jeandet's destination. The book was enthusiastically received by the French public.[17] Jeandet did not mention having read the book but, given his character, it would be surprising if he had not. Like other literary works of the period, the book presented Africa as a cruel continent cursed by a brutal climate and horrifying illnesses. The continent would lure the white man, just like the African woman who enchanted Jean Peyral, the main protagonist in Loti's book, to his fatal end.[18]

So why did Jeandet opt for a colonial career in the least desirable region of the French empire? In his letter announcing to his father his decision to become a colonial administrator, Jeandet wrote: 'Dear beloved father, this letter will reach you on your birthday. It is both important and sad, because it discusses my departure, our separation.' He then told his father about his ambition to walk through the gates that Brazza and Soleillet[19] had opened. He wrote that the glorious history of his family compelled him to follow in his ancestors' footsteps, and that his proud and courageous mother would be happy to see a 'a ray of glory shine[ing] above over her child.'[20] He assured his father that he was confident he was doing the right thing: 'I trust my star and myself, feeling like a man in the midst of our sickly generation.'[21] Jeandet ended his letter with the idea of the civilizing mission that was the primary justification for the brutal French conquests overseas: 'And you my beloved father, you will be happy, because your only son will be one of the pioneers of this civilization and this progress for which you have always fought. On this flag of France, which my hands will plant, the word "Liberty" will be inscribed for eternity.'[22]

In this letter, then, Jeandet declared that the main motive for his decision to leave for the colonies was patriotism. Jeandet no doubt saw himself as a true patriot, in contrast to most politicians of the Third Republic, whom he regarded as corrupt and hedonistic. This was the type of patriotism that characterized the French Right at the time, the same as that proclaimed by Maurice Barrès, the author who would later write the preface to Jeandet's memorial book. Like Barrès, Jeandet was not particularly fond of the republican regime nor of the capital, Paris. His patriotism was deeply rooted in the soil of his home region, Burgundy. The empire attracted him because serving it corresponded with his kind of patriotism. This was a non-hedonistic patriotic mission that fulfilled the duty to civilize so-called primitive people and disseminate French culture and norms among them. Patriotism was, of course, the noblest motive for joining the colonial service—a motive that would be strongly emphasized after Jeandet's death. It is no wonder, then, that Gausseron chose to quote the letter announcing Jeandet's decision to opt for a colonial career in full. It was a letter that fitted perfectly with the idea of the patriotic Frenchman who risked his life to bring French civilization to Africans and glory to his fatherland.

Another related motive to become an administrator, and which Gausseron also emphasized in his book, was Jeandet's wish to become 'a real man.' One of the main contradictions between Jeandet's apparent agreement with French thinkers of his time who criticized the Third Republic is that most of them fiercely objected to French colonial expansion up until World War One. Nevertheless, as Ariel Roshwald shows, some right-wing nationalists, foremost Barrès, although hesitant about the colonial project that distracted France from taking its revenge on Germany, believed much earlier that the empire might provide a space that could produce a new breed of men—men who acted and not only talked, who rejected the hedonism of French society and embraced a life of adventure, heroism, and

Figure 1.1 Jeandet caressing a lion cub

self-sacrifice. He and other nationalists thought that the colonial elite could become part of the vanguard of a national recovery.[23]

Just like those nationalists, Jeandet saw the empire as the place where his masculinity could flourish. As he wrote to his father, he wanted to be a man among the sickly members of his generation. In his essay on the 'colonial man,' Robert Aldrich draws the image of this type of masculinity that French men searched for in the empire. The empire was some sort of recompense for the defeat of masculinity in France brought about by its rout by Prussia. It was an outlet from the supposed mediocrity and debauchery of France, an escape from fear of decadence and new cultural and social ideas. From the late 1800s, these new ideas included attacks on traditional manhood. So, while Europe was the birthplace of the 'new woman,' the colonies were where the old-fashioned man thrived. Serving in the colonies allowed those who went there to distil the 'essence of Frenchness.'[24]

According to Aldrich, the colonial man was supposed to be healthy, courageous, and energetic. He had to be able to face challenges, use weapons, hunt big animals, and thus subordinate nature. He had to be loyal to his country, implement the values of his 'race' and yet he had the right to enjoy wine and women.[25] Almost all these characteristics and challenges appear in some form in Jeandet's letters. He discusses his good health incessantly, comparing it to others around him who were apparently constantly sick. Even when he described episodes of sickness, he framed them in heroic masculine terms, emphasizing that his illnesses did not stop him from fulfilling his duties.[26]

Unlike these descriptions of Jeandet's developing manhood, the patriotic tone of the first letter he sent his father, and the reference to the 'civilizing mission,' do not recur in his later letters sent from Senegal. In them, we can find a series of other, perhaps less 'noble' motives, that Gausseron did not bother to mention in his book. Jeandet mentioned money in every one of his letters. His financial motives, including salary, and quick promotion are obvious, as he kept sending money to his parents to cover their debts and explained how he intended to advance and earn more.

Jeandet was indeed determined to promote his career and even saw himself one day as a governor. During his stay in Senegal, he took upon himself difficult missions and unusual workloads.

In June 1887 he wrote that his position entailed too many responsibilities, which caused him excessive fatigue, but he had to take them on because such missions might help him advance his career.[27] Jeandet translated almost every mission his superiors assigned to him into promotion in colonial ranks. When he happily announced to his parents in 1887 that he had won the position of director of political affairs (directeur des affaires politiques), he added that it entailed a lot of work, but this was worthwhile as the position was a milestone on his way to a brilliant future.[28]

Jeandet's hope that he would be promoted without having to resort to intrigues reflected his negative opinion of France and the values that reigned there. This recurrent theme in his letters is crucial to our understanding of Jeandet's perception of his colonial mission. On many occasions, Jeandet lamented the treatment his father had received from the French authorities, the lack of respect and the obstacles to his father's career progression. In what seems like Jeandet's attempt to attenuate the insult to his parents, he complained about the avalanche of distinctions the politicians of Paris heaped upon 'mandarins,' without finding a position for one brave man. 'Let us drop the crosses and favours upon the unworthy—nowadays man is mad.'[29] The empire, thus, not only offered Jeandet the chance to earn well and be promoted according to his merits. It also provided refuge from the metropolitan political, social, and cultural life that Jeandet often treated with disdain.

Within the expanding empire, Jeandet found Senegal to be the most useful for all these motives. It offered fierce battles against yet unconquered people, remoteness from what he saw as French nepotism, difficult conditions to enhance his masculinity, and more opportunities for advancement and raises in salary. When Jeandet's mother tried to convince him to move to a more 'convenient' part of the French empire, such as Oran in Algeria, he responded in detail, contradicting each of her arguments. Among other claims, he explained to his mother that his chances of becoming a governor in Senegal were much greater than in Algeria, where the corrupt politics of the republic had greater influence. Senegal, therefore, despite, and perhaps even thanks to, its remoteness and hard conditions was the perfect colony for him to flourish in.[30]

Let us now follow Jeandet's career and physical itineraries within Senegal, and see how his encounter with the colony, combined with his mindset and background, shaped his perceptions about colonialism and the ways in which it should be implemented.

Saint Louis, Senegal—Jeandet's encounter with the colonial scene

Located at the mouth of the Senegal River, Saint Louis, Jeandet's destination, was the colony's capital and remained its most important coastal settlement until Dakar took over in the early twentieth century. On 5 November 1886, less than two months after announcing to his father his decision to join the colonial service, Jeandet boarded a ship in Bordeaux heading for the colony assigned to him. At the time, Senegal was a rather complex territory that incorporated the old and the new aspects of the French empire. Its coastal settlements of Saint Louis and Gorée dated back to the seventeenth century. They were founded as trading posts (*comptoirs*) and were licensed to trading companies, mostly from Bordeaux and Marseilles.[31] During the brief period of British occupation of the region (1758–1779), the European traders along the Senegal River became more independent of any central control. They began to hire liberated African 'slaves' and other 'free Africans' to run their businesses. They created a system of trade that worked with local rulers in the West African hinterland. When the French reoccupied their Senegalese outposts in 1816, the administration made efforts to gain more control over the commerce on the river and make it more lucrative for France. Nevertheless, the French and métis traders remained the main economic agents in the region and negotiated directly with local chiefs.[32] Ten days after leaving Bordeaux, with two stops in La Coruña (Spain) and Lisbon (Portugal), Jeandet arrived in Dakar. After purchasing a hat to protect himself from 'the infamous Senegalese sun,' Jeandet had a quick lunch in the city before consulting the train schedule to Saint Louis.[33] The French inaugurated this railway line with grand pomp just one year before Jeandet's arrival. The local newspaper, *Moniteur du Sénégal et dépendances*, reported enthusiastically on the inauguration ceremony that took place on 6 July 1885. It included speeches, a military band, and a lavish banquet. The new line, according to the *Moniteur*, was the way of progress, 'progress without a shock, without violence, without protest, and without revolt.'[34]

The various speeches of the director of works, M. Blondelet, Governor Génouille, and the priest of the church of Saint Louis, all reflected this theme of progress and civilization through French technology. The governor even went as far as declaring that 6 July would remain a commemorated day in the history of Senegal.[35] The new railway line mainly contributed to the elevation of Dakar's status at the expense of Saint Louis as it dramatically enhanced the position of the Dakar port. By the early twentieth century, this harbour enabled Dakar to dominate the waters between France and West Africa, and only Lagos port presented any meaningful competition.[36]

At the time of Jeandet's visit to the city, Dakar was still in its very early stages of development. Governor Pinet-Laparde designed a plan for the city in 1862, hoping that Dakar might one day become the capital of the French empire in West Africa. This plan included a port, administrative headquarters, and military and commercial facilities. As for other cities in the French colonial empire, Dakar's planning allowed its designers broad architectural freedom that was inconceivable for metropolitan architects. Dakar indeed became the capital of the federation of French West Africa (Afrique occidentale française) in 1902. It then became a model for sub-Saharan urban planning. Its role was to become international rather than local, and Parisian architectural elements were incorporated in its design.[37]

But in 1886 all this was a distant dream. Jeandet described the future capital of the federation of French West Africa (the federation would be established five years after his death) in these words: 'It is a city still to be built and of which the plan is made; it is located in front of Gorée and has hardly more than twenty European houses, most of them made of wood.'[38] After leaving Dakar at 2 a.m. that night, Jeandet arrived in Saint Louis almost 12 hours later. In a letter to his parents, he described it as follows:

> St Louis is, in a way, an Arab town with galleried and terraced houses. It is located on an island in the Senegal River and separated from the sea by a narrow strip of sand called the Langue de Barbarie; three bridges connect the city to the Langue de Barbarie, including a pontoon bridge more than 600 metres long, built by Faidherbe. The black quarter includes the two suburbs, a southern one and a northern one, of Guet N'dar and N'dar Tout; finally, two villages, those of Bouetville and Sor, are part of St Louis.[39]

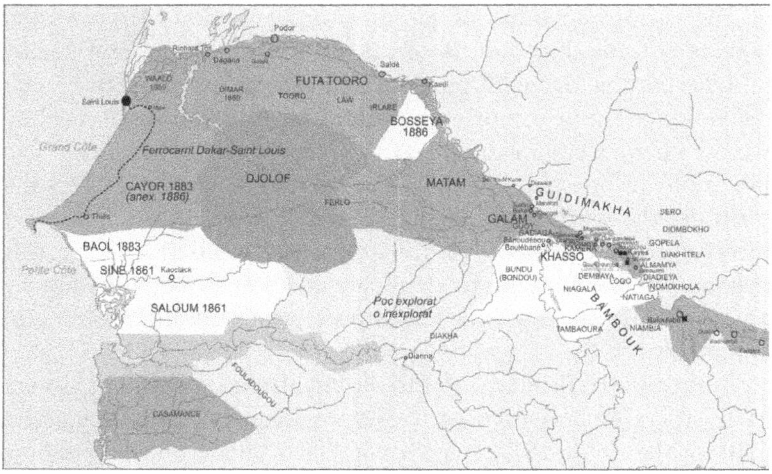

Map 1.1 Senegal in the nineteenth century

Saint Louis impressed Jeandet much more than Dakar, as indeed this town was the centre of the French territories in West Africa. The governor and the main administrative departments were located there. It had the largest population in Senegal, the best French schools, and the headquarters of the main representative body in colonial Senegal—the General Council (conseil général). Most seats on this council were occupied by representatives of the city's inhabitants.[40]

The population of Saint Louis was racially hierarchical. In the mid-nineteenth century around 15,000 Africans lived in the city. Only about half of them were free, while the others were indentured servants: French traders had bought them from their enslavers after the French government abolished slavery in the colonies in 1848, and turned them into domestic servants or colonial soldiers. The working conditions of these so-called 'freed slaves' did not improve much, though. The free African populations, of which some were descendants of indentured servants, were predominantly ethnically Wolof and their faith was Islam. Many of them controlled the trade along the Senegal River. Some financed their own trading operations and even competed against the big French and métis firms, but most borrowed funds from the big trading houses and conducted small-scale operations.[41]

The city of Saint Louis was one of the four French strongholds on the coast of Senegal known as the four communes (*les quatre communes*). In 1816, when the French regained control over their Senegalese possessions, after a period of British occupation, the governor reluctantly agreed to preserve the position of a local mayor in Saint Louis. But he refused to allow the elected mayor to serve until his death, rather making their tenure dependent upon the governor. The municipal elections continued until the end of the Second Empire, although occasionally mayors were dismissed by governors. This was a form of limited democracy that the people of Saint Louis, especially the Creoles and assimilated Africans, were accustomed to. In 1871, Senegal's seat in the Chamber of Deputies had been restored after it was abolished in 1848 by Napoleon III. A year later, the inhabitants of Saint Louis, Bordeaux merchants, métis, and Africans succeeded in getting Paris to restore both the general council and the municipal council, which had also been abolished by Napoleon III. A decree of 10 August 1872 gave the communes of Senegal the rights of French municipalities. Elections were held by the end of 1872, and municipal government controlled by the local population was once again a reality in Senegal. In 1880, Rufisque was given the same form of government, and in 1887 Dakar was separated from Gorée and made a full commune.[42]

This political system was unique in the African territories that later came under French control, as it accorded certain political rights to Africans who had inhabited the four communes at the time and to their descendants. They became known as *originaires* and held invaluable privileges in the yet to be established French African empire. In 1916, Blaise Diagne, who two years earlier had become the first African representative of Senegal in the French parliament, managed to guarantee these citizenship rights.[43]

The remaining population of Saint Louis was European in its culture and orientation and included Europeans and métis (who were the descendants of French men and African women). The métis, who played a crucial part in the Jeandet Affair, dominated the politics of the colony until the early twentieth century. As there is no accurate data regarding their numbers during that period, it is only possible to provide vague estimations. These vary from several hundred to 1,700. Many of the métis were Catholic and linked by blood or by business interests to prominent trading firms in Bordeaux. They accumulated much political and economic influence during the eighteenth and nineteenth centuries. The métis worked with networks of African traders, many of whom were Muslim, and who maintained headquarters in Saint Louis.[44] Finally, at the top of this racially hierarchical pyramid were the Europeans, a predominantly male population that included between 400 and 800 administrators, who usually stayed in Senegal for only a few years, and approximately 200 merchants. The latter ran the big commercial houses, most of which were also linked with Bordeaux.[45]

Jeandet remained in Saint Louis for training until March 1887. He soon stood out among his peers, and the governor wished to appoint him as a district commander. As there was no open position for this promotion, the governor came up with an original solution—he simply created a new district, especially for Jeandet to rule, around the small town of Louga, about 75 kilometres from the capital.

Figure 1.2 Saint Louis, view from the Senegal River (photo: Eyal Ginio)

Jeandet as a special envoy

Even though an entire district was established especially for him, Jeandet served as a district commander of Louga for only six months. He was desperately needed for the complex task of subjugating local rulers and facilitating the French expansion into the West African hinterland. After promoting Jeandet to administrator level 2 (administrateur nivau 2), the governor appointed him on 19 June 1887 as a special envoy (envoyé extraordinaire). In this capacity, Jeandet was responsible for implementing the French policy of expansion into the hinterland of the Senegalese coast by creating alliances where possible and through military campaigns.

In September 1887, Jeandet described this expansion to his parents in surprising detail: Gallieni[46] headed a military column in French Sudan (nowadays Mali); a second column was sent to Niami, Niger, to fight Mamadou Lamine who, according to Jeandet, 'played at being a Mahdi [joue au Mahdi]'; Jeandet ensured the collaboration of Abdul Bokar, the ruler of Bossea; in Baol, a third column was required to avenge the death of Captain Minet; in Sine the ruler's nephew caused some difficulties; and in yet another district the British managed to seduce the ruler with their gold.[47]

This long list of missions well reflects the complexity of implementing the French policy of expansion at the end of the nineteenth century. Administrators and military officers had to deal with resistance almost everywhere. Even when they managed to establish alliances, these soon proved extremely fragile. Friends could easily become foes under religious and charismatic leadership, due to British attempts to lure African leaders, or simply because the situation had changed, and the French were perceived to be weaker.

The Senegal River, like other African rivers, was the main channel through which the French expanded their rule into the African hinterland. But even before it began to serve as a means of expansion, the river was the focus of French interest in the region. The colonial administration aimed to control African leaders because of its interest in trading along the river and in the trading posts (*escales*) that fed the maritime trade linking Saint Louis to France and the Atlantic world. This region attracted various groups of agents, traders, and interpreters from the French, métis, and African communities of Saint Louis. The ethnic groups that lived along the river also aspired to make some profit from this trade. Since the end of the eighteenth century, social and commercial relations between these various groups evolved, first through the trade in enslaved people and later the gum trade. Until the mid-nineteenth century, peanuts became the most profitable export product on the southern bank of the river. Chiefdoms that became centres of peanut production, such as Cayor, began to interest the French. The river was also the living thread linking the political entities and ethnic groups that predated the colonial era.[48]

The French colonization of West Africa was not a unitary process. It fluctuated. One conquest served as the starting point for the next. Paris was not supportive at the time. To get authorization for military campaigns, they had to be presented as defensive and as a reaction to hostility. Even then, the ministry in Paris focused on caution or even retreat.[49] Between 1817 and 1854, 30 governors ruled Senegal. Therefore, only the commercial elite of Saint Louis had any ongoing consecutive knowledge regarding local politics, and they were thus able to influence the policy of the under-secretary of the colonies (sous-secrétaire d'Etat aux colonies) in Paris.[50] Until the mid-nineteenth century, this elite managed to profit from the trade along the Senegal River while paying taxes to local leaders. Their profits then began to dwindle due to conflicts and wars that broke out along the river. These traders approached Paris and pressured for a strong and aggressive governor to be sent to Senegal with sufficient budget to return the river to order. Paris obliged and sent the governor who became known as the founder of French Senegal, Louis Faidherbe. The French conquest of Senegal relied on previous experience and knowledge gained in Algeria. Faidherbe had served in Algeria and implemented in Senegal what he had learned there. He changed the image of the European along the river from trader to soldier.

Along the lines of military expansion, Faidherbe also introduced some reforms in the administration and changed its relations with the Wolof on the coast. He gave the African soldiers serving the French a name—*Tirailleurs Sénégalais* (Senegalese Riflemen)—as well as a framework and *esprit de corps* that turned them into a force that later helped colonize West and Equatorial Africa as well as Madagascar on the other side of the continent. Faidherbe also established a school for chiefs' sons and interpreters and thus managed to train local manpower that expanded the colonial administration and assisted in its functioning. Faidherbe's major achievement was the creation of a Muslim francophile and self-confident community in Saint Louis.[51]

The area into which Faidherbe expanded French rule along the Senegal River was the Senegalo-Mauritanian zone, as David Robinson has termed this region, on the two banks of the river. Despite the ethnic division between Mauritania and Senegal and the paternalistic view of the groups living in Mauritania towards those living south of the river, this was one space in which cultural and commercial relations took place for several centuries, continuing into the twentieth century. This was the hinterland of the French colonial centre of Saint Louis, and this city served as the capital of both Mauritania and Senegal until the mid-twentieth century when the two colonies gained their independence.

In terms of social structure, before the French conquest the region was characterized by a hierarchical society headed by a political elite that provided protection to the inhabitants in return for taxes, while at the same time fighting with other groups in the region and enslaving people during these battles. Alongside the political elite, a commercial elite also headed this society. Under them were the artisanal classes or castes who worked with different materials, such as metal, wood, and leather. The griots, who were responsible for transmitting oral traditions and history, also belonged to this social layer. They had close ties with the ruling elites. At the bottom of the social structure were the enslaved people, but they possessed some degree of social mobility. It was possible to exit this class by emancipation, emigration, or escape. It was also possible to fall into it through defeat in battle. Even powerful rulers could become enslaved. Some enslaved people worked as bodyguards to important people and possessed much power. These warrior-soldiers were called *tiéddos* in Wolof and Pulaar and became notorious for their violent raids and alcohol-fuelled anarchic behaviour. The *tiéddos* were the antithesis of productive and pious Muslims. Occasionally, they managed to deploy their fighting abilities and their weapons for the benefit of powerful elites that were independent of their patrons.[52]

The entire system in the Senegalo-Mauritanian Zone was constructed on patron–client relations. Patrons needed supporters and the political and commercial elites kept forming coalitions and were constantly challenged by other competing alliances, often having to deal with secession or revolt. The only religion in the region was Islam, but it expressed itself in a variety of forms. There was no single religious and political authority. The scattered *marabouts* were those who held religious authority.[53]

After Faidherbe, there was a relatively quiet period in the region. The combination of political turmoil in France following the defeat by Prussia and outbreaks of diseases that slowed down French progress along the Senegal River forestalled the process of colonization. Nevertheless, the French continued to strengthen their institutions. They established the Division of the Interior (direction de l'intérieur), which mainly controlled the four communes, while the Division of Political Affairs was responsible for the protectorates.

In 1876, Brière de l'Isle was appointed governor of Senegal. He saw himself as Faidherbe's successor, and received much support from Paris. Brière de l'Isle focused on expansion to the east, and his successors completed the occupation and the creation of the territory known today as of Senegal. During the 1880s the railway line between Saint Louis and Dakar put an end to the semi-independence of the chiefdom of Cayor. The telegraph lines along the coast and the Senegal River and the opening of a steamboat line between Dakar and Bordeaux enforced French control over the colony. The final pockets of resistance in the Senegalo-Mauritanian Zone were finally defeated in 1890–1891, around the time Jeandet was assassinated. Fouta Toro was one of the regions that drew French attention and was deemed problematic.[54] This was the region in which Jeandet was most needed, and the one that sealed his fate.

During his work as a special envoy, Jeandet disclosed to his parents his personal view regarding several aspects of the French colonial policy that were not compatible with that of his superiors. He was especially critical regarding the French attitude to Islam, which was highly relevant to the turmoil in Fouta Toro. As a deeply religious man, he despised the secularism of the Third Republic and believed that the policymakers in Paris simply could not understand any religion, including Islam. Jeandet did not see Islam in general as a problem. His abhorrence of secularism and contempt towards the philosophers of the enlightenment influenced his ideas about Islam. In his letters, he often mentioned faith as one of the pillars upon which France was built, a true value, perhaps more than those of the

Third Republic—Liberty, Equality, and Fraternity. When Jeandet spoke of religion, he meant the Catholic faith. It is obvious that he saw his religion as inseparable from his patriotism. Religion for him was true patriotism. He kept asking his parents to pray for him and believed that their faith was keeping them strong in his absence.[55] But any religion for Jeandet, even Islam (as long as it was not fanatical according to his convictions), was superior to the values of the enlightenment, which he saw as the evil of his time. Thus, for example, in the following letter he expressed specific disdain for the two prominent philosophers of the enlightenment—Jean Jacques Rousseau and Voltaire. He saw his generation as badly influenced by their ideas, which made them unhealthy and alienated from their motherland. Faith in the will of God, for him, was the only answer to his parents' problems, as may be seen in the following quotation:

> I apply myself to the knowledge of the soul of the Koran which with the Gospel are the two books dictated by God through the voice of prophets, I become almost a philosopher—nothing of that dreadful J. Jacques [Rousseau] nor of that abominable Voltaire. For Muslim does not mean fatalist—which would be equivalent to an idiot, but a man subject to the will of God.—The more I go, the more I learn, the more I find myself ignorant and the more I think that this world is hardly worth the trouble that we give ourselves to hold a place [in it].[56]

In this pessimistic paragraph, we can see that Jeandet put religion (even Islam) above the politicians of the Third Republic who reward the undeserving and neglect the deserving—foremost, his parents. He also considered the holy books of both religions to be superior to the 'abominable' ideas of Rousseau and Voltaire.

Jeandet's sympathy for what he saw as non-fanatical Islam was reflected in his relationships with some of the local rulers, such as that of Diambour, who even offered him a beautiful Koran made of goat skin. Interestingly, this Koran somehow found its way to the Brandeis University library, where it can be found today along with a short note mentioning that it was offered to Jeandet by the ruler.[57] Jeandet also revealed much appreciation of the *tiéddos*, mentioned above, and heavily criticized French policy towards them.

The *tiéddo* warrior soldiers, as noted above, managed to accumulate power, and became notorious for violent raids and drinking alcohol excessively. According to an interview conducted by David

Robinson in 1968 in the Fouta region, the *tiéddos* had long roots in local history and were perceived by society in different ways. Some saw them as courageous; some simply treated them as having a specific skill: hunters or horsemen. Others saw them as mean people who became angry quickly but also forgot quickly. They were also seen as those who were the latest to convert to Islam.[58] Jeandet, in any case, admired the *tiéddos*. He was not deterred by their love of alcohol, despite the Muslim prohibition, but rather appreciated it. He told his parents how he shared his excellent cognac with the ruler of Diambour, explaining that, as a *tiéddo*, the latter could enjoy a glass of cognac without inhibition.[59] In another letter, he described the *tiéddos* as proud, adventurous, brave, and free. In other words, they were exemplars of the qualities that Jeandet believed to be essential for 'real men.' He emphasized again the *tiéddo* love for alcohol and their disobedience of Islamic leaders. He lamented the fact that French policy had been tending toward the destruction of the *tiéddos*, while encouraging their enemies, the *marabouts*. In 50 years, so he predicted, the *tiéddos* would disappear, and the French would be left with the fanatical, treacherous, horrible *marabouts*.[60]

Jeandet was certain that the French Islamic policy was wrong and even disastrous. He believed that the colonial authorities in Senegal as well as in Paris did not understand, as he did, the minds of the region's inhabitants. One of their gravest mistakes, in his opinion, was related to the issue of the migrations to the east encouraged by al-Hajj Umar and later by his son and successor, Sheiku Amadou. Both had encouraged the inhabitants of Fouta Toro to leave their lands, distance themselves from the French infidels, and join the Islamic state in Nioro (nowadays in the territory of Mali), which Umar had established. This migration worried the French as it undermined the stability in this region. Jeandet was convinced that the inhabitants of Fouta Toro did not leave their homes because they were fanatical Muslims who followed the call of al-Hajj Umar without thinking. He maintained that the only reason they were leaving was because of the cruelty of their ruler, Lam Toro Sidick.[61]

When Jeandet was assigned to administer the region of Fouta Toro from Podor in December 1887 he tended to blame Sidick for everything that he saw as wrong in the area and insisted that he had to be dethroned. He soon initiated a policy aimed at dismissing Sidick and weakening his successors.

Colonial arrogance and the turmoil in Fouta Toro

Jeandet arrived in Fouta Toro for the first time in December 1887 and stayed there until his first and only vacation in France, ten months later. After returning from France, he was posted in Saint Louis and other regions. In July 1890 he was sent to Fouta Toro again to replace Administrator Pagès, who was losing control over the situation, at least according to his superiors. Jeandet's decisions during his first stay in Fouta Toro were crucial to understanding the circumstances of his assassination five weeks after he was sent to save the day in 1890. These decisions need to be examined in view of the history of this region.

The Fouta region is a 400-kilometre long and 20-kilometre wide area along both sides of the Senegal River. The western side is called Toro, or Fouta Toro, and this is the area that was ruled by the Lam Toros. The central region of Fouta included other chiefdoms, such as Bossea, which Jeandet was trying to conquer at the time he was murdered. The land of Fouta Toro was extremely fertile, and the region was (and still is) agriculturally the richest in Senegambia and Mauritania. It had two growing seasons every year and, during its history, it exported grain to other regions. This territory was, therefore, highly attractive to outsiders. The Fouta Toro was located along the Middle Valley, an area difficult to rule due to its narrow geography and the frequent raids at the hands of its nomadic neighbours. Fear of these raids led most inhabitants to reside on the Senegalese side of the river, even though the Mauritanian side was just as fertile.[62]

Ethnically speaking, the region of Fouta Toro was diverse. It attracted fragments of several ethnic groups that sought protection for various reasons: Soninke from the east, Wolof from the west, Moors from the north and Fulbe from the south. The combined fragments of these groups gave birth to a new ethnic group, Tokolor, that formed the majority of Fouta Toro's population. Around the period under discussion, about 260,000 people inhabited the Middle Valley, of whom 60 per cent were Tokolor, 30 per cent were Fulbe, and the rest were divided among the other ethnic groups. These numbers are probably significantly lower than those of the mid-nineteenth century, as the population dwindled due to migrations to the north and the cholera epidemic of 1868–1869.

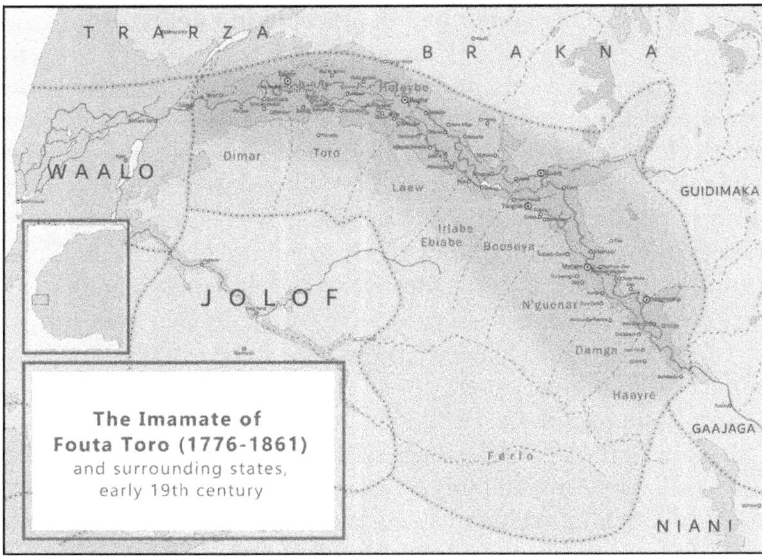

Map 1.2 Fouta Toro

The Tokolor were sedentary Pulaar-speakers, different from the pastoralist Fulbe. The ruling elite of Fouta Toro came from among them. The members of this elite were called TorodBe. They viewed non-Pulaar speakers as inferior to them and referred to them as 'blacks.'[63]

As mentioned above, one of the most serious concerns of the French during the second half of the nineteenth century was the attempt by al-Hajj Umar to encourage the inhabitants of Fouta Toro to migrate to the east to his state, Nioro, away from the French presence and trade. Although he encountered some resistance initially, he eventually succeeded in persuading many to leave Fouta Toro. These migrations worried the French, as they eroded the population they were trying to rule, brought hunger, and damaged trade. As noted, after Umar's death in 1866, his son and successor Sheiku Ahmadou continued to encourage these migrations.[64]

The migrations and the weakness of Fouta Toro encouraged the French to establish protectorates in the eastern and western parts of the chiefdom. As discussed, the protectorate was an inexpensive form of administration, in which the French could be in charge yet leave local leaders with all the hard work of daily administration. Legally speaking, it was also very convenient, as French law did not apply in the protectorates. A commandant was sent to the town that the French saw as the centre of a protectorate with a local garrison. This commandant served as the administrator of the protectorate. He enjoyed some autonomy as it was difficult for the central administration in Saint Louis to control all his actions and decisions.

The protectorates were established with the cooperation of local chiefs who agreed to respect the rights of French subjects in their respective areas. In theory they would also elect the ruler of the area, who would control it according to custom. In practice, however, things were quite different. In one of Jeandet's letters he describes the process of election, emphasizing that the final choice had to be confirmed by the administrator.[65] The elected chief, therefore, was often controlled by the French administrator and ruled according to French interests. The elected chief's legitimacy was often fragile as he usually came from a lineage that the TorodBe regime opposed, and therefore was left no option but to collaborate with the French.[66]

The region of Western Fouta, in which the chiefdom of Toro was the most important stronghold, drew French attention. The concentration of French interests in the Lower Senegal and the direct relations of the area with the Wolof states made the French consider it as part of their effective sphere of influence.[67] Therefore, in April 1859 the French signed a treaty with the main leaders of Toro that recognized the independence of the province from the Islamic dynasty known as the Almamate that was responsible for selecting its rulers. The treaty also obligated these leaders to refuse asylum to the enemies of the French administration in Saint Louis. In the mid-nineteenth century, the Lam Toro of Guédé, Toro's capital, exercised limited power over the Tokolor and the Fulbe. He was chosen from either branch of the Sall family. In theory, the two dynasties, Dethye and Hamady Ngaye, were supposed to alternate in power, but the Dethye dynasty was more powerful in the nineteenth century.[68] When Jeandet arrived in Podor in 1887, the elected ruler of Toro was Lam Toro Sidick Sall from the Dethye branch. He ruled the area from 1882. Jeandet saw Sidick as a major threat to French efforts to control the region and blamed him for being cruel to his subjects. He therefore saw Sidick's dismissal as his main task.[69]

'Yesterday at five o'clock in the evening I had smashed a king, this morning at eight o'clock I will have made another; the old one was Lam Toro Sidirek [sic], the new one will be Lam Toro Amady Notago! I am, as you see, Warwick on a small-scale.'[70] With these words, Jeandet opened his letter where he proudly told his parents how he had managed to dispose of an unwanted ruler for the sake of another, whom he had preferred. He compared himself to Richard Neville, the earl of Warwick who demoted Henry VI in 1461, putting Edward IV on the English throne. Nine years later, Warwick reversed his actions, restoring Henry VI—only to be defeated by Edward IV at the Battle of Barnet in 1471.[71]

This pompous comparison to a fifteenth-century English earl reflects Jeandet's sense of power as an administrator in Senegal. He went on to describe to his parents how he performed his shrewd plan and changed the political reality in Fouta Toro. Only nine days after arriving in Podor, so he bragged, he reunited the 18 chiefs in charge of the Lam's election, listened to dignitaries, clarified a tangled situation, released four free men who had been enslaved, and imposed a certain order around Fouta Toro. And he achieved all this, in his view, without committing any gross injustice towards any of the chiefs. The elections, according to Jeandet were peaceful, unlike those of French radical politicians. 'I worked as an artist' (Je l'avais travaillée en artiste), so Jeandet wrote. He went on to describe the election process. He gathered all voters in his living room to ensure their liberty to vote as they chose. Each chief wrote his name and the name of his candidate on a piece of paper, folded it in four and inserted it in Jeandet's helmet. His preferred candidate, Hamady Nogato, won 16 votes while his adversary, whom Jeandet disliked, won two. None of the electors voted for Sidick.[72]

In a formal report that Jeandet sent to the director of political affairs after these improvised elections, he elaborated on the situation that caused him to displace Sidick and the process by which he had chosen to do so. He explained that Lam Toro Sidick committed many unjust acts towards his chiefs and the entire population of Fouta Toro. According to Jeandet, Sidick revived old customs that the French had abolished, and extorted exaggerated sums of money from the village chiefs. He also enslaved people who were supposed to be free according to local customs or by French decree. All these acts were made possible because Sidick knew how to take advantage of the political rivalries between various families to reinforce his position and overcome resistance. Jeandet explained in his report that the Lam Toro was chosen from the two rival families. The four most recent Lams came from the Dethyé Sall family and, therefore, Sidick felt that his family was to rule Fouta Toro forever. Jeandet conveyed his conviction—one he had also shared with his parents—that the true motive behind the emigration from Fouta Toro was the desire to escape Sidick's supposedly cruel rule. He was certain, therefore, that Sidick's dismissal would not cause rebellion, but rather joy.

It is most likely, though, that Sidick was no crueller than any of the other local rulers with whom Jeandet enjoyed sharing a glass of cognac. The hostility Jeandet developed towards Sidick was probably a result of the latter's power and status as well as his refusal to play by the French rules. While there were obviously local people and chiefs who were happy to see Sidick go, there were others who felt resentment toward the French following his dismissal. These were not only his African supporters but also Gaspard Devès, whose commercial business depended on Sidick. We must also doubt Jeandet's enthusiastic description of the elections he had conducted and his claim that they were more just and free than those in Metropolitan France. Jeandet was considered a powerful administrator, and the threat of violence, if not actual violence, was always in the air. Elections conducted in the administrator's living room, with his helmet, which he used in military campaigns, as a ballot box, were far from assuring free choice.[73]

Jeandet was not content with Sidick's dismissal. Although he had trusted Nogato, he did not want to allow him the same power as his predecessor. He therefore reduced his authority in several ways. He limited the Lam Toro's right to extract gifts from his chiefs. The Lam Toro was no longer allowed to dismiss chiefs without the administrator's permission. The colonial administration could veto appointments of village chiefs. Finally, Nogato had to accept any changes that the administration might wish to make to the treaty of annexation of 1 September 1863.[74]

Towards the end of the 1880s, the French began to feel more confident and replaced their policy of collaboration with local rulers—such as Abdul Bokar, who ruled eastern and central Fouta, and who was mentioned in Jeandet's list of missions that he shared

Figure 1.3 The district commander's house in Podor—view from the fort (photo: Eyal Ginio)

with his parents—with direct conquest and the establishment of protectorates. By the end of 1888 all western Senegal, except Jolof, was in French hands, and protectorates were established along the northern valley of the Gambia River. At this stage, Clément Thomas, who held an expansionist policy, became governor and was supported by Louis Archinard, the superior commandant of Senegal who was a leading figure in French imperialism.[75]

Jeandet remained in Podor until September 1888, occasionally leaving on short missions in the area. In October 1888 he was at last entitled to a vacation and he left for France. In March 1889, while his parents were still enjoying the last days of his company, Jeandet's favourite Lam Toro, Hamady Nogato, died suddenly; the French suspected that he had been poisoned, although no proof was provided to support this view. Sidi Abdul, Sidick's cousin, was nominated in his stead and the situation in Fouta Toro became unstable. Fearing loss of control, the governor sent Jeandet back to Podor in July 1890 to replace Pagès, the métis district commander in whom the governor of Senegal had lost confidence.[76]

In his last letter, sent to his cousin Amédée on 31 August 1890, Jeandet wrote that he was about to leave on a military campaign against Abdoul Bokar, the ruler of Bossea.[77] This was an attempt to finally subdue Fouta Toro and bring it firmly under French control. Two days later Baidy Kaccé shot Jeandet to death. The administrator's assassination was a severe blow to the French administration in Senegal and constituted a real challenge to their authority in the region. The next chapter examines the French reaction to the murder and the process that led to the brutal executions on the bank of the Senegal River.

Notes

1 Henri Bernard Gausseron, *Un Français au Sénégal* (Paris: Librarie Ancienne Honore Champion Editeur Edouard Champion, 1913), 2.
2 *Ibid.*
3 Alphonse Bertillon invented a system of identifying lawbreakers according to the measurements of their facial features and the distances between those features. He fell from fame after testifying in the Dreyfus trial that Dreyfus had indeed written the *bordereau*, even though his expertise did not extend to graphology. See Ruth Harris, *Dreyfus: Politics, Emotion, and the Scandal of the Century* (New York: Metropolitan Books, 2010), 23.
4 Gausseron, *Un Français*, 4.
5 Gausseron, *Un Français*, 14.
6 Archives de Saône-et-Loire, François Joseph Etienne Abel Jeandet, F 1413, Saint-Louis, 8 June 1889.
7 Gausseron, *Un Français*, 203.
8 Archives de Saône-et-Loire, François Joseph Etienne Abel Jeandet, F 1413, Saint-Louis, 20 December 1886.
9 Gausseron, *Un Français*, 9.
10 On General Van der Meere, see: Auguste Louis Nicolas Vandermeere, *Mémoires du général comte Van der Meere* (Bruxelles: C. Muquardt, 1880).
11 Archives de Saône-et-Loire, François Joseph Etienne Abel Jeandet, F 1413, Saint-Louis, le 7 April 1888.
12 Gausseron, *Un Français*, 12–13.
13 Robert Aldrich, 'Colonial Man,' in *French Masculinities. History, Culture and Politics* (2007), 124.
14 William B. Cohen, *Rulers of Empire: The French Colonial Service in Africa* (Stanford: Hoover Institution Press, 1971), 13–15.
15 Cohen, *Rulers of Empire*, 16.

16 Claire Zalc and Tal Bruttmann, *Microhistories of the Holocaust* (New York & Oxford: Berghahn Books, 2022), 4–5.
17 Hélène de Burgh, *Sex, Sailors and Colonies* (Bern: Peter Lang, 2005). www.peterlang.com/view/title/9707, 13.
18 Pierre Loti, *Le roman d'un spahi* (Paris: Calman-Lévi, 1881).
19 Brazza and Soleillet represent two different types of colonial explorers. While Brazza signed contracts with local leaders and transferred their sovereignty to the French government, Soleillet wished to open Africa to trade by peaceful means without colonial oversight. For both explorers, see: Julien Gauthier, 'La société de géographie commerciale de Bordeaux: sur les traces des explorateurs entre 1874 et 1911,' *Dynamiques environnementales. Journal international de géosciences et de l'environnement*, no. 39–40 (2017).
20 Un rayon de gloire briller au front de son enfant (all translations are mine).
21 J'ai confiance en mon étoile et en moi, me sentant un mâle au milieu de nos générations maladives.
22 Et toi, père bien aimé, tu seras heureux, car ton fils unique sera un des pionniers de cette civilisation de de ce progrès pour lesquels tu as toujours combattu. Sur ce drapeau de la France, que mes mains planteront, sera inscrit pour le bon le mot de Liberté! Gausseron, *Un Français*, 12–13 (a letter from Jeandet to his father, 15 September 1886).
23 Aviel Roshwald, 'Colonial Dreams of the French Right Wing, 1881–1914,' *The Historian* 57 (1994), www.tandfonline.com/doi/abs/10.1111/j.1540-6563.1994.tb01334.x.3 (Accessed 2 April 2025).
24 Aldrich, 'Colonial Man,' 124–125; 136.
25 Aldrich, 'Colonial Man,' 129.
26 See, for example: Archives de Saône-et-Loire, François Joseph Etienne Abel Jeandet, F 1413, 12 February 1890.
27 *Ibid*, 19 June 1887.
28 *Ibid*, 22 June 1887.
29 Laissons tomber les croix et les faveurs sur les indignes—aujourd'hui l'homme est fou! *Ibid*, 12 November 1889.
30 *Ibid*, 15 March 1890.
31 Elizabeth Foster, *Faith in Empire: Religion Politics, and Colonial Rule in French Senegal* (Stanford: Stanford University Press, 2013), 13.
32 Alain Sinou, *Comptoirs et villes coloniales du Sénégal: Saint-Louis. Gorée, Dakar* (1993), 82–84.
33 Archives de Saône-et-Loire, François Joseph Etienne Abel Jeandet, F 1412, 27 November 1886.
34 Du progrès sans secousse, sans violence, sans protestation et sans révolte. 'Inauguration du chemin de fer de Dakar à Saint Louis,' *Moniteur du Sénégal et dépendances, Journal officiel*, 186.

35 *Ibid*, 187.
36 Liora Bigon, 'Urban Planning, Colonial Doctrines and Street Naming in French Dakar and British Lagos, C. 1850–1930,' *Urban History* 36, no. 3 (2009), 431. On the debate between investment in the railway from Dakar and Saint Louis and the reliance on waterways, see: Margaret O McLane, 'Railways or Waterways: The Dakar Railway Network and the Senegal River in the "Mise En Valeur" of French West Africa' (paper presented at the Proceedings of the Meeting of the French Colonial Historical Society, 1992).
37 Bigon, 'Urban Planning,' 431.
38 C'est une ville encore à construire et dont le plan est fait; elle est située en face de Gorée et ne possède guère qu'une vingtaine de maisons européennes, la plus part en bois. Archives de Saône-et-Loire, François Joseph Etienne Abel Jeandet, F 1412, 27 November 1886.
39 *Ibid*, 7 December 1886.
40 David Robinson, *Paths of Accommodation: Muslim Societies and French Colonial Authorities in Senegal and Mauritania, 1880–1920* (2000), 98.
41 David Robinson, *Chiefs and Clerics: Abdul Bokar Kan and Futa Toro, 1853–1891* (Oxford: Clarendon Press, 1975), 33.
42 G. W. Johnson, *The Emergence of Black Politics in Senegal: The Struggle for Power in the Four Communes, 1900–1920* (Stanford: Stanford University Press, for the Hoover Institution on War, Revolution and Peace, 1971), 44–45.
43 Sheldon Gellar, *Democracy in Senegal: Tocqevillian Analytics in Africa* (New York: Palgrave, 2005), 39; Hilary Jones, 'Rethinking Politics in the Colony: The Métis of Senegal and Urban Politics in the Late Nineteenth and Early Twentieth Century,' *The Journal of African History* 53, no. 3 (2012), 334. The other three communes were Dakar, Gorée, and Rufisque.
44 Foster, *Faith in Empire: Religion Politics, and Colonial Rule in French Senegal*, 14.
45 Robinson, *Chiefs and Clerics*, 31–32.
46 Joseph-Simon Gallieni (1849–1916) was a distinguished French army officer who successfully directed the occupation of French Sudan and Madagascar during this period. More on Gallieni see: C. M. Andrew and A. S. Kanya-Forstner, 'The Groupe Colonial in the French Chamber of Deputies, 1892–1932,' *The Historical Journal* 17, no. 4 (1974).
47 Archives de Saône-et-Loire, François Joseph Etienne Abel Jeandet, F 1412, 25 September 1887. On the figure of Abdoul Bokar and the challenges he presented to the French see: Robinson, *Chiefs and Clerics*.

48 Tamba M'bayo, *Muslim Interpreters in Colonial Senegal, 1850–1920: Mediations of Knowledge and Power in the Lower and Middle Senegal River Valley* (Lanham: Lexington Books, 2016), viii–ix.
49 Robinson, *Paths of Accommodation*, 58.
50 Until 1894, the colonies were under the ministry of the navy, and an under-secretary was responsible for them. Robinson, *Paths of Accommodation*, 60.
51 Robinson, *Chiefs and Clerics*, 33; Robinson, *Paths of Accommodation*, 61.
52 Robinson, *Paths of Accommodation*, 11–15.
53 *Ibid*, 16.
54 *Ibid*, 63.
55 See, for example: Archives de Saône-et-Loire, François Joseph Etienne Abel Jeandet, F 1413, 20 December 1886, 13 January 1888.
56 *Ibid*, Tivavouane, 12 November 1889.
57 I am grateful to Sean Beebe who wrote to me after hearing a presentation I had delivered in the FCHS meeting in Montreal in 2019 about this Koran that is in the possession of Brandeis's library in which he had worked at the time.
58 Special Collections, Michigan State University, David Robinson's Collections, Box 8, Folder 2.
59 Archives de Saône-et-Loire, François Joseph Etienne Abel Jeandet, F 1413, Saint Louis, 21 January 1887.
60 *Ibid*, 5 May 1890.
61 *Ibid*, 13 January 1888.
62 Robinson, *Chiefs and Clerics*, 1–3.
63 *Ibid*, 5–7.
64 *Ibid*, 46–51.
65 Archives de Saône-et-Loire, François Joseph Etienne Abel Jeandet, F 1412, 5 January 1888.
66 Robinson, *Chiefs and Clerics*, 51–52.
67 *Ibid*, 79.
68 *Ibid*, 79.
69 Daha Chérif Ba, Crimes *Et Délits Dans La Vallée Du Fleuve* Sénégal *De* 1810 à 1970 (Paris: Editions L'Harmattan, 2010), 235.
70 Hier à cinq heures du soir j'avais brisé un roi, ce matin à huit heures j'en aurai fait un autre; l'ancien était le Lam Toro Sidirek, le nouveau sera le Lam Toro Amady Notago! Je suis vous le voyez un vrai Warvick au petit pied. Archives de Saône-et-Loire, François Joseph Etienne Abel Jeandet, F 1412, 30 December 1887.
71 On the Earl of Warwick see: Michael K. Jones, 'Edward IV, the Earl of Warwick and the Yorkist Claim to the Throne,' *Historical*

Research 70, no. 173 (1997), 342–352. I would like to thank Denis Charbit for his assistance in following Jeandet's reference.

72 Archives de Saône-et-Loire, François Joseph Etienne Abel Jeandet, F 1412, 30 December 1887.

73 According to Saddick Sall, Sidick was one of the voters. Therefore, the fact that no one supposedly voted for him, not even he himself, makes these elections quite dubious. Interview with Saddick Sall, Dakar, 21 March 2024.

74 Archives de Saône-et-Loire, François Joseph Etienne Abel Jeandet, F 1412, 5 January 1888.

75 Robinson, *Chiefs and Clerics*, 149–158.

76 CAOM, Sénégal I 90, 5 August, 1890.

77 See note 45.

2

The murder and its consequences

Jeandet's murder came as a shock to the French administration in Saint Louis. As we have seen, he was no usual administrator. His credentials were much better than any other administrator at the time, and he was certainly an unusual candidate for this difficult job. When the situation in Fouta Toro became unstable, the only person considered suitable to solve the crisis was Jeandet. His murder, then, left a big hole in the administrative machinery of the growing French empire at a time when administrative talent was extremely needed. The French administration at the time was not in a strong position. Such an act of open resistance as the murder of an administrator put it in a very fragile place. There was great concern that this was just the beginning of a large-scale rebellion. It was this fear and relative weakness that led to the excessive response to the murder. The French were operating in a new territory away from Saint Louis, which had been under their rule since the seventeenth century. They believed that they operated under different rules and therefore acted as they never would have in their old empire. To understand the scandal and the legal debates around it, it is therefore necessary to examine closely the administrative actions that followed Jeandet's murder—the investigation and the eventual illegal executions that led to an 18-month-long scandal and a real challenge to the French colonial administration.

The murder and its investigation

In August 1890, Governor De Lamothe ordered Jeandet to open a military campaign against Abdoul Bokar, the ruler of Bossea. This campaign was supposed to be decisive in the French attempt to control the entire area of the Fouta. As we have seen in Chapter 1, Jeandet mentioned his success in attaining Bokar's cooperation in one of his letters to his parents. But this achievement was limited. Bokar was not an easy challenge. He had wielded significant influence in Fouta Toro's political landscape prior to French conquest, thanks to his proclaimed personal attributes, such as generosity and political insight, as well as his status in Bossea, a region controlling Fouta. His esteemed dynasty further bolstered his prominence. Despite being encouraged by al-Hajj Umar to join the emigration from Fouta Toro, Bokar declined, recognizing that he would be marginalized in any reform movement. Instead, he envisioned his most optimistic future in Fouta, utilizing the network of alliances created by his grandfather and father. Following the Umarian exodus, Bokar found himself strategically positioned to participate in Foutanke politics. The departure of leaders in the 1850s created a vacuum, and their successors, influenced or compromised by the exodus from Umar or acceptance of French expansion, had diminished impact.

Bokar reached the apogee of his power in 1885. The French were paying him an annual sum of 2,500 francs so that he would allow them to construct a telegraph line through his territory. They acknowledged him as the dominant ruler of central and eastern Fouta. When Clément Thomas became governor in April 1888, his conquest ambitions led him to confront Bokar, who refused to cooperate. This refusal drove the French to physically subdue territories that were not yet under their direct rule, including those Bokar ruled.[1]

On 2 September 1890 Jeandet was on his way to confront Bokar. According to a report formulated three months after the murder, Jeandet began this campaign on the first day he had regained his forces after a long period of sickness that had confined him to bed. The moment Jeandet felt better, Clément Thomas had sent him to the campaign against Abdoul Bokar, who had found refuge on the Mauritanian side of the river. The governor was concerned that Bokar was planning to push the French away from the region with the help of Sheiku Ahmadou (al-Hajj Umar's son) and the people of Guédé and saw this campaign as a good opportunity to examine the effects of Jeandet's reform in Fouta Toro. He ordered Jeandet to assemble the Toro contingents near the telegraph post of Aeré and, from there, onto the other side of the river in Bossea. Jeandet assembled 400 troops from among the local villages within four days.[2]

Jeandet's recruited force was camping in Aeré in anticipation of the governor's instructions and due to the difficult weather conditions. It is impossible to know what exactly happened that morning, but there are several facts all accounts agree on. Around 9 a.m., while Jeandet was in his cabin, taking refuge from the heavy rain, an interpreter by the name of Boubakar Abdoul appeared along with one of the force's soldiers, a man called Baidy Kaccé. The exact conversation that followed remains unclear, but the visit's aim was to report to Jeandet that Kaccé was acting in a rebellious manner. Jeandet imposed a certain punishment on Kaccé. In some accounts Kaccé was sent to join the porters for the day. In other accounts, Jeandet had ordered that Kaccé, in addition, be flogged. What is relatively certain is that Kaccé was indeed sent to join the porters and was asked to leave his weapon behind. Instead of obeying, Kaccé shot Jeandet several times—there are different versions as to how many times, varying between three and seven. It is also unclear whether Jeandet returned to his hammock before Kaccé came back to kill him or just stood with his back to the entrance smoking a cigarette.

The shooting caused a commotion, and several people rushed into the cabin. According to some witnesses, Boubakar Abdoul prevented a policeman by the name of Karounga from shooting at Kaccé, thus allowing the latter to escape. As we shall see, one of the greatest mysteries around the murder, in addition to Kaccé's real motive, was the role Boubakar Abdoul played in it. Abdoul had worked as an interpreter for Jeandet in the past but was replaced by Abdoulaye Kane, who was pivotal in the subsequent investigation of the murder.[3]

According to the official report, Abdoulaye Kane was the one who rushed to Jeandet, trying to extinguish the flames on his shirt—ignited by the gunfire—and making a desperate but unsuccessful attempt to save his life. At his order, several chiefs, including Abdoul Sidi, the Lam Toro, who was Sidick Sall's cousin, went on horseback after the killer. Kaccé was caught 24 hours later in Golléré, a village between Podor and Matam, by one of these chiefs, a man called Ardo Mbantou.[4]

At the time of Jeandet's murder, there was in Senegal no established apparatus for investigating crimes. The only justice system was that of Saint Louis, which was a replica of the French metropolitan system. The Jeandet murder was, therefore, one of the first cases, if not the very first, in the newly conquered territories, that the French administration had to investigate. According to Thaïs Gendry, in later years, after the establishment of a parallel justice system for colonial subjects in 1903, murder investigations were under the responsibility of the district commander, who was heavily dependent on members of local society. Gendry argues that the canton or village chief usually reported to the district commander when a suspicious death took place. These chiefs were also the intermediaries between the commander and the population, and they conducted the investigation on the commander's behalf. The chiefs interviewed witnesses, located suspects, and usually decided who among them should be brought before the commander. Based on these chiefs' inquiries, declarations, and testimonies—which the district commander rarely disputed, unless he suspected that the confessions were obtained through violence—he decided whether a suspect should be brought to trial, over which he himself presided. Usually, as Gendry demonstrates, the only thing left for the district commander to do was to bring a medical expert to examine the body. All the rest was done by the village or canton chief. The commander had to judge the case according to the information the canton chief provided him with.[5]

The investigation of Jeandet's murder was even more questionable than those described by Gendry. An autopsy was out of the question, not only because of the lack of means to conduct it, but also because the identity of the murderer was no mystery. Chiefs could not be used as intermediaries because they were mostly not trusted by the French administration. The time dedicated to the entire investigation was especially short. When a designated team, headed by a 35-year-old marine captain by the name of Pineau, arrived at Podor on 6 September, the investigation was in fact already concluded. All Pineau was left to do was write his report.[6]

The key figure in the investigation was Jeandet's interpreter Abdoulaye Kane. One of the suspects was the interpreter, Boubakar Abdoul, who had brought Kaccé to Jeandet on that fatal morning. As interpreters were so dominant in the investigation, and later when the murder turned into a full-blown affair in Saint Louis, before we delve into how the dubious investigation unfolded, it is vital to pay attention to these intermediaries' important role during the French colonization of Senegal.

Jeandet and the other administrators could not operate without the assistance of interpreters. Despite French presence on the coast of Senegal since the seventeenth century, they never bothered to learn the local languages. Out of concern with this situation, the influential governor of Senegal, Louis Faidherbe, established a division of local interpreters and translators in 1856 to work for the administration, as well as a school aimed to train them. He also deployed another means to overcome the linguistic and cultural divide between French administrators and the local population. He established a form of marriage which he termed '*mariage à la mode du pays*' and encouraged administrators to take an African wife. This was a temporary alliance, valid only as long as the French husband remained in the colony. Faidherbe practised what he preached and took a 15-year-old Peul wife who bore him a child.[7]

Faidherbe's school was at first called Ecole d'Otages (School of Hostages) because it was intended for the children of African chiefs' families who had been sent to Saint Louis according to the precolonial practice of holding relatives as guarantees in financial or political transactions. The school was closed in 1871 and later reopened in 1894 under the more respectable name of Ecole des fils de chefs et des interprètes (School for Chiefs' Sons and Interpreters).[8] The primary mission of the school's graduates was to help French trade along the Senegal River. However, the French administrators also used them in courts and as assistants in their daily work and in military campaigns. In northern Senegal most, if not all, interpreters were Muslim, but they came from different ethnicities and social backgrounds. They also possessed different levels of competence, proficiency in languages, and integrity.[9]

During the early stages of French colonial expansion, interpreters held enormous power, as most of the African population had not yet learned French. As knowledge of French slowly expanded, the interpreters lost some of their control, but remained critical intermediary figures in the colonial system. In the period under discussion, hardly any Africans living in the hinterland could speak or understand French. French administrators remained ignorant of local languages throughout the colonial period. The lack of proficiency in African languages was not only the result of arrogance or paternalism. The French system of transferring administrators every few years from one post to another, sometimes even on a different continent, made the effort of learning an African language seem pointless. Once an administrator had learned to say a few sentences in the local language, his superiors might send him where this language was of no use.[10]

The interpreters who operated in Senegal in the second half of the nineteenth century were figures who could traverse the colonial divide. They mediated between French interests and competing African interests during a politically unstable period characterized by deep uncertainty. While working for the French colonial administration, they also tried to maintain their own interests as well as those of their communities. In this sense, they were not simply collaborators with the colonial regimes.[11] Interpreters were also cultural brokers. They not only transferred words and sentences from one language to another. In the colonial scenario, they became the bridge between cultures. While this is true for any translation work, for interpreters in colonial Senegal, mediating between French and Africans involved the transmission of ideologies, concepts, and moral principles.[12]

Our knowledge of interpreters in the French colonial sphere is limited, as archival documents on interpreters are slim and incomplete. Also, most of the manoeuvres that African interpreters could perform were unknown to administrators. They often suspected interpreters, but had no way of knowing whether they were being misled and, if so, how. The colonial administrators, who produced the sources that we now find in the archives, could not have known the most intriguing information about their interpreters. They had no idea how interpreters chose to translate cultural ideas, whether they omitted or changed the narratives of both sides while mediating between them, whether they were loyal to their employers, to their communities or to themselves alone.

This lacuna in the colonial archives turns Amadou Hampaté Ba's semi-autobiographical novel, *The Fortunes of Wangrin,* into a significant source for understanding the role and figure of the interpreter.[13] Tamba M'Bayo, the author of the most extensive study on interpreters in the French colonial system, maintains that this well-known novel, describing the manipulations of an interpreter at the early stages of French colonial rule, distorted the image of the colonial interpreter. It generalized an idea of the dishonest interpreter who thinks only of himself. M'Bayo attempts to offer a more detailed analysis of the colonial interpreter's roles, activities, and characteristics.[14]

The role of Jeandet's personal interpreter, Abdoulaye Kane, in the investigation of his patron's murder was crucial. He had the power of deciding how to translate to the French administrators the testimonies of witnesses and suspects. He was also the one who translated Baidy Kaccé's confessions. Abdoulaye Kane replaced Jeandet's personal interpreter, Boubakar Abdoul, whom Jeandet had dismissed in 1887. Kane was trained in Saint Louis and was highly appreciated by Jeandet. A few months before his murder, Jeandet described Kane to his parents: 'My interpreter is a very intelligent young man, son, and brother of interpreters. I think he will be a good servant, and I am pleased with him.'[15] It is evident from the letters Kane sent Jeandet when the latter was on vacation in France that he felt quite at ease writing to his superior. The letters he wrote also demonstrate his strong command of French, a skill not shared by all interpreters at the time. An interpreter by the name of Silly Diawar from Thiès, for example, had to use Kane's services to write his own letter to Jeandet in February 1888.[16]

Kane was crucial in the investigation, both as a witness and an investigator although he was hardly the neutral person needed for the job. He had family relations with some of the people involved in the affair. As we have seen, Boubakar Abdoul, Jeandet's former interpreter, who was one of the main suspects, was his rival. He was therefore far from being an impartial investigator. His unsuitability for the job did not bother Captain Pineau, the French officer assigned to conduct the investigation.[17] Kane was apparently the only person he was willing to entrust with this delicate mission.

Kane talked to witnesses but also to people who were absent from the scene of the crime. He asked them for their views about the ostensible involvement of Sidick Sall and Mamadou Yoro in the alleged conspiracy. The information he gathered from informants in Fouta Toro helped the French establish their case against the two dignitaries.[18] We have no way of knowing whether the translation of Kaccé's confession was accurate. Perhaps it was, but Kane had incredible power to formulate the information he gathered in any way he pleased. The trust that he had earned from Jeandet influenced the way other administrators saw him. They all believed he was beyond suspicion. Aubry-Lecomte even emphasized in his report Kane's deep shock and sorrow at the time of the murder. He was so devastated that he was unable to escort Jeandet's body to Podor; he followed four hours later. Kane's decision to stay behind for four hours could have been interpreted as suspicious, perhaps as a way to get rid of evidence or compare testimonies with other witnesses. But no suspicions were aroused. Abdoulaye Kane's innocence was beyond doubt. The French trusted him, maybe in part because they could not manage without him.

Pineau had arrived in Podor on board the boat *Richard Toll*, with an administrator by the name of Martin, on 6 September at 4 PM. He then learned from Riquetty, an interim administrator, who was formerly a post employee, that Jeandet's funeral had taken place the day before, and that Kaccé was held in the administrative post of Podor having already been interrogated by Riquetty with the help of Jeandet's interpreter Kane. Before Kaccé was caught, immediately after the murder, an earlier interrogation of the people who had witnessed the event had taken place. Immediately after Kaccé's confession, Kane was sent on a mission to collect testimonies from local dignitaries to verify Kaccé's claims. This was not a thorough or well-organized investigation. Kane conducted it while travelling during the night from Aeré to Podor. He then provided Pineau with materials to base his report on. Pineau, who was not present in any of the investigation's stages, combined the materials in his report and added some analysis of his own of the main suspects and their motives.

According to Pineau's report, Baidy Kaccé confessed in several stages. The first time was even before he was interrogated. When Ardo Mbantou, a village chief from the Toro region, who was one of the people who had chased Baidy Kaccé after the murder, finally caught him, Mbantou tied Kaccé's hands with extreme force, hurting Kaccé, who then cried out that he had not acted alone, and that Ardo Mbantou had given him the bullets. While he was led to Podor, Kaccé was reported to have shouted: 'May God curse Boubakar Sidick' (Que Dieu maudisse Boubakar Sidirck!), a shout that was interpreted as accusing the ex-Lam Toro.

When Kaccé was brought to Podor, Riquetty conducted the interrogation and Kane was present as an interpreter. At first, Kaccé bragged about killing an infidel, but later he changed his testimony. Pineau did not mention the measures taken during the interrogation, but we can assume it was not conducted in a very polite manner. Violence was probably exercised. Nevertheless, the confessions were probably not invented nor extracted through violence alone. According to Pineau, Kaccé mentioned three names in his confession—Ardo Mbantou, who had captured Kaccé, Sidick Sall, and the latter's cousin Mamadou Yoro. Kaccé repeated this confession several times, the last time being just an hour before the execution, when Pineau told him he was to be decapitated and therefore would not reach heaven.[19]

There is some reason to suspect that Kaccé's confession was genuine. Only two of the people mentioned were accepted as true culprits and one, the interpreter who brought Kaccé to Jeandet, Boubakar Abdoul, was added by Pineau to the list of suspects even though he was not mentioned at all. Pineau did not believe Ardo Mbantou was involved, but he was certain that Abdoul was. If Riquetty had invented the confession or extracted it by force from Kaccé, then why include in it a person Pineau was convinced to be innocent and remove one he had suspected?

Pineau opened his report by analysing the figure of the murderer. It is obvious that he had felt some sort of admiration for Kaccé, at least physically. He opened his description with these words: 'Baidy Kaccé is about 24 years old, big, well built, muscular, this is an athlete with a herculean force.' But the admiration ended there. He continued to describe Kaccé's character without mentioning his sources, which were probably rumours conveyed to him by Kane. Pineau portrayed Kaccé as a person who had lost his mind following a wrestling match. He noted that everyone considered him to be crazy, and that he used to go into villages pretending he was a lion. This assertion should be taken with a grain of salt, as lion might have been Kaccé's nickname, or the animal that was associated with him. Although Kaccé had recovered from his insanity at some point, according to Pineau, he continued to terrify everyone, entering huts, beating up the men, and raping the women. The Lam Toro punished him for these actions with lashes, but Kaccé bore no grudges against the Lam Toro and did not seek revenge. Pineau probably emphasized that to prevent anyone from reaching the conclusion that Kaccé tried to frame Sidick Sall as revenge. Pineau noted that Kaccé had become Sidick's servant and moved to Guédé from his native village, Giya. He was an orphan and was known to be a man who could execute any order of his masters.

Pineau then analysed the possible motives of the three people Kaccé mentioned in his confession, as well as the one he had added to the list. He began by dismissing Kaccé's accusation of Ardo Mbantou, saying that this was pure vengeance for being caught by him. He described Mbantou as an insignificant and powerless chief, who could not have obtained control over Guédé and therefore had nothing to gain from Jeandet's murder. On the contrary, he had much to lose as the murdered administrator, according to Pineau, liked and respected Mbantou.[20]

After removing Mbantou from the suspects' list, Pineau turned to those he was convinced were to blame, despite the lack of any substantial evidence against them. Pineau stated that Sidick's dismissal in 1887 had left him frustrated and full of hatred towards the administrator. Sidick was certain that, by eliminating Jeandet, he would be able to regain his position as Lam Toro. Pineau also wrote, again without providing any shred of evidence, that Sidick was slowly poisoning the incumbent Lam Toro, Sidi Abdoul.

As for Mamadou Yoro, Pineau could not provide a convincing motive, as the former was in line to inherit Sidi Abdoul. Pineau therefore claimed that Jeandet preferred another royal from his family, and getting rid of Jeandet would have enhanced Yoro's chances to inherit the throne. One could wonder, though, whether it would not have been much simpler to get rid of Jeandet's favourite candidate rather than assassinate an administrator.

Pineau therefore accepted Kaccé's accusations of Sidick and Yoro without any evidence, while rejecting, again with no evidence, the accusation of Mbantou's involvement. But there was another person whom he had good reason to believe was involved because of his suspicious conduct right after the murder—Jeandet's former interpreter Boubacar Abdoul.

The suspected interpreter was the son of a Lam Toro. His maternal brother, Sidi Abdoul, replaced the supposedly poisoned Lam Nogato. Boubakar and Sidi's mother, Mbowba N'Diack, was an influential woman who controlled Sidi Abdoul's actions. An administrative report stated that Sidi Abdoul had acted upon the advice of his powerful mother and had also listened to his brother, Boubakar.

Jeandet was not pleased by this situation, as their advice did not always correspond with his own interests and plans.[21]

Until Jeandet became displeased with Boubakar, the latter held an important position. In 1889, he became a member of the Senegalese delegation to the Universal Exhibition in Paris—he served there as an interpreter. He visited Jeandet in hospital in Saint Louis on his way back from Paris after the latter fell ill. The best proof of his elevated status was the distinguished title of Officier de l'Académie that the administration accorded him. Further supporting evidence of Abdoul's prestige among the French administration was the fact, according to one of my informants, that his father had perished in the war against Prussia in 1870. My informant's explanation for Abdoul's dismissal in 1887 was that Abdoul was 'a man who did not tremble before a white person.' He looked at administrators straight in the eye, and they did not like that. According to my informant, Jeandet preferred to employ someone more malleable.[22]

And, indeed, Pineau described Abdoul as one of 'our most relentless enemies and certainly the most skilful.' He claimed that Abdoul had political ambitions. He wanted to inherit his brother's title and position. Therefore, Jeandet's reforms and the new constitution limiting the Lam Toro's authority were severe blows for him. This, according to Pineau, gave Abdoul a motive to get rid of the administrator.[23]

In addition to this motive, the investigation concluded that Abdoul's conduct before the murder, and immediately following the shots that put an end to Jeandet's life, was highly suspicious. Aubry-Lecomte, one of the two administrators who had supervised the illegal executions, described this questionable conduct in the final investigation report. Having interrogated Abdoul, Kane, Karounga (the gendarme who tried to shoot the murderer), Kaccé, and two other witnesses, Aubry-Lecomte concluded that the chain of events was as follows. When the shot was fired at Jeandet, all the individuals in the hut were seized with panic and fright and got up and jostled each other. Smoke filled the cabin, and no one could see a thing. They had no idea what had just happened. Someone cried: 'the commandant was killed.' Abdoulaye Kane testified that some people told him that Boubakar Abdoul was the one who had shouted, but the administrator was unable to corroborate that. Everyone tried to grab a weapon, and both Karounga and Abdoul attempted to seize the same rifle that was leaning against the wall next to Jeandet's sword. When Aubry-Lecomte asked Karounga why he thought Abdoul wanted to take the gun from him, he replied that he believed Abdoul wanted to run after the killer. Everyone began shouting: 'Catch him! Catch him!' But only one person, Ardo Mbantou, managed to progress from words to action and ran after the killer.[24]

Pineau's suspicion against Abdoul was influenced by Kane. It is apparent that Kane did not like Abdoul, and that he tried to project to the other members of the investigation a negative image of this interpreter. Kane told Aubry-Lecomte that, ever since his colleague returned from the Universal Exhibition, he had kept bragging that he had caused the dismissal of a French administrator, Ernest Noirot, Jeandet's superior upon his arrival in Senegal.[25] Kane also told the administrator that Abdoul convinced the local population that he was far more important than any administrator—even more highly valued than one as senior as Jeandet.[26] Furthermore, Abdoul had clear political aspirations. After his return from Paris, he came to Fouta Toro aiming to become a chief like his father.[27]

In his testimony, Abdoulaye Kane mentioned his surprise that Abdoul had not warned Jeandet that Kaccé had left his gun just outside the hut's door. He also stated that Abdoul made a mistake by warning Kaccé that Jeandet would punish him severely, as this only provoked Kaccé, making him more inclined to violence. Nevertheless, he confirmed the view of one of the French investigators that Abdoul was not part of the conspiracy to kill Jeandet, and that he had not meant for Kaccé to respond as he did.[28]

Aubry-Lecomte was sure that Abdoul had provoked Kaccé before the murder. He believed that Abdoul was lying when he had said he was unaware of Kaccé's tendency to anger, as Kaccé's reputation was well known everywhere in the region. As Kaccé never mentioned Abdoul, Aubry-Lecomte concluded that if Abdoul had indeed provoked Kaccé to murder Jeandet, he had done so without Kaccé being aware of it, thus ensuring that Kaccé would not implicate him if caught.[29]

Both Pineau and Aubry-Lecomte seemed confident about Abdoul's guilt. They concluded that Abdoul contributed to the conspiracy by leading Kaccé to Jeandet and warning Kaccé before he entered that the administrator would humiliate him, thus provoking his rage in advance. He also prevented Karounga from shooting at Kaccé, claiming that he took the gun for the purpose of going after Kaccé, a declaration Aubry-Lecomte doubted.[30]

Nevertheless, Abdoul was not executed together with the other suspects and was released after the investigation ended. The only explanation for this decision that the documents offer is that Abdoul escaped execution due to the lack of evidence against him. This assertion is bizarre, as the same lack of evidence did not prevent the administrators from decapitating the two implicated dignitaries along with the murderer. One explanation can be found in a letter Admiral Vallon, the French representative of Senegal in the French parliament, sent to a person by the name of Dalmas on 18 September 1890. Vallon wrote that Abdoul was going to be executed at a later stage, but in the meantime the investigation about the illegality of the executions had started, so the administrators decided to let Abdoul go.[31] An article in the metropolitan *La Cocarde* seems to corroborate the suggestion that the administrators indeed planned to execute Abdoul at a later stage. According to the article's author, Lucien Rabuel, a few minutes before the execution of Sall and Yoro, the administrators told Abdoul: 'We keep you for later.'[32]

Three of my informants offered a different explanation for Abdoul's release. What helped Abdoul, according to them, was being the cousin[33] of Captain Mamadou Racine Sy, the first African officer in the French army. Born in 1842, Sy joined Faidherbe's forces of the *Tirailleurs Sénégalais* after a quarrel with his father. He later learned French and managed to be sent to the 1878 Universal Exhibition in Paris. There he learned the manners of colonial officers and impressed them with his knowledge of French and acquaintance with French culture and habits. He was soon appointed an officer and reached the highest rank possible for an African soldier at that time. The French administration also employed Sy as an interpreter, and he helped in the conquest of massive parts of the new West African empire.[34] When Sy heard about Jeandet's murder and the ensuing investigation, he intervened on behalf of his cousin. He pleaded with the French to send Abdoul to him, promising to supervise him and make sure he did not cause any trouble. The French had no choice but to agree because they needed Sy desperately.[35]

It is evident from Aubry-Lecomte's report that releasing Abdoul was not an easy decision. The administrator seemed convinced of Abdoul's guilt and regarded him as a dangerous person. He saw him as a wildly ambitious person, and ambition was not something he expected from Africans. The dubious proof he presented attesting to Abdoul's devious character was the fact that Abdoul owned two charms with Arabic letters. One, according to Aubry-Lecomte, designated the killing of a chief loyal to the French and the other, Abdoul's own success.[36]

We can see, then, that Abdoul's primary sin in the eyes of the French was his ambition. A powerful African who held high aspirations was considered dangerous unless he was indispensable, like Abdoul's cousin, Racine Sy. In a biography that Sy's grandson wrote, he referred briefly to his grandfather's role in the Jeandet Affair. He mentioned an ongoing argument between his own family and that of Abdoulaye Kane, Jeandet's interpreter, about who had saved Abdoul from execution—Captain Racine Sy or Abdoulaye Kane. He concluded that there was no doubt that his grandfather was the one who had saved Abdoul as the two interpreters were rivals. While Abdoul was more influential than Kane, the latter knew better how not to upset the administration. Abdoul lost his status because he had become too powerful; but, even as he lost his footing, he still managed to use his family connections to save himself. In contrast, the Lam Toro and his cousin, who were supposedly much more powerful, failed to escape their fates even though the only evidence the administration had against them were mere rumours.[37]

Even allowing for the low standards of crime investigations in French-ruled West Africa, the one that led to the illegal executions of the three suspects was completely unprofessional. It lasted barely a week, relied mostly on rumours and hearsay intermediated by people who had their own interests, and was in no way backed by evidence of any sort. Baidy Kaccé's confessions were the main basis for the accusation of the two ostensible accomplices, but a third person who Kacce had accused was dismissed as a serious suspect. Abdoul Boubakar, on the other hand, who was not mentioned in the confession, was added to the list of suspects, only to be removed from it without any serious explanation. Pineau reported about the information gathered by Kane, most of which would have probably treated as hearsay had there been a proper trial. An inhabitant of one of the villages he passed on his way told him, for example, that he had heard from the brother of a local griot that the people of Guédé had decided to join Jeandet in his campaign, but stressed that if Jeandet annoyed the Guédé men who joined his forces, they would kill him. Such vague statements convinced Pineau that Jeandet's murder was a result of a political conspiracy and not a personal act of vengeance.

A letter containing instructions for the interrogation team that Tautin sent on 7 September, on the morning of Pineau's arrival in Podor, before he had even had a chance to receive information about the ongoing investigation, demonstrates how flawed and biased it had been. Tautin wrote:

> You must, despite everything that the interrogations can teach you, pretend to believe only in personal revenge, otherwise we will not achieve effective repression. Shorten it as much as possible and, when you have nothing more to get from Baydi [sic], have him beheaded, his body thrown into the river. We must neither hang him nor shoot him, but rather cut off his head in order to deprive him of the prospect of paradise in the eyes of his fellow citizens and accomplices. Once again, beware of indiscretions and everyone's ears.[38]

Tautin instructed the interrogators to pretend that they believed the version of personal vengeance, which meant it was already decided, before any witness had been interrogated, that the murder was not a result of an individual fury, but rather part of a political conspiracy. The pretence was meant to mislead the population and the ostensible culprits, so that they could not prepare for the administration's retribution. The instruction to behead Kaccé when there was nothing left to get from him insinuates a direction to employ violence against Kaccé and make him admit what the investigators already presumed. This document also proves that not only was Tautin aware of the execution's planned protocol, a fact he later denied, but he was also the one who dictated it.

Although we cannot know what exactly happened and whether Kaccé had acted alone out of rage or had been seduced to commit the crime, an alternative version to that described by Pineau can be found in the letter from Vallon cited above. Vallon offered a very different description of Jeandet's character than that given by his superiors or that which emerges from his letters. Vallon described Jeandet as a violent and capricious man, who lost his nerves easily and regularly. He administered justice by extreme punishments of lashes, but the next day he would offer his prayers to the punished person if necessary and would deeply regret the punishment he had inflicted on him the day before. Vallon plainly suggested that Jeandet's behaviour sealed his own fate. He added an important detail to the exchange with Kaccé just before the murder, saying that Jeandet ordered that Kaccé receive a hundred lashes. This detail is not mentioned in other reports about this exchange, and it might have been confused with a similar punishment that Kaccé ostensibly received from Lam Toro Sidick in the past. In any case, Vallon insisted that Kaccé acted on his own accord, and that he was pressured to give his confessions about an ostensible political conspiracy, while in fact it was obvious that this was an act of vengeance in response to Jeandet's typical violent conduct. He noted that, just before the executioner wielded his sword, Kaccé admitted that he had lied and that the people he had implicated in his confession were not involved in the murder at all. This claim was also mentioned later, when the scandal reached Paris, in the French daily, *La Cocarde*, established in 1888 by a supporter of Boulanger and later run by Maurice Barrès.[39] Vallon concluded that while Kaccé's execution with no legal procedures was unacceptable, the other two executions that were based on dubious confessions were simply outrageous.[40] Let us now examine these illegal executions that were at the heart of the scandal.

The executions

Kaccé's execution and, even more so, that of Sall and Yoro, were the focal point of the Jeandet Affair. Two main issues, later debated in Saint Louis and Paris, concerned the executions—their brutality and their illegality. I will examine the executions that took place on 10 and 15 September 1890 in the context of the practice in metropolitan France and in the British African colonies, to understand why these executions concerned and horrified the judicial elite in Saint Louis to the extent that it opened an investigation against the administrators who had ordered and supervised them.

Baidy Kaccé's execution was one of the first to take place in the French African colonies. The aim of this execution, and of the one that followed a few days later, was not only to punish the condemned but to instil fear in the local population and deter anyone from being tempted to emulate those who were executed. To achieve this goal there were two conditions that the executions had to fulfil. First, they had to be brutal and performative, a display of extreme violence, in a kind of horrifying ceremony. Second, they had to be public, and therefore they had to be performed in a place where a substantial audience could attend. The village of Aeré, the small village remote from any large population centre, where Jeandet had been murdered, was not a suitable location for such a purpose. Podor, on the other hand, was a perfect spot. It was a central commercial town on the river, and a decent crowd could be gathered there to watch the violent spectacle of death.

It is therefore easy to understand Podor's attraction for the administrators who performed the execution or, more accurately, supervised it, as the French always preferred assigning the actual violence to African auxiliaries. However, this decision turned out to be disastrous, as it turned the executions into a legal scandal. The main motive for opening an investigation against those who ordered and those who supervised the executions was that they inflicted capital punishment with no legal procedure whatsoever, and this was done in a location where French law applied. While the brutality of the execution, to which I will shortly refer, was also a cause for criticism, this alone would unlikely have created a scandal. The illegality was clearly the exception in the French colonial setting. Within the territories that the French controlled along the coast, since the seventeenth century, the death penalty could not have been inflicted without a proper trial.[41]

This was also true for British colonies. As Stacey Hynd shows, the British had been debating the form executions should take in their African colonies. While they saw the death penalty as a crucial tool of control, especially in the early stages of colonial rule, they were aware of the contradiction posed by a cruel public execution for the ideal of the civilizing mission. Quite simply, public cruelty was not civilized.[42]

At that time in Europe, cruel killing methods had been replaced with more 'humane' ones, and executions were performed behind prison walls away from curious and bloodthirsty crowds. In France specifically, public executions using brutal methods were the rule under the old regime. Their aim was to prove to the crowd watching the ceremony with horrified fascination that it was not worthwhile to sin, either against God or, even worse, against the King. The ritual also had religious significance. Just before being killed, the suffering criminal could atone for his sins and return to the bosom of his society. He thus died as part of his community rather than as an outcast.

The philosophers of the enlightenment challenged these two ideas. First, they saw the publicity and cruelty of the punishment as contradictory to civilization. The death penalty was acceptable as long as it was not cruel and did not become a spectacle. Secondly, enlightenment thinkers saw the criminal as the ultimate 'other.' Therefore, no religious ritual could save him (or her) from leaving this world as an outcast.[43]

The French Revolution that ended the old regime in France was, in a way, a corridor to post-revolution 'civilized' executions. The ritual was still public, as it was important to warn the population against counter-revolutionary ideas, but the guillotine, which was the main tool for these public executions, was presented as a symbol of civilization. It was a sophisticated machine that brought an instant and painless death to the executed person.[44]

At the time of Jeandet's murder, executions in France and other parts of Europe had changed their character completely and were no longer a spectacle of horror. But the empire was an entirely different story. While the British deliberated over whether to use similar methods to those used in Britain, mostly hanging, and to stop public executions in their colonies despite their intimidating effects on the population, the French held no such discussions, at least not at the beginning of colonial rule. As for the French, the empire was a territory where different rules applied. The necessity for public executions stemmed from the fact that, in the eyes of the administration, all colonial subjects were like the executed person. They were all potential criminals who had to be deterred from emulating the condemned person. The execution, therefore, had to be public and cruel, even if this was no longer the case in the metropole. According to Daha Cherif Ba, in the four years prior to Jeandet's assassination the practice of summary executions began to accompany that of military expeditions in West Africa. These executions were performed in secret with no spectators around. Their aim was to dispose of people considered dangerous and thus prevent rebellions.[45] Jeandet's murder necessitated a different approach. The punishment's aim was to instil terror among the population and therefore the executions could not be secret, and its sordid details had to be meticulously planned.

On 13 September, Tautin gave Aubry-Lecomte very specific instructions regarding the execution of the people Kaccé had implicated:

> From the landing of the temporary garrison in Podor, you will have the three [sic] princes of Toro executed under the same conditions as their instrument Baydi Catié [sic], the true culprits of Mr. Jeandet's assassination. In other words, they will be beheaded, their bodies thrown into the river, quite far downstream, and their heads will be displayed. However, as it is important that the memory of this punishment lasts a long time and that it be well-known to natives of all regions, after a one-day display, the heads will be buried[46] to be later sent to the Division of Political Affairs where they will remain on view, with an Arabic sign explaining to whom they belonged and for what reasons they were executed.[47]

Tautin, therefore, gave much thought to the form of the planned spectacle. Obviously, such a spectacle could only have been performed in front of a substantial audience, and so could not have been carried out in Aeré. The gruesome instructions regarding the desecration of the culprits' bodies—the beheading, the prevention of a dignified burial, the display of the severed heads, first in Podor for an entire day and then in Saint Louis—were all aimed at terrifying the population and humiliating the condemned men. Like the executions of the Old Regime in France, these also had a ritual aspect, but they were opposite in aim from the Christian rituals. The French believed that, according to Islam, a person could enter paradise if his or her body was not intact. The beheading for them held additional value as it denied the condemned person religious redemption. While there is no such Islamic tradition, it is important in Islam for the dead body to be brought to burial unviolated. Nevertheless, there is no mention anywhere in the Koran that a person cannot enter paradise if his or her body is not intact. It is possible that some such local traditions existed in pre-colonial Senegal, but it might also purely be a French invention. The French had many misconceptions about West African Islam and, in this case, the theory could have been meant to disguise pure brutality as a rational act.[48]

The brutality of the executions was not an exception in the French empire. In his article on late nineteenth-century Vietnam, for example, Michael Vann argues that while, according to Michel Foucault, public punishments and tortures ceased in Europe in the modern era, in the colonies they persisted against non-whites. Although the French authorities were aware of the contradiction between their own barbaric punishment methods and the idea of the civilizing mission, they continued with this practice. They saw it as vital for deterring potential violence and contributing to the settlers' sense of security. Public executions were not only performed in the centre of Hanoi in front of large audiences, but they were also visualized in postcards, which French tourists would enthusiastically purchase in the markets of Indochina.[49]

We can, therefore, assume that the barbarity of the two executions carried out in Senegal in September 1890 would not have sufficed to create a scandal. Their illegality, however, did. The decision to perform the executions in Podor, so that they would be seen by a substantial number of colonial subjects, was not taken by the highest authority in the colony, and certainly did not emanate from Paris. At the time of the executions there was no governor in Senegal. Clément Thomas had already left for Dakar and was preparing to leave the colony, while his successor, Henri de Lamothe, had not yet arrived. The man who filled this position was Paul Fawtier, the director of the division of interior affairs who served as an interim governor until de Lamothe arrived in the colony on 23 September 1890. The telegram he sent to Tautin on 15 September could not have been clearer about the illegality of the second execution: 'Suspend all execution. Hand over the accused to the judicial authority of St. Louis with instructions given by you, and report to me in writing everything you have done regarding the assassins of Jeandet.'[50]

These clear orders were not fulfilled, either because they did not reach their destination on time or because they were ignored. The illegal executions started a scandal that lasted about 18 months.

According to one of the French metropolitan newspapers, the task of decapitating the two implicated culprits fell on Sidick's servant, who had to strike his patron's neck several times until he managed to detach the head from the body.[51] Perhaps it was this difficulty killing Sidick that led to the belief of my informants that the French shot Sidick, but that the bullets only 'tickled' him. According to this myth, Sidick finally told his executioners that the only way to kill him was to stab him behind the ear with a special kind of thorn daubed with some substance. One can see this tradition as an African version of the Achilles myth.[52]

The practice of the death penalty was thoroughly transformed after the reform in the justice system in French West Africa in 1903. From then onwards capital sentencing became an imperial process, with final sentencing decisions made in Paris.[53] In 1890, however, the only justice system available in colonial Senegal was the metropolitan one. The cruel penalty inflicted on the three men, without a trial, was unacceptable in this justice system, and soon an outraged Antillean judge by the name of Ursleur fired the first salvo that began a long and alarming scandal.

Figure 2.1 The remains of Jeandet's monument erected in Podor in 1894 at the spot of the executions and demolished after Senegal's independence (photo: Eyal Ginio)

Notes

1 Robinson, *Chiefs and Clerics*, 59–61; 125; 138–139.
2 CAOM, Sénégal IV 66a, 25, letter from Tautin, the Director of Political Affairs to the governor, 4 December 1890.
3 The different versions can be found in official correspondence (CAOM, FR ANOM Sénégal IV 66a), metropolitan newspapers reporting on the events of 2 September 1890, and were also collected in interviews.
4 CAOM, FR ANOM Sénégal IV 66a, Rapport du Capitaine Pineau, 17 September 1890. The different versions I mention will be discussed later.
5 Thaïs Gendry, 'Le droit de tuer: la peine de mort au service de L'ordre colonial en Afrique occidentale française, 1900–1950 (PhD dissertation, EHESS UNIGE, 2020), 159–166.
6 CAOM, FR ANOM Sénégal IV 66a, Le Capitaine Pineau, chef de la mission du Toro, à M. le Colonel, Commandant Supérieur des troupes au Sénégal à Saint Louis, September 1890.
7 Benjamin N. Lawrance, Emily Lynn Osborn, and Richard L. Roberts, *Intermediaries, Interpreters, and Clerks: African Employees in the Making of Colonial Africa* (Madison: University of Wisconsin Press, 2006), 12.
8 *Ibid*, 12.
9 M'bayo, *Muslim Interpreters*, 5–8.
10 Lawrance, Osborn, and Roberts, *Intermediaries, Interpreters, and Clerks: African Employees in the Making of Colonial Africa*, 13.
11 M'bayo, *Muslim Interpreters*, 1.
12 *Ibid*, 19–20.
13 Ralph A. Austen, 'Colonialism from the Middle: African Clerks as Historical Actors and Discursive Subjects,' *History in Africa* 38 (2011).
14 M'bayo, *Muslim Interpreters*, 8.
15 Mon interprète est un jeune homme très intelligent fils et frère d'interprète. Je pense en faire un bon serviteur et j'en suis content. Archives de Saône-et-Loire, François Joseph Etienne Abel Jeandet, F 1413, 14 May 1889.
16 *Ibid*, 1 February 1888.
17 Pineau's first name is not mentioned in the documents.
18 FR ANOM Sénégal IV 66, 5 October 1890.
19 CAOM, FR ANOM Sénégal IV 66a, Le Capitaine Pineau, chef de la mission du Toro, à M. le Colonel, Commandant Supérieur des troupes au Sénégal à Saint Louis, September 1890.

20 *Ibid.*
21 *Ibid.*
22 Interview with Cheick Baba Sall, 14 February 2020.
23 FR ANOM Sénégal IV 66a, September 1890 Rapport de Capitaine Pineau.
24 FR ANOM Sénégal IV 66a, Adminstrateur Aubry-Lecomte en mission à Affaires Politiques—St. Louis, 16 September 1890.
25 Noirot and Jeandet were apparently close, as Jeandet gave his address to his mother so that Noirot could help her navigate Paris when she visited the universal exhibition in 1889. It is unclear how Abdoul caused his dismissal. Noirot was involved in a scandal due to his lack of control of his interpreter and was consequently dismissed, but that was only in 1905. On the Noirot Affair see: Emily Lynn Osborn, 'Interpreting Colonial Power in French Guinea: the Boubou Penda-Ernest Noirot Affair of 1905,' in Lawrance, Osborn, and Roberts, *Intermediaries, Interpreters, and Clerks: African Employees in the Making of Colonial Africa*.
26 Fond ancien AOF série G 13G 135, 16 September 1890.
27 This information was revealed during Abdoul's interrogation after Ba's filed her complaint against the administrators who had ordered the execution. ANOM, Sénégal IV, 66a, 20 November 1890.
28 Fond ancien AOF série G 13G 135, 14 September 1890.
29 *Ibid*, 16 September 1890.
30 FR ANOM Sénégal IV 66a, 16 September 1890, Administrateur Aubry-Lecomte en mission à directeur des Affaires Politiques.
31 *Ibid*, 18 September 1890,
32 Lucien Rabel, 'Exécutions sommaires,' *La Cocarde*, 16 June 1891.
33 The term 'cousin' does not necessarily mean first cousin, but it does indicate a familial relation.
34 Abdoul Sow, *Mamadou Racine Sy: premier capitaine noir des tirailleurs sénégalais (1838–1902)* (Paris: Éditions L'Harmattan, 2010).
35 Interviews with Abdourahmane Niang, Podor, 7 February 2020; Haruna Diop, Dakar, 14 February 2020; Cheikh Baba Sall, Rufisque, 14 February 2020.
36 Fond ancien AOF série G 13G 135, 16 September 1890.
37 Seydou Madani Sy, *Le capitaine Mamadou Racine Sy, 1838–1902: une figure sénégalaise au temps des tirailleurs* (Paris: Editions Karthala, 2014).
38 FR ANOM Sénégal IV 66a, 7 September 1890, Affaires Politiques à Administrateur et à Commission enquête—Podor.

39 Lucien Rabuel, 'Exécutions sommaires', *La Cocarde*, 16 June 1891. On Boulanger see Chapter 3, note 25.

40 FR ANOM Sénégal IV 66a, 18 October 1890. The author of this letter might be Admiral Vallon, as at the beginning of the affair the content of the letter reflects his view, which he declared several times at the time. This will be further discussed in Chapter 3.

41 *Ibid.*

42 Stacey Hynd, 'Killing the Condemned: The Practice and Process of Capital Punishment in British Africa, 1900–1950s,' *The Journal of African History* 49, no. 3 (2008), 403–418.

43 Michel Bée, 'Le spectacle de L'exécution dans la France d'ancien régime,' *Annales. Histoire, Sciences Sociales* 38, no. 4 (1983), 851.

44 Jürgen Martschukat, 'Nineteenth-Century Executions as Performances of Law, Death, and Civilization,' in *Cultural Lives of Capital Punishment: Comparative Perspectives* (2005), 57.

45 Ba, *Crimes et délits dans la vallée du fleuve Sénégal de 1810 à 1970*, 349.

46 It is likely that the heads were to be buried to prevent decomposition until they could be sent to the Division of Political Affairs.

47 FR ANOM Sénégal IV 66a, 13 September 1890, Affaires Politiques à Chef poste—Richard Toll.

48 On French misconception of West African Islam see: Rüdiger Seesemann and Benjamin F. Soares, '"Being as Good Muslims as Frenchmen": On Islam and Colonial Modernity in West Africa,' *Journal of Religion in Africa* 39, no. 1 (2009), 91–120.

49 Michael G. Vann, 'Of Pirates, Postcards, and Public Beheadings: The Pedagogic Execution in French Colonial Indochina,' *Historical Reflections/Réflexions Historiques* 36, no. 2 (2010), 44–45; 52–53.

50 Suspendez tout exécution, remettez accusés à l'autorité judiciaire de St Louis avec instruction faire par vous et rendez-moi compte par lettre de ce que avez fait au sujet des assassins de Jeandet. FR ANOM Sénégal I 90, 15 September 1890.

51 Lucien Rabel, 'Exécutions sommaires,' *La Cocarde*, 16 June 1891.

52 Interview with Aliou Sall, 9 March 2017, Dakar. The warrior Achilles is one of the great heroes of Greek mythology. According to legend, Achilles was extraordinarily strong, courageous, and loyal, but he had one vulnerability—his 'Achilles heel.' His mother, Thetis, who was concerned about his mortality dipped him in the river Styx whose waters were said to bestow the invulnerability of the gods. As she had to hold him by his heel, this was the only spot through which he could be hurt. As an expression meaning 'area of weakness'

or 'vulnerable spot,' the use of Achilles' heel dates to 1840. See: P. Grimal, *The Dictionary of Classical Mythology*, translation A.R. Maxwell-Hyslop (Oxford: Blackwell, 1996), 5.

53 Stacey Hynd and Thaïs Gendry, 'African Women, Colonial Justice and White Man's Mercy,' *Histoire & Sociétés / Crime, History & Societies* 27, no. 1 (2023), 111.

3

An affair is born

Among the first to be horrified by the illegal and brutal executions of Kaccé and of Sall and Yoro was Conrad Frédéric Ursleur, a judge who originated from French Guiana, and who in 1890 was the chief justice of Senegal. Born in 1853 in Cayenne the son of a lawyer, Ursleur completed his studies in 1876. He joined the judicial service in Senegal in 1879 as the public prosecutor in Gorée. He later moved to Saint Louis, where he became the head of the colony's judicial service, the highest position available. Ursleur represented a whole group of Creole members of the colonial administration in Senegal who had been appointed to high-ranking positions in the colony's justice system. As we shall see later, these judges had a particular perception of the law influenced by the struggles against slavery in their places of origin. Ursleur's personal file, located in the French National Archives, contains the annual reports of his superiors both before and after the affair. All these reports of him are excellent. They all emphasize Ursleur's integrity, professionalism, expertise, and sensitivity. Just a year before Jeandet's murder, in 1889, Clément Thomas, the same governor who was anxious to get rid of Ursleur when the latter initiated an investigation against the administrators who had supervised the executions, recommended offering him the knight's cross of the Legion of Honour (légion d'honneur) and wrote the following professional evaluation:

> Mr. Ursleur directs the administration of justice with the utmost distinction. A magistrate brilliantly gifted, he knows how to command the respect owed to the judiciary through his integrity, firmness, tact, and impartiality. The population has confidence in him. Personally, I have nothing but praise for the enlightened support I have always found from this head of administration.[1]

It is difficult to imagine a better evaluation than that Clément-Thomas provided of Ursleur only a year before he became the main enemy of the colonial administration. In fact, the qualities that his superior recognized in Ursleur—his integrity, professionalism, and strong character—were precisely and ironically those that made him the governor's enemy. Just two days after the executions, Ursleur sent the governor the following telegram:

> Capital executions committed on French territory, outside of any judicial procedures, cannot, under the pretext of a political matter, be exempted from the knowledge of the judicial authority—Powers of governors are clearly defined.—They have no authority to condemn anyone to death.—Orders given in this regard should not be executed, and those who obey them, failing in their duty, do so at their own risk because they commit a crime.—If the events that occurred in Podor were tolerated, there would be no more guarantee for those residing in colonies on French soil who are entitled to the protection of the laws. I am giving the order today to the public prosecutor to pursue the matter.[2]

Ursleur could not have been clearer. The executions were a crime, even if such an order was given, and those who had committed this crime should be prosecuted. In another telegram he sent a day later, Ursleur emphasized that, in the 11 years in which he had served in Senegal, an execution had never been carried out by administrators without a trial. He added that justice was meant to protect everyone and that there was no point in keeping Senegal as a colony if the law was not upheld.[3] On the same day, Clément Thomas, who was still in Dakar, responded to Ursleur's telegram. He rejected the judge's accusations and his decision to open an investigation against the administrators who had presided over the executions. He added that if there were deep emotions in the colony, they were not because of the executions, which ensured European safety and satisfied the African population, but rather due to measures that had compromised French domination and influence.[4] Clément Thomas thus pointed an accusing finger at the judge, saying that he, rather than the administrators who had performed the executions, was the one destabilizing French colonial rule in the colony. The governor demanded that Ursleur put an end to the investigation against the administrators and, when the latter refused, the governor asked the colonial under-secretary to remove him from Senegal:

'I request the immediate transfer of Ursleur, who cannot remain the Chief of the judicial administration in the colony where his conduct in the Jeandet case has aroused general disapproval.'[5]

As the colonial under-secretary was absent at that time, his representative in the ministry reassured Clément Thomas on the same day that he would receive the backing of the ministry and that his request would be fulfilled. A day later, Ursleur was invited to Paris to 'offer explanations,' and a replacement was found for him—Henri Larrouy from Guadeloupe. While the governor was initially very happy to receive Larrouy into the colony and to dispose of Ursleur, he was soon to find that in fact this was not a good deal for him. As we shall see, Larrouy's position regarding the affair was no different from that of his predecessor.

When de Lamothe took over the colony from Clément Thomas in September 1890, he asked Tautin to prepare a file with all the documents regarding the executions, a request that Tautin had refused earlier when asked by the interim governor, Fawtier. To ensure that no one else in the judiciary could decide to reopen the investigation, the new governor declared that only a person of interest, meaning someone impacted personally by the executions, could open a judicial procedure. With this de Lamothe hoped to ensure the end of the affair. However, behind the scenes, Gaspard Devès was preparing the stage for the second act.[6]

Devès as the administration's nemesis

Devès was clearly the main engine that drove the Jeandet Affair forward, and the administration was certainly aware of this. He was probably the one who had informed Ursleur about the illegal executions in Podor, and the one who had asked him to open an investigation. He had both the motivation and the means to instigate the scandal and to maintain it for a year and a half, during which the governor and the ministry of the colonies were struggling to find ways, both legal and extra-legal, to extinguish the fire that Devès had started.[7]

Well before the Jeandet Affair, the French administration had already treated Devès with suspicion. He and his sons or, as they became known, the 'Devès clan,' (*clan de Devès*) were significant and highly influential figures in nineteenth- and early twentieth-century Saint Louis. They established a trade network in the Senegalo-Mauritanian zone, and used their economic power to establish their political influence in the capital. Devès created shifting coalitions with French, métis, and African supporters. His attempts to curtail French power over their area of trade eventually failed but, for several decades, including the period under examination here, they were able to mobilize significant human and financial resources. They managed to turn electoral institutions to their advantage in a manner that deeply concerned and upset the French administration. They thus earned the administration's trenchant hostility.[8]

Born in 1827, Gaspard was the son of Bruno Devès and his Fulbe mistress from Dagana (a town on the Senegal River, not far from Podor), known as Sylvie Bruno and originally named Coumbel Peul Ka or Coumbel Ardo Ka.[9] It was through his mother that he had close relations with people from Fouta Toro. By the 1850s Gaspard had established his own company, obtained the right to supply the French administration with grain, and developed an elaborate network along the Senegal River, in what was known as the peanut basin. His marriage to Catherine Foy, daughter of a local rich métis merchant, only enhanced his position. After she died in childbirth, Gaspard married a Fulbe woman, Madeleine Tambe Diop, who gave birth to his three sons, Justin, Hyacinthe, and François, who followed in his footsteps in later years.

In the 1850s, Devès opposed the expansion policy of Governor Faidherbe and then continued to resist the policy of later governors. At the same time, he kept profiting from the French presence and military expeditions. In the 1870s, Devès entered politics and served on several occasions as mayor of Saint Louis and councillor in the General Council, the main representative institution in Senegal. Jean-Jacques Crespin was his most important ally. Together they formed a political clan that rivalled another influential métis trader by the name of Descemet, who supported the French governors. Devès's immediate intervention in the Jeandet Affair stemmed from his close relationships with the Fouta Toro chiefs who had consulted him often. His involvement in the affair increased the natural hostility of the French administration towards him, turning it almost to paranoia.[10]

To understand Devès's motives in keeping the affair alive, we must look into the complex political scene of Saint Louis in the late nineteenth century. With the expansion of electoral politics to Senegal during the first decade of the Third Republic, the métis became significant actors in the political arena. With their French education, commercial experience, and deep ties with the local African population—whom they often married—the métis were in an excellent position to capitalize on the expanding democratic institutions in the colony. The main institution they dominated was the General Council. Unlike the Advisory Council (Conseil Privé), which was elected solely by the governor and which served only to advise him, the General Council held real power. Its control over part of the colonial budget enabled its members to shape colonial policy and hinder French agendas. The General Council also managed the budget of the territories under direct administration, to which the town of Podor belonged, thus enhancing its importance in the interior. At the time of the affair, the General Council had 16 members, of whom ten were from Saint Louis and six from Gorée. Members could serve an unlimited number of six-year terms.[11]

The expansion of electoral politics in Saint Louis coincided exactly with the opposite process—the often-brutal colonization of vast territories in the West African hinterland. This brought an additional large population under French rule, one that had no part in the electoral scene and was devoid of any civil or political rights. The French administration was therefore deeply worried that the growing power of the métis might hinder their colonization efforts. It must be emphasized, though, that the political scene in Saint Louis was very complex and often fluid. Furthermore, unlike what is usually expected in a colonial situation, this was by no means a system divided along racial lines. Not all métis were enemies of the administration. In fact, the different coalitions that emerged during the last decades of the nineteenth century were formed according to the way each saw the future of colonial rule in Senegal. The métis were divided on this subject and, as the unfolding of the Jeandet Affair shows, not all members of the administration were aligned either.

The debate centred on two main colonial visions. The first was whether the territories considered then as the colony of Senegal should remain a mere commercial enterprise—which therefore did not really need a democratic metropolitan-style political system—or whether it should become a colony like the other old French colonies with institutions that would safeguard 'Senegalese interests.' The first view was held mainly by the Bordeaux commercial companies who traded in Senegal. The main champion of the second, was Gaspard Devès. Senegalese interests for him were not only those of the métis, but also of Africans. He soon realized that to fulfil his vision of Senegal as a vibrant colony, he also had to protect the rights of its African population, both in Saint Louis, which was part of the electoral system, but also his allies and intermediaries in the territories that France was trying to subdue. This idea of defending the African population was the one that often put him in conflict with the colonial administration.

The second main colonial vision under debate that affected the emergence of coalitions within the political life of Saint Louis was around the status of the territories in which there was already a French presence. Maintaining the influence of various African political entities in these territories motivated Devès to support African rulers in some of their struggles against the administration. One such struggle which annoyed the administration greatly was his opposition to the construction of a railway line through the territory of Cayor, to which its ruler, Lat Dior, was opposed, knowing that it would harm his autonomy. Devès thus positioned himself in opposition to colonial progress in the eyes of the French, who saw the railway as one of the main symbols of the civilizing mission. But the debate went even further. One of the most sensitive issues in the forming of political alliances was the question of slavery. The French abolished slavery in the regions under their direct rule in 1848 but, in practice, it was very difficult for them to implement, as many of their local allies were enslavers and the French did not want to alienate them. The French protectorate regime was a perfect solution to this quandary. As French law did not apply to the protectorates, the administration's allies could safely keep their enslaved people. Devès, as well as the Bordeaux companies, also had a problem with the issue of abolition because of their close relations with French parliamentarians from overseas territories who were ardent abolitionists, such as Alexandre Isaac, who later supported Ba's lawsuit. The only way Devès and the Bordeaux companies could maintain their alliance with these French parliamentarians was by supporting the existence of protectorates and objecting to the annexation of African kingdoms and other territories.[12]

The Jeandet Affair highlighted this debate and added the legal perspective to it. This will be discussed in greater depth in Chapter 4.

A few months after Devès revived the affair by persuading Ndiereby Ba to sue the administrators who had executed her husband, Governor de Lamothe wrote a long letter to Eugène Etienne, the colonial under-secretary, to complain about Devès's annoying involvement. This letter well reflects Devès's image as a clever and devious enemy of the administration. It is obvious from the letter that de Lamothe saw Devès as a highly intelligent and very powerful man. De Lamothe explained to the under-secretary that Devès acted as he did in the Jeandet Affair to win the votes of the African population of Saint Louis. But this was not the whole story. According to the governor, Devès wished to maintain his relations with African rulers and with his intermediaries in the hinterland, and he therefore attempted to present himself as the protector of their rights and interests as well. That was the governor's explanation for Devès's opposition to the construction of the Cayor railway. In the Podor Affair, according to the governor, Devès tried to demonstrate to the Tokolors that he was able to punish administrators for carrying out their duties and, in doing so, enlarge his clientele in Toro.[13]

In this letter, the governor presented Devès's involvement in the Jeandet Affair as being all for his own personal interest. Devès wanted to augment his clientele in Toro and his political power in Saint Louis. While this was probably part of his motivation, it is hard to imagine that it would have been enough to fuel Devès's long and tenacious struggle against the administration. The issue at stake was not only Devès's personal gain. His determination to keep the Jeandet Affair alive also stemmed from his vision of the colonial project and the form it should take. Devès did not think that the violent occupation of inland territories and their annexation to the colony was the right way to pursue the colonial project. He had hoped that a legal scandal would show the administration that such a future for the colony was not viable. To do that, he had to find a way of prosecuting the administrators who had ordered and supervised the illegal execution.

Devès's main interest in stirring the scandal after the executions was his close relationships with African rulers whose power was being undermined by railroad construction and violent military campaigns, such as the one Jeandet was in the process of conducting

Figure 3.1 Devès's grave in Saint Louis (photo: Eyal Ginio)

at the time he was murdered. As many of the métis had legal training, the legal arena was the perfect one to challenge the administration, and the illegal executions provided an excellent opportunity to do so. It is not surprising that Ursleur was persuaded by Devès to open the investigation. Local métis in Saint Louis, including Devès, maintained close relations with members of the judiciary in the city, including Ursleur. In addition, Ursleur was related to Pagès, whom Jeandet had replaced, and who until then maintained good relations with Lam Toro Sidick, which aligned with Devès's interests.

Searching for a plaintiff

With the removal of Ursleur from his post in Senegal, Devès had to find an alternative way to continue the legal struggle. His only option was to find a party in interest who would be able to sue the administrators. With the help of his close allies, Africans from Toro or originating from there, he began looking for a suitable candidate. The search that Devès conducted in the month following Ursleur's removal demonstrates very well his influence in Toro and his ability to work closely with his African allies. Who were these people who helped with the search that eventually brought Ndiereby Ba into the picture?

The main information about these men and women comes, unfortunately, from a very dubious source: a long letter that Tautin, who had ordered the executions, wrote after Ndiereby Ba arrived in Saint Louis. In this letter, Tautin describes the people who helped Devès persuade Ndiereby to sue the administrators, and who brought her to Saint Louis, in very negative terms. His views on Devès's allies are, of course, biased and filled with contempt and hatred. Nevertheless, it is possible to get some idea about these people by reading his letter with his biases in mind.

Tautin mentioned ten people in his letter—eight men and two women. To some he allocated more space, explaining their flawed characters by offering examples of their conduct before the affair. Some he described as working for Devès, such as Chadelle (Ndiereby Ba's future lawyer) and Crespin. Some were related to Sidick Sall, like Aco Faye, who lived in Saint Louis and was one of Devès's most influential electors. Others were Suleyman Diop, a post office employee, Samba Fall, an interpreter, who would be very active later on during the affair, Lamine (no last name is mentioned), a liberated enslaved person of Sidick Sall, and several traders who worked with Devès.

I would like to focus here on one of the two women mentioned in the letter—Bitti Lokho. It seems that her role in persuading Ndiereby Ba to go to Saint Louis and to sue the administrators was crucial. She later offered Ndiereby support while in Saint Louis, and even hosted her in her home for a while. Lokho was connected to the affair in multiple ways. She was related to Ndiereby, Suleymen Diop, and to Rosso Sidi, the other woman Tautin mentioned, who worked as a nanny for Crespin. Lokho's character and involvement in the affair sheds light on the vital participation of women in this legal struggle.

Tautin allocated a substantial part of his letter to Lokho. Of all the people he described, she seems to have annoyed him the most. He started his description of her with these words: 'Bitti is a woman of bad conduct, a drunkard, pretending to adopt the practice of a devout Islamist. She is the owner of the house she lives in thanks to a real scam at the expense of her divorced husband, Blandin Diop.'[14] From this opening alone we can understand the level of hatred and concern that Lokho aroused in Tautin. He also obviously resented the fact that Lokho owned a house in Saint Louis. But his criticism did not end there. To demonstrate Lokho's evil character, Tautin referred to May 1889, when the Universal Exhibition in Paris took place. Crespin, who employed Rosso Sidi, Lokho's relative, headed the committee of the Senegalese delegation to the exhibition and, in this capacity, sent his nanny's cousin to Paris as part of the delegation. His aim, according to Tautin, was to make her an influential and active electoral agent for him there. In Paris, so Tautin wrote, Lokho's behaviour was deplorable. She was constantly half drunk and spent her time harassing the visitors, demanding money from them and reacting aggressively when they refused.[15]

As with other descriptions of Africans who were involved in the affair, we cannot, of course, take Tautin's report at face value. It is obvious that Tautin intended to present all those who defied the administration, be they African or métis, as despicable and immoral. Nevertheless, we can assume that Lokho did indeed cause some problems for the exhibition organizers. She might have refused to play by the rules and become an exhibit. She might also have enjoyed the food stalls on the exhibition grounds that sold wine at reduced prices and were open to all—visitors and participants alike.[16] Perhaps she took advantage of the visitors' habit of throwing coins at the people exhibited, and maybe she tried to extract more generous sums from them. Her behaviour might have reflected her frustration and disappointment at her trip to Paris, which ended in an enclosed space from which she was not allowed to venture, nor which allowed her to explore the attractions of the city of lights.

We cannot know for sure what went on in Lokho's mind, but the fact that she was later willing to take the risk of playing an active part in Ba's legal struggle demonstrates that she was indeed rebellious. She certainly was not motivated by alcohol nor fanatic religious zeal. The dissonance between the treatment she received as an 'exhibit' at the exhibition and her position as a well-to-do woman who owned a house in Saint Louis was probably the likely motive that prompted her behaviour both at the exhibition and during the Podor Affair.

Tautin described Lokho in his letter as having a crucial role in the mission to bring Ndiereby Ba from Guédé to Saint Louis. While his aim was to denigrate Devès and his African accomplices, their actions emerge in his description as being quite impressive.

They certainly demonstrate both Devès's influence and his allies' courage and determination. Both Tautin's report, as well as the series of telegrams Devès's agents exchanged during their search for a candidate to sue the administrators, give us a good idea of how this difficult mission was accomplished.[17]

On 14 or 15 October, Aco Faye, one of Devès's associates, arrived in Podor to start looking for a suitable candidate. In the meantime, Devès's allies in Saint Louis put some pressure on Boubakar Abdoul, the interpreter who had managed to escape the fate of Sidick Sall and Mamadou Yoro, to submit a civil lawsuit against the administrators. Being a relative of Sidick Sall, this was a viable option. As Abdoul seemed quite hesitant to do this, Devès's team attempted to find an alternative candidate in Toro. Faye had in mind a young woman, Sall's niece. She was a suitable candidate, as she was the fiancée of a trader who worked with Devès. She had also lived in Saint Louis for a while, so knew the city well. This woman came to Saint Louis, but then seemingly had second thoughts and decided it would be prudent for her to back out of the suit. Faye had no choice but to approach Sidick's widow, Ndiereby Ba.[18]

We do not know how old Ndiereby was at the time but, according to one of my informants, she probably married at the age of 14 or 15. As Sall was executed about seven or eight years later, Ndiereby was most likely in her early 20s.[19] Apart from being very young, Ndiereby could not speak French and had never set foot in Saint Louis. She was therefore ostensibly less suitable for the mission than Sall's niece. Another problem with Ndiereby Ba's candidacy was the local custom according to which a widow had to mourn her husband for four months—she could not leave her house during the mourning period. By early November, only about half of this period had elapsed.[20]

On 4 November, it became clear that Abdoul had decided not to press charges against the administrators. This decision seems logical as, having barely escaped the death penalty, it would have been quite risky for Abdoul to 'draw fire' by again attracting attention to his role in the murder. Suleyman Diop, the postal employee that Tautin denigrated in his report, sent a telegram to Demba Sarr, who also worked for Devès, asking him to pass an urgent message to Guédé instructing Ndiereby and Lamine, Sall's emancipated enslaved person, to come to Saint Louis immediately. The next day, Sarr wrote back confirming that he had acted accordingly. Ndiereby, accompanied by Lamine, arrived in Podor on 6 November, but it apparently still required some persuasion to get her on a boat to Saint Louis. Bitti Lokho wrote from Saint Louis urging Demba Sarr to send the widow to the capital. On 10 November, Suleyman Diop wrote to say that Ndiereby and Lamine must board the *Germaine*, a 70-ton ship that belonged to Devès's commerce house, and that the expenses of the trip would all be covered. He added the words: 'Sommes pressés' (we are pressed) and asked Demba to inform him when they left Podor. Finally, Ndiereby boarded the ship and arrived in Saint Louis on 14 November. She was welcomed by her cousin, Lokho, who hosted her in her home. It took Ndiereby only three more days to present herself in court. The scandal was reawakened, and Devès was back in business.[21]

After Baidy Kaccé's bullets halted Jeandet's campaign to eliminate the final resistance to French rule in Fouta Toro, the French administration found itself facing a very different kind of resistance to colonization. This was a much less violent form of resistance than that represented by Jeandet's murder, but it was, in a way, also much more challenging. As we shall soon see, the administration reached a state of panic and acted aggressively to block this new form of resistance. Let us now alight from the *Germaine* together with the young widow arriving in the capital, Saint Louis, in search of justice.

The legal scene in Saint Louis and the unfolding of the affair

One of the most important aspects of the affair was the complex colonial legal system in Senegal. It was the complexities of this system that turned the executions into a scandal, and it was also this system that allowed the lawsuit to take place. Members of the judicial system, mainly from among the métis, but also some French, defended Ba's right to sue the administrators who had ordered her husband's execution, and took a firm stand against the governor and other senior administrators. To understand the importance of the legal aspect of the affair some explanation is necessary about the development of the colonial legal system until the end of the nineteenth century.

The process of establishing a legal system in Senegal began before the French expansion into the West African hinterland and was heavily influenced by Napoleon Bonaparte's Egyptian campaign, which established the principle of the protectorate, by his legal reforms in France that directly contradicted this principle, and by the French colonial experiment in Algeria. Finally, the conquest of Western Sudan, which paved the way for the colonization of a huge part of Western and Equatorial Africa, set the stage for the great struggle over the nature of French colonialism. Law played a central role in this struggle, which ended in 1903 with the establishment of a parallel native legal system for non-citizens that enabled the colonial administration to avoid implementing French law in the African colonies.[22]

The concept of a French colonial legal system in West Africa thus evolved around a fierce debate between two notions—that of the protectorate in which French law was not applicable and that of a unitary concept of justice based on the Napoleonic code that elevated the idea of the natural rights of the individual and framed them in universal terms. This latter idea became problematic when the French conquered Algeria in 1830. This conquest was not planned, and as soon as it began the French encountered fierce resistance. This situation advanced the military model of colonialism together with a reluctant respect for Islam and the resilience of Muslim institutions. The French established the Arab offices (bureaux arabes) in Algeria to explore local customs and introduced Muslim courts into the colonial administration.[23]

Algeria was also the terrain on which the *indigénat*, discussed in the introduction, was first implemented. This repressive tool, which bestowed upon administrators and, in fact, any European, the power to inflict punishments on colonial subjects without trial, contradicted the basic principles of French metropolitan law and influenced the administrative and judiciary organization of all the future French colonies in Africa.[24]

The struggle over the shape of the colonial legal system was also connected to the debate between military and civilian approaches to colonial rule. While in Senegal, unlike Algeria, there were no settlers, and the army had much less influence over the shaping of colonial policy, the same legal contradictions were nevertheless present and affected the debate around the concept of colonial justice.

During the period between 1879 and 1893, the French military expanded extensively into western Sudan, taking over vast territories in West Africa. General Louis Archinard, the supreme military commander (commandant supérieur) at the time, was pivotal in shaping the military concept of functional justice, designed to support the new colonial order. According to Archinard, the administrators on the ground were to be given unlimited power. Justice was supposed to be swift, harsh, and public. Capital punishment was the preferred tool to implement this form of practical justice. It was the most unambiguous expression of power. Indeed, justice in the expanding French empire was definitely swift and harsh, and it usually took place in the most public place possible.

Despite the rapid military conquest of West Africa, the National Assembly (assemblée nationale) in France was not happy with the implementation of military rule in this vast territory. Richard Roberts refers to a conflict over colonialism that positioned Archinard's model of indirect rule against the colonial idea of the republican civilizing mission that saw direct rule and establishment of French metropolitan institutions as pivotal to colonial rule. During the 1880s the Third Republic was becoming increasingly anti-militaristic. Many republicans, though undoubtedly not all, if we define Jeandet's family as republicans, saw the army as an outdated and anti-republican, even monarchist, institution. The Boulanger Affair (1886–1889) also influenced the Third Republic's impatience towards military actions in western Sudan.[25] The military influence over West Africa largely decreased with the establishment of a separate ministry of the colonies in 1894. Until then it was combined with the ministry of the navy and had an under-secretary rather than a minister of its own. This separation reinforced the civilian agenda at the expense of the military.[26]

Yet, despite the republican objection to the military model of justice, we must bear in mind that republicanism was hardly ever consistent, and it was not systematically implemented in the colonies. Paris seldom had much influence over the newly colonized territories or the people who ruled them in its name. In addition, the Jeandet Affair demonstrates well that this struggle over the concept of colonial law was not neatly divided along military/civilian lines. While most, if not all, military officers in West Africa supported Archinard's model of colonial justice, many civilian administrators supported it as well.

Unlike the legal situation in France's new territories occupied from the mid-nineteenth century until World War One, the legal scene in Saint Louis followed the metropolitan pattern from the beginning of the nineteenth century. With the reoccupation of Senegal in 1816 after a period of British rule, the French instituted a metropolitan justice system in the colony as part of its wider reorganization. The Gorée tribunal convened for the first time in 1822 and, 15 years later, this tribunal and the one in Saint Louis became tribunaux de première instance, the principal courts of the French judicial system. Until 1840, the magistrates of these courts were French commandants of the cities, assisted by a senior French employee and a local notable. From that year, the French started recruiting professional judges to preside over the two tribunals. They also established appeals courts in the colony. Under Faidherbe, in the 1850s, the judicial system grew stronger, but it was only in 1891 that the French created the position of attorney general (procureur général), who would control the first instance and the appeals courts administratively. Both types of courts heard civil and criminal cases involving French citizens or *originaires*. This judicial system did not provide for any African who was not an *originaire*, an assimilated French citizen or involved in a case against French citizens. In 1857, as part of his 'Muslim policy,' Faidherbe established a Muslim court in Saint Louis, which heard only civil cases of Muslim French nationals.[27]

This new court contradicted the Napoleon Code and the French idea of equal justice for all citizens. Most French judges viewed any refusal to apply French legislation to Africans as contrary both to natural law and to the policy of assimilation. They often confronted the administration on this subject trying to limit, and occasionally succeeding in limiting, the authority of the Muslim tribunal.[28]

One of the similarities between the justice system in Saint Louis and metropolitan France was the important role lawyers played in political life. Lawyers were a central aspect of the Jeandet Affair. The affair involved several attorneys who played important roles in it. And, indeed, lawyers played an important role throughout the Third Republic, which was even termed by one historian as 'the republic of lawyers.'[29] Attorneys' skills in reaching compromises made them crucial in the establishment of the Third Republic. At the end of the nineteenth century, many members of parliament and civil servants had trained as lawyers. In 1881, for instance, 41 per cent of the members of parliament were trained lawyers. Lawyers often saw their role as natural protectors of the underdog.[30] This approach to their role might explain Chadelle's continued support of Ba's case despite constant harassment on the part of the colonial administration.

Just like their French metropolitan peers, young métis in Saint Louis were attracted to the profession of law during the first decades of the Third Republic. The Devès brothers all studied law in Bordeaux. As a barrister, Crespin earned the reputation of a great orator, who never tired of passionately protecting his clients. Upon Crespin's untimely death on 2 January 1895, speeches in his honour emphasized the importance of law in Saint Louis, and the close relationship between law and politics. They praised his struggle on behalf of Senegalese interests, highlighting the divide between the administration's view of Senegal as a colony and the métis who practised law to defend local interests. The tendency of lawyers in France and in Saint Louis to leverage their professional standing to champion politically controversial matters is well reflected in the Jeandet Affair. As lawyers, the métis felt obligated to defend democratic principles and to challenge administrative officials. While Devès and perhaps other métis obviously also served their commercial and political interests by challenging the administration, the struggle over the form of the colonial legal system was at the heart of the affair.[31]

In this struggle a very important role was played by judges who originated from the Caribbean. Ursleur, Larrouy, Simoneau and other members of the Senegalese judiciary were those who presented the administration with its most difficult obstacle. They knew the law and believed in the myth of French republicanism ostensibly to uphold the principle of equal justice for all. A few words are therefore needed about this group of relentless judges.

From 1848 to 1946, when Guadeloupe, Martinique, and Guyana won the status of French overseas departments (départements d'outre-mer), their inhabitants held the ambiguous status of colonized subjects who had become citizens, much like the inhabitants of the four communes of Senegal. The difference was the long legacy of slavery that existed in the Caribbean, and the French determination to promote a new social group, designed to be an intermediary group between the French administration and settlers and the majority of the population. The republican schools became a dominant tool for this new elite and for social mobility. The struggle against slavery in the Caribbean contributed to the determination of this new elite to uphold the values that brought about its end.[32] While the French administration in West Africa tried to present the continued existence of slavery in this region as essentially different from the type of slavery abolished in its ancient colonies, as Hilary Jones demonstrates, this argument did not persuade those who believed all slavery should be abolished in the colonies. The creoles who served in the colony's justice system saw the struggle against slavery in the newly conquered territories of West Africa as their moral duty, a position that brought them closer to their métis allies and put them in conflict with the colonial administration, whose main African allies were enslavers.[33]

As we have previously seen, the French had difficulties in recruiting administrators for their expanding African empire. The colonial administration soon became the main attraction for Caribbean creoles who wanted to get away from plantation work. Those who agreed to serve in the colonial administration outside their place of origin, and especially in Africa, gained many advantages, such as social promotion, high salaries, and guaranteed pensions. Higher education, in particularly in Law, opened many doors for this new social group.[34]

The creoles who served in the administration of the African colonies often supported republican values and in fact embodied them. They soon forged strong relations with African and métis politicians. Many of the creole members of the judiciary system married local métis women. They also encouraged and supported political struggles led by métis politicians. The Jeandet Affair is a perfect example of this kind of cooperation. The creoles were linked to the liberal and republican movement in France and were descendants of those who had been fighting for the establishment of the republic since the days of the French Revolution.[35] Nevertheless, they had an ambiguous status as colonized people who colonized Africans. Their presence within the ranks of the administration underlined the incoherence of the colonial system and called into question republican politics. The position of most of these judges in the Jeandet Affair highlights the challenges they presented to the republican colonial politics of the time.[36]

The French colonial expansion beyond the four communes of Senegal, discussed in Chapter 1, started a legal debate. The administration looked for repressive tools that would allow it to control the newly conquered territories effectively. The French legal system was certainly not suitable for this aim. The excuse that was found for these non-democratic devices, as well as for the brutality of punishment, was that the colonial population outside the areas controlled by France since the seventeenth century was unprepared for the principles of French justice. They were still uncivilized, and therefore it was impossible to subject them to civilized law. This view was reinforced by racial theories that flourished in Europe in the late nineteenth century. The conclusion was that inferior and superior races should be governed by different and even opposed political and judicial regimes.[37]

The Jeandet Affair brought a woman who was not entitled in principle to the protection of French metropolitan law into the legal milieu of Saint Louis, which was supposed to be a replica of that same law. The situation was unprecedented, and opened the door for possibilities that the French administration viewed as a nightmare.

Let us now follow the main stages of the affair in Saint Louis before we try to understand the debate on the shape of the colonial legal system in Senegal and beyond. While it might seem that the various stages spanned a long period of time, in fact the entire process between Ba's first attempt to file her complaint and the end of the legal process in Saint Louis took exactly one week. Nevertheless, it was an unusually busy week for the justice system in Senegal's capital.

Ndiereby Ba alighted from the *Germaine* after her long voyage on the Senegal River on 14 November 1890. Her relative Bitti Lokho was waiting for her. Bitti took Ndiereby to her house, where Ndiereby began preparing for her legal struggle. Ndiereby and the people who accompanied her were not alone. They were constantly followed by spies sent by the director of political affairs, Tautin, who reported to him on every move the widow made while in Saint Louis. As we shall see in Chapter 5, this surveillance continued during the entire period Ndiereby spent in Saint Louis.

Three days after Ba's arrival in the city, on 17 November at 4 p.m., the only notary working in Saint Louis, a man called Louis Rivet, was sitting in his office when an unusual group of people entered. He later described their visit in these words:

> The woman [Ba] presented herself, accompanied by Mr. Chadelle, another woman [probably Bitti Lokho], three or four individuals of African descent, and the interpreter to the Government, Samba Fall. Assuming it was just an ordinary matter, I invited everyone to leave except Mr. Chadelle, proposing to use as instrumental witnesses the individuals who usually assist me. However, when I learned about the nature of the act I was being asked to perform, I informed Mr. Chadelle that I wished to have two specific witnesses to verify the identity of this woman who was a stranger to St. Louis. He then brought in two of those who had accompanied her, a merchant, and an Arab schoolmaster.[38]

As we shall see later, the interpreter Rivet mentioned, Samba Fall, played a crucial role in preparing Ndiereby for the mission ahead. The reason for the visit was straightforward and was supposed to be simple. Ndiereby asked to appoint Chadelle as her lawyer and to file a complaint against Aubry-Lecomte, Tautin, and Edward Martin, who, according to her, all played a part in the assassination of her husband. After verifying Ba's identity, Rivet started to work on the required document and asked Chadelle to return later to collect it. But when he came to write down the word '*assassinat*' (assassination) he stopped. He called Chadelle back and told him that he refused to register the complaint.[39]

Ba, Chadelle, Fall, and the others who accompanied the widow were not alone when they marched towards Rivet's office. As usual, Tautin made sure they were followed. In a telegram he sent the governor after the meeting at the notary office, he related that his African spy reported that Ba was acting as a civil party in a criminal complaint.[40] To understand Tautin's alarm when he realized what the widow had requested, a brief explanation of the French system of filing private complaints is needed. A victim of an offence can initiate an action by filing a 'civil party criminal complaint' (un procès au criminel, se portant partie civile) before an instructing judge or trial court. In this manner, the person filing the complaint had a large measure of control over the following action of pressing charges.[41]

It took Chadelle exactly two days to respond to Rivet's action. He sued Rivet for refusing to register his nomination as Ba's attorney and her complaint against the administrators. Chadelle claimed that as Rivet was the only notary in Saint Louis, and therefore the only person who could register him as Ba's attorney and open the procedure for filing her complaint, his refusal to do so caused his client great harm. The resultant trial against Rivet is interesting as it was the only one that actually took place during the affair. In all the other cases, the colonial administration succeeded in preventing the complaints from ever reaching trial. It was also the only legal victory that Ba's side managed to achieve. On one side was the plaintiff, Ba, represented by her lawyer, Chadelle. On the other side was the accused Rivet and his lawyer, Jules Couchard. Couchard would later play a central role in the affair. He was a French lawyer, who represented the interests of the small European population of Saint Louis, and was an ardent supporter of the administration. In February 1892 he would become Ba's lawyer, probably without her genuine consent, and would put an end to the scandal. But at this early stage Couchard defended Rivet in court and lost. One of the main arguments of the defence was the intention of one of the administrators Ba complained against, Aubry-Lecomte, to leave Senegal as part of a delegation to the Gambia. The administrator was supposed to board the ship *Brandon*, on 20 November, so time was short. Chadelle stated that Aubry-Lecomte was trying to evade interrogation and that his absence would harm his client's case. He brought legal references to prove that Rivet should not have refused to register the complaint, and added that his actions obstructed justice. He asked that Rivet be fined the heavy sum of 10,000 francs for the serious damage caused to his client. Couchard agreed that Rivet was indeed obliged to register the complaint, but claimed that the damage caused to Ba was not that serious and did not justify the fine. Finally, the court accepted Couchard's claim, but demanded the immediate registration of the complaint and imposed a fine of 100 francs for each day of delay. It also imposed the court costs on Rivet.[42]

This legal victory terrified the governor as well as the accused administrators. As they suspected, Chadelle did not waste any time and, on the following day, he filed Ba's complaint. While the examining magistrate, Auguste Raymondon, agreed to open an investigation against the accused, according to French law, he had to demand Ba pay a sum of 500 francs in advance to cover the court's expenses in case she lost.[43] This rule applied to any foreigner who pressed charges within the French legal system. While the governor hoped that this would be an obstacle for Ba's complaint, she paid the sum, which was probably given to her by her métis supporters. The road was now opened for a criminal investigation against the administrators and even the possibility of their arrest. The governor was in panic. His state of mind is revealed in a telegram he sent to Etienne, the colonial under-secretary on the same day Ba's complaint was filed. After recounting to Etienne what had happened so far, he wrote the following:

> This affair is already having a deplorable effect on public opinion, and its developments could seriously compromise authority over indigenous populations. It is urgent, above all, that if debates are to take place, they should occur outside Senegal. I request immediate instructions, either for the measures indicated in the letter of November 5th, or to issue an order without the advice of the Advisory Council, or finally, for any measures necessary to stop the scandal.[44]

The governor had one hope. He counted on Larrouy, who had replaced Ursleur as the president of the tribunal of Saint Louis, to prevent the scandal by issuing a decree that would stop the legal procedure or by finding another legal solution to the problem. To end the legal procedures against the administrators and to prevent a scandal on that same day, the governor convened the Advisory Council, of which Larrouy was also a member. In the meantime, to prevent the mortifying scene of colonial administrators being arrested and questioned following the complaint of a young woman from Fouta Toro, the governor asked Larrouy to suspend all procedures for three days, until he had received instructions from the ministry in Paris. The governor seemed to be positive that Larrouy, who had initially agreed to the request, would keep his promise, although the warning he had received the day before from his chief secretary, who had been present at Rivet's hearing, should perhaps have alerted him: 'I attended the hearing; the judgment was postponed until four o'clock. All of this is a shameful plot by the magistrates, including, of course, the head of the Judicial Service, whom one must be wary of.'[45]

The Advisory Council was appointed by the governor and its members were supposed to offer him advice on matters falling under their expertise. Apart from the governor, its session on

20 November 1890 included nine men in various positions, including Larrouy, the head of the judicial service, Fawtier, head of interior affairs, De Kersaint-Gilly, head of the administrative service, Boistel, commander of the marines, Colonna, superior commander of the troops, and Farques, the secretary and archivist who had previously alerted the governor to Larrouy's possible attitude. During this turbulent week, the council convened twice, and its meetings were long and full of tension. In Chapter 4, I will discuss in depth the main insights that these long debates provide, and that shed light on the legal aspects of the affair. Here I will confine myself to outlining how these two meetings sealed the fate of Ba's complaint and prevented it from coming to trial in the colony.

The first meeting of the Advisory Council began at 10 a.m. and continued until 5:15 p.m. According to the French tradition of taking a long lunch break, even during emergencies, the discussions paused between 11:45 a.m. and 2:00 p.m. The protocol, which probably omitted some of the more difficult expressions voiced during the session, as protocols usually do, still reflects the tense atmosphere and the animosity between some of the council's members. The main person who was under constant pressure to align himself with the majority of the council's members was Ursleur's replacement, Larrouy. As we shall see, he did not succumb to this pressure and refused to divert from what he saw as the clear word of the law.

During the session, the governor proposed several options to end the procedures against the administrators, all of which will be reviewed in Chapter 4. Every proposal was rejected by Larrouy. The only person in the room who supported Larrouy and voted in line with his statements was the head of interior affairs, Fawtier. This was the same person who tried in vain on 15 September to stop the illegal executions of the Lam Toro and his cousin. During the heated debates, the head of the administrative service, De Kersaint-Gilly, asked several times for three people to be brought before the council, who, according to him, could shed light on the dubious motives behind the complaint and its immorality. These were Ndiereby Ba, the interpreter Boubakar Abdoul, who was initially one of the suspects in the so-called conspiracy to murder Jeandet, and the notary who had refused to register Ba's complaint, Rivet. Larrouy objected to this proposal, asserting that there was nothing to be gained from talking to these people; but most of the members supported the proposal. As we shall see in Chapter 5, the three interviews shed light on the administration's attempts to present Ba as a puppet of powerful men who were not interested in justice but only in embarrassing the administration and weakening French authority in the colony and beyond.

After Larrouy had rejected all the governor's legal solutions, de Lamothe asked him again to suspend the procedures for three days to allow him to ask the colonial under-secretary in Paris to approve his last suggestion—declaring the tribunal of Saint Louis incompetent to judge a case of a political nature. Although Larrouy asserted that this solution was legally invalid, he agreed to suspend the procedures for three days.[46]

Soon, however, the governor discovered that this promise had not been kept. The next day Chadelle heard that Aubry-Lecomte was about to board a ship on his way to the Gambia. He wrote to the governor demanding the prevention of the administrator from leaving the colony. He also notified the examining magistrate, Raymondon, about Aubry-Lecomte's plans, and he ordered the investigation to resume immediately. Raymondon then summoned the three suspects to his office. In response, the governor transferred the case from Raymondon to de Montlanqua, the president of the Saint Louis tribunal, but the latter refused to cooperate. The enraged governor had no option but to summon his Advisory Council again to prevent the imminent arrest of his administrators.

The council convened the next day, on 22 November. This time, Colonel Alfred Amédée Dodds, who was absent from the first meeting, was present. Dodds was a métis who had advanced well in the French army. He had supervised repressive colonial wars in various parts of the French empire. In Senegal, Dodds commanded the forces that defeated Lat Dior, the ruler of Cayor, and took part in the final campaigns to suppress resistance in Fouta Toro.[47] The strong position Dodds took against Ba's complaint and her métis supporters demonstrates that race was not always the crucial element in the debate around the law in the colony.

The governor opened the session with an explanation for summoning the council's members only two days after the previous meeting. He expressed his shock and anger at Larrouy's failure to fulfil his promise to delay the procedures against the administrators for three days while he awaited instructions from Paris. He was also upset that Larrouy did not recognize that the request for delay came from the council and was not just the governor's wish. Larrouy responded that he had indeed promised a three-day delay, but was not aware at the time that Aubry-Lecomte was planning to leave Senegal. The moment Raymondon heard from Chadelle about this, he had no choice but to open the inquiry. The governor did not accept this explanation and saw it simply as an excuse. He said that Aubry-Lecomte had left for a reason and was not trying to escape justice, and that he would return immediately if instructed to do so.

This assertion was a lie. In the letter de Lamothe sent to the minister in Paris in early November, mentioned previously, he explained the steps he would take if his administrators were in danger of arrest: 'Perhaps the best solution would be the more or less prolonged absence of the officials against whom the new procedure would obviously be directed. Mr. Aubry-Lecomte will be in Gambia in about a fortnight. I could grant Mr. Tautin administrative leave to return to France.'[48] So, while Aubry-Lecomte was indeed supposed to go to the Gambia, his departure coincided fortuitously with the governor's intention to send him, as well as Tautin, away in any event, to avoid an embarrassing arrest.

At a certain point, some of the council members wanted to summon Raymondon to the meeting so that he could be persuaded to suspend the legal procedures against the administrators, but Larrouy insisted that he go alone to speak to Raymondon. The council recessed for 45 minutes, but the result disappointed the governor. The judge refused to suspend the investigation. One wonders if Larrouy even tried to convince Raymondon. He did not seem to think that Raymondon should succumb to this demand, and his insistence to go to talk to him alone reinforces the likelihood that he made little attempt at persuasion.

When Larrouy returned to the meeting with a negative answer, he was attacked from all directions. Dodds even warned him that his attitude might lead to his dismissal, to which Larrouy responded that he was not impressed by threats. Again and again, the governor and the other council members urged Larrouy to approve legal measures to declare the court incompetent, which had been suggested in the first meeting. Larrouy insisted such a measure would obstruct justice. He suggested trying to delay the investigation until 25 November, but this time he did not promise he would succeed, and the governor could not put much hope in his suggestion. The situation, according to de Lamothe, was alarming. Tension in the city was high and troubles were on their way.[49]

The governor did not hesitate much and went into action. He allowed Aubry-Lecomte to leave for the Gambia the next day[50] and, despite Larrouy's objection, he declared the Saint Louis tribunal had no jurisdiction in the affair related to Ba's complaint.[51] It took him three more days to get rid of Larrouy and send him back to Paris. The governor also dismissed the other judiciary members who supported Ba, thus giving himself more latitude in which he could freely operate.[52] This purge legally ended the affair, but there was still one person the governor had not managed to dispose of—the widow, Ndiereby Ba. She insisted on staying in Saint Louis and, as long as she was there, the governor could not sleep well at night. Eventually, the governor's fears materialized. Ndiereby's insistence on staying in Saint Louis led to a final act in this legal drama, which took place in Paris. Before we look at the special role Ndiereby played in the affair and its final stage in the metropole, Chapter 4 examines more deeply the two main opposing positions regarding the affair, as well as the two main tactics de Lamothe resorted to while trying to end the scandal and prevent its revival. These tactics can shed light on the effectiveness of the law as a tool of administrative authority in Senegal, as well as its limitations.

Notes

1 Archives Nationales, Paris, BB/6(II)/603, 25 September 1889.
2 CAOM, Sénégal IV, 66 a, 17 September 1890. A telegram from Ursleur to the Governor of Senegal.
3 *Ibid.*
4 ANS, Fond ancien AOF série G 13G 135 Bobine 275, A telegram from Clément Thomas to Urseur, 18 September 1890.
5 CAOM, FR ANOM Sénégal IV 66a, Telegram from Clément Thomas to the Minister of the Colonies in Paris, 19 Septempber 1890.
6 CAOM, FR ANOM Sénégal IV 66a, Télégramme, Fawtier à Gouverneur Clément Thomas, 19 September 1890.
7 Manchuelle, 'Métis et colons,' 490.
8 Robinson, *Paths of Accommodation*, 108.
9 Jones, *The Metis of Senegal*, 140; 232n3.

10 Robinson, *Paths of Accommodation*, 109. It is interesting to note that Descemet, despite his support for the French, also assisted Lam Toro Sidick, who he met in 1886. Nevertheless, in the Jeandet Affair he chose to side with the governor. See: Jones, *The Metis of Senegal*, 151.
11 Jones, *The Metis of Senegal*, 128.
12 Jones, *The Metis of Senegal*, 139–155; Manchuelle, 'Métis et Colons,' 477–504.
13 CAOM, Sénégal IV, 66 a, 16 January 1891.
14 Biti [sic] est une femme de mauvaise conduite, ivrognesse affectant la pratique étroite d'un islamisme bigot. Elle est propriétaire de la maison qu'elle habite grâce à une véritable escroquerie aux dépens du traitant Blandin Diop, son mari divorcé. CAOM, Sénégal IV, 66 a, undated (probably December 1890).
15 CAOM, Sénégal IV, 66 a, undated (probably December 1890).
16 Van Troi Tran, 'How "Natives" Ate at Colonial Exhibitions in 1889, 1900 and 1931,' *French Cultural Studies* 26, no. 2 (2015).
17 CAOM, Sénégal IV, 66 a, undated (probably December 1890).
18 *Ibid.*
19 Interview with Haruna Diop, Dakar, 13 February 2020.
20 CAOM, Sénégal IV, 66 a, undated (probably December 1890); 20 November 1890.
21 This description is based on a series of telegrams exchanged between Saint Louis and Podor from 4 to 11 November 1890: CAOM, Sénégal IV, 66 a. Jenadet mentioned the *Germaine* in one of his letters to his parents and said that it usually carried gum between the commerce stations along the river. Archives de Saône-et-Loire, François Joseph Etienne Abel Jeandet, F 1412, 13 January 1888.
22 Richard Roberts, *Litigants and Households: African Disputes and Colonial Courts in the French Soudan, 1895–1912* (Portsmouth: Heinemann, 2005), 35–36.
23 Roberts, *Litigants and Households*, 37–40.
24 Samp, 'Affaire Albert [Sic] Jeandet: la peine de mort sans procès,' 225.
25 Roberts, *Litigants and Households*, 44–47. George Ernest Jean-Marie Boulanger was a French general and politician nicknamed 'Général Révanche' because of his support for a war against Germany to retrieve Alsace and Lorraine. His charisma and popularity, which reached its zenith in January 1889, alarmed the French government, which feared he could topple the Third Republic and become a dictator. His movement failed later that year due to his lack of consistency and weakness. He finally killed himself in 1891 beside his lover's grave. See: William D. Irvine, *The Boulanger Affair Reconsidered:*

Royalism, Boulangism, and the Origins of the Radical Right in France (Oxford: Oxford University Press, 1988).
26 Roberts, *Litigants and Households*, 56.
27 Kristin Mann and Richard Roberts, *Law in Colonial Africa* (Portsmouth: Heinemann, 1991), 12.
28 Dominique Sarr and Richard Roberts, 'The Jurisdiction of Muslim Tribunals in Colonial Senegal, 1857–1932,' *Law in Colonial Africa* (1991), 133–134.
29 Gilles Le Béguec, *La république des avocats* (Paris: Armand Colin, 2003).
30 Roberts, *Litigants and Households*, 50.
31 Jones, *The Metis of Senegal*, 113–114.
32 Véronique Hélénon, *French Caribbeans in Africa: Diasporic Connections and Colonial Administration, 1880–1939* (New York: Palgrave Macmillan US, 2011), 2–6.
33 Hilary Jones, 'Fugitive Slaves and Christian Evangelism in French West Africa: A Protestant Mission in Late Nineteenth-Century Senegal,' *Slavery & Abolition* 38, no. 1 (2017).
34 Hélénon, *French Caribbeans in Africa*, 15.
35 François Manchuelle, 'Le rôle des antillais dans L'apparition du nationalisme culturel en Afrique noire francophone,' *Cahiers d'études africaines* (1992), 376–377.
36 Hélénon, *French Caribbeans in Africa*, 31–32.
37 Olivier Le Cour Grandmaison, 'The Exception and the Rule: On French Colonial Law,' *Diogenes* 53, no. 4 (2006), 36–37.
38 CAOM, Sénégal IV, 66 a, the Advisory Council session of 20 November 1890.
39 *Ibid.*
40 CAOM, Sénégal IV, 66 a, telegram from the director of Political Affairs to the governor, 18 November 1890.
41 P. M. Bakshi, 'Continental System of Criminal Justice,' *Journal of the Indian Law Institute* 36, no. 4 (1994), 424.
42 CAOM, Sénégal IV, 66 a, Tribunal de 1ère Instance de Saint-Louis, 19 November 1890.
43 CAOM, Sénégal IV, 66 a, 22 November 1890.
44 CAOM, Sénégal IV, 66 a, telegram from the governor of Senegal to the Ministry of the Colonies, 20 November 1890.
45 CAOM, Sénégal IV, 66 a, telegram from the chief secretary to the governor, 19 November 1890.
46 CAOM, Sénégal IV, 66 a, the Advisory Council session of 20 November 1890.
47 Jones, *The Metis of Senegal*, 136–137.

48 CAOM, Sénégal I 90, 5 November 1890. Letter from de Lamothe to the Under-Secretary of State in the Ministry of the Colonies.
49 CAOM, Sénégal IV, 66 a, the Advisory Council session of 22 November 1890.
50 ANS, Fond ancien AOF, 13G 135 letter from Chadelle to the governor, 23 November 1890.
51 CAOM, Sénégal I 90, Déclinatoire de compétence, 23 November 1890.
52 CAOM, Sénégal IV, 66 a, 22 November, 27 November 1890.

4

The affair in Saint Louis

The late nineteenth century was a time of transformation in Senegal. From a small colony consisting of four strongholds on the coast, in which all inhabitants, including Africans, were subject to a French legal system, with all its rights and benefits, French territory was becoming much wider. With the massive colonization and penetration deep into the hinterland, vast populations were added to the growing West African empire. Legally, the game had changed and therefore its rules had to be revised. The affair and the crisis it caused left no time for long theoretical debates. As we saw in Chapter 3, the governor was under immense pressure to prevent his administrators from being arrested and the colony from falling into dangerous turmoil. The scandal thus exposes, in a very clear and distilled manner, the two main opposing positions regarding the idea of 'colonial justice' at a time of massive expansion of French territories and the inclusion of new populations within them. The scandal also highlights the extent to which the higher administrative authority in the colony could overcome a legal challenge using legally dubious tactics. The chapter thus examines the two main tactics the governor used in his efforts to end the affair. As long as de Lamothe still thought he could convince the judiciary to stop the legal procedures against his administrators, he opted for the manipulation of the law. After realizing he could not win this way, he turned to the removal of his opponents.

But before we delve into the heated debate that took place during the brief stage of the affair in Saint Louis, a few words are needed about Henri Félix de Lamothe, the governor who presided over these discussions and who had acted fiercely to put a quick end to the affair. Born in Metz in 1843, de Lamothe lived a long and eventful life, of which five years were dedicated to serving as governor of Senegal (1890–1895). He held three different careers during his life. His military career spanned nine years from 1862 to 1871, during which he fought in the Hungarian legion in Italy.[1] His subsequent journalistic career lasted the next 15 years from 1871 to 1886, during which he served as a correspondent for various journals, including *Le Temps*, which focused on diplomatic affairs. As a journalist, de Lamothe was sent to various cities in the Balkans, and even reached Canada, where he wrote an essay titled 'Excursion au Canada et à la rivière Rouge du Nord' (Excursion in Canada and the Red River of the North).[2] De Lamothe's third career was as a colonial administrator. He started this career relatively late, aged 43. His first posting, the one immediately before Senegal, was as the commander of the islands of Saint Pierre and Miquelon, located in the north-western Atlantic Ocean, where he served from 1886 to 1890. After his five-year term in Senegal, de Lamothe was sent to Guiana, the Congo, Cochin-China, and Cambodia, his last posting before his retirement in 1907. He died in Paris in 1926.

While in Senegal de Lamothe resisted any attempts at criticizing the administration. He opposed the revival of the local press, after four years of closure due to its criticism of the violence that characterized the French military campaigns under Governor Genouille. De Lamothe also used his position to investigate individuals or institutions that impeded the administration's initiatives. He tried to limit the power of the democratic institutions in Saint Louis and he developed a deep animosity towards the Devès clan and their allies. In February 1891, for example, he ordered the municipality to be dissolved, and removed Crespin, Devès's ally, from the mayor's office.[3] De Lamothe's dislike of Crespin was so great that, when the latter died unexpectedly in 1895, rumours circulated around Saint Louis—following the suspicions of Crespin's aunt—that de Lamothe had poisoned him. These rumours might have been the reason for de Lamothe's sudden departure from Senegal before the official end of his term as governor.[4] Nevertheless, the governor gave a moving speech at Crespin's funeral. Finally, de Lamothe was enthusiastic about the policy of disannexation, discussed in the Introduction, which meant demoting territories under direct French rule and therefore subject to French law to the status of protectorates, in which French law did not apply.[5]

De Lamothe's arrival in the colony coincided precisely with the moment of crisis that followed the illegal action taken under his predecessor, Clément-Thomas, who had already left the colony's capital. De Lamothe's repressive stance partially emerged from this crisis, but it probably also reflected the views he held prior to his arrival in Saint Louis in September 1890. In any case, his strong resolve to put a quick end to the affair at any cost, shaped the debate over colonial justice.

The desired extent of French law

The debate over the concept of 'colonial law' revolved around one main question. Given that French colonial territory was rapidly expanding, and new populations had thereby come under French rule, was it still desirable, or even possible, to implement French law in the newly acquired colonial territories and to allow the new colonial subjects to receive the full protection of French law? This debate highlights the real French approach to the idea of assimilation. While the local population in Senegal was manageable and limited to the four communes, this idea could survive the basic administrative hostility towards it. When the French expanded their territory and ventured into vaster areas, taking over large populations, this idea could no longer hold water. From grudgingly accepting this ideology in the French communes, the French administration fully rejected it in its growing empire. Assimilation could no longer work and had to be replaced by a set of vague and often meaningless concepts put under the umbrella term 'association.'

The two opposing sides in this debate were aligned mainly according to profession and/or role within the colony. Many of the representatives of the Saint Louis judiciary believed that French legal principles should be maintained at all costs. An illegal action had occurred in a territory where French law applied, therefore legal procedures should be taken against those who had committed the act. They maintained that if no legal action were taken against the administrators who had broken the law, no person in the colony, be they European, métis, or African would feel legally protected. Most of the administrators and military personnel disagreed. As we shall see, the colonial administration acknowledged the formal illegality of the executions. Nevertheless, they claimed that this was insignificant, and only served as an excuse for people who wanted to destabilize the colony—that is, Devès and his supporters. In short, the governor and most of the administration saw the scandal as a matter of political manoeuvring rather than as a genuine struggle for justice.

The Advisory Council's debate around the term '*assassinat*' (assassination), which was mentioned in Ba's complaint and prompted Rivet's refusal to register her complaint, sheds some light on the different ways in which each side viewed the scandal. According to Dahl's legal dictionary, the French definition of the term '*assassinat*' is as follows: 'Any murder committed with premeditation or ambush is classified as assassination (Penal C. Art. 296).'[6] Rivet maintained that this term was shameful and had nothing to do with the administrators. Jeandet was the one who had been assassinated; accusing French administrators of assassination put them in the same category as Kaccé and his associates. For Ba's lawyer, Chadelle, who most probably formulated the complaint, his client's husband was indeed murdered, as extra-judicial execution with no due legal process, not to mention a fair trial, was equivalent to murder.[7]

During the first meeting of the Advisory Council that took place a day after Rivet lost his case, the head of the administrative service justified Rivet's refusal to register the case, stating that the administrators had only followed orders and therefore could not be referred to as assassins. Larrouy responded by emphasizing that a civil party could use any legal term he or she wished to use. Moreover, he justified the choice of the term by quoting the above-mentioned legal definition of '*assassinat*':

> Now, this act is classified as 'assassination,' as can be easily seen in Article 296 of the Penal Code, which states that 'any murder committed with premeditation or ambush is classified as assassination.' In this case, the murder was indeed committed with premeditation, according to the complaint of the civil party, and there is no doubt about it. Therefore, no other legal term could be found other than that of assassination.[8]

Larrouy then embraced Ba and Chadelle's definition of the crime that had been committed by the administrators. During the second meeting, two days later, Colonel Dodds expressed his rage about the use of this term that made criminals of the administrators. To highlight his anger, he proclaimed: 'I support them, that makes me a criminal!' (Je les approuve, donc je suis un criminel!).[9]

This argument is important because it demonstrates that, for the administration, conquest and colonial stability were ends that justified the means. It was impossible to achieve these goals while adhering to French law that had nothing to do, according to this view, with the people and territories that were being colonized. Therefore, administrators acting against people who had murdered or conspired to murder an administrator could not be termed assassins. Using this term was, for de Lamothe, a savage attack on the essence of French colonial rule. The entire scandal, for him, was putting at risk every European in the colony and undermining colonial authority in the territories the French were in the process of colonizing.

A report written by Tautin a week or so after the heated debate in the meetings of the Advisory Council clarified the administration's position regarding the affair, and its justification of an action they knew was illegal. In his report, Tautin tackled the Saint Louis judges' three criticisms of the administrators' actions after Jeandet's murder: the lack of due legal process, the problematic location of the executions, and their brutality.

As for committing the executions in a territory under direct French rule, Tautin explained that, after Jeandet's murder, the people of Guédé felt that they had won. They said to all those who supported France: 'we have killed your commander, now you are left without protection.' According to Tautin, the traders along the river, who due to Jeandet's policy had begun to feel safe again, were so afraid that they refrained from joining Jeandet's funeral, even though they loved him. The Tokolor bragged that they had killed a Christian. So the governor did not hesitate to order the burning down of Guédé—as he argued that no one was innocent there—and the execution of the murderer and his two accomplices. In fact, as we shall soon see, the order did not actually come from the governor. As for the burning down of Guéde, this collective punishment ultimately did not take place, perhaps due to the start of the judicial investigation.

Tautin acknowledged that the executions were performed in a manner that was later criticized, and pointed out that they should have been performed outside the annexed territory by a protected local chief. He nevertheless claimed that it was necessary to perform the executions in Podor in order to maintain the governor's control over the territory.

Tautin provided an interesting explanation for the location of the executions. He wrote:

> Podor is the district's capital; Podor has a position that could guarantee our security; Podor is the only point where we could gather all the leaders to make them witnesses to the punishment. In Podor, we clearly, squarely assumed responsibility for the execution; elsewhere and otherwise, we hid. Given the way it was done, we carried out an execution and we punished; otherwise, we would simply have resorted to assassination.

In this short paragraph, Tautin exposes the hypocrisy of the Saint Louis judges. They would not have protested against an execution outside French direct rule, even if it were clear that it was done to punish the murderers of an administrator. Therefore, what bothered them was not that three men were executed brutally without a trial but, rather, that it was done in a certain location and thus tainted the French legal system. In practice, so Tautin claimed, carrying out the executions in Podor represented justice, while doing the same by hiding behind a local chief in a foreign location would have been murder.

Tautin not only justified the location of the executions but also the lack of any proper trial. He maintained that the legal procedures, thought to be essential by Ursleur, were impossible to implement under the circumstances:

> But if we had proceeded, as Mr. Ursleur, Chief of the Judicial Service, has claimed we should have, through the criminal investigation and the Assize Court, [already] long ago anything even remotely related to Europeans would have been looted and slaughtered! What do these punishments, which only occur after several months, mean in the eyes of the Blacks, to whom their civilized or semi-civilized friends rightly promise escape? Because in regular justice, the guilty would have inevitably escaped: foreign subjects having committed a crime on foreign territory, they would have challenged the jurisdiction of the court, which would have inevitably accepted their challenge.[10]

Tautin was sure that a trial would only have resulted in setting the culprits free. He blamed their supporters in Saint Louis, both the civilized, probably of European origin, and the semi-civilized, presumably referring to the métis who had supported Ba's complaint. He went on to ask: 'Since when, moreover, have the constantly recurring political difficulties in these countries, which are merely subject to our influence, been resolved through legal means?' Tautin claimed that Ursleur was aware of this and, at first, did not think to interfere, but later he had understood that this was an opportunity to denigrate the administration, so he acted out of political motives rather than in the interests of seeking justice. 'Justice,' so he wrote, 'which is not otherwise prepared for this category of affairs through constant study, would be blind and always limping.'[11]

Tautin mentioned that only by combining the location, the swiftness, and form of the punishment could the administration return Toro to tranquillity. By form he meant the brutal way Kaccé, Sall, and Yoro were executed, as detailed in Chapter 2. To counter the judiciary's criticism on this issue, Tautin explained that the fact that a Muslim had killed a Christian was crucial, especially in a region in which the Muslims belonged to what he described as the intolerant order of the Tidjaniya. The agents of Abdoul Bokar and Ahmadou would not hesitate to offer paradise to the authors of such murder.[12] Here Tautin excused the brutality of the executions with the so-called Muslim superstitions according to which an unwhole person could not enter paradise. He noted that the only way to prevent murder of Europeans in the future was to prove to the Africans that by killing a European their road to paradise would be closed.[13]

The administration's position, then, was that only by acting exactly as they had done could the administrators restore peace and order to the turbulent region of Fouta Toro after Jeandet's murder. A recurrent point that the supporters of this view raised during the meetings was that, by proceeding with Ba's complaint and summoning the administrators for interrogation, which could even lead to arrest, the judiciary would return Fouta Toro to a state of turmoil, and perhaps even bring chaos to the capital Saint Louis.[14] Furthermore, legal proceedings against the three administrators would undermine the confidence and sense of security of every administrator serving in distant outposts. In this regard, Tautin wrote that the administrators who were in an 'un pays non-assimilé' (unassimilated country) among hostile populations had only their prestige to protect them.

> But this prestige is a very weak bulwark. The death of Jeandet, perhaps the most beloved among us, at the same time as one of those who enjoyed the greatest influence and authority, the death of Jeandet, by overturning this cardboard barrier, would have shown weakness, even futility, to all our subjects if repression had not come immediately.

He added that if it were possible freely to murder an administrator representing French authority no one along the river would be safe.

Finally, Tautin summed up the administration's position by stating that the continuation of the affair would set a dangerous precedent. 'Today the court accepts the lawsuit made by Sidick's widow against those who took part in the executions (or more correctly, advised it). The result may be that we will have to bombard Guédé to restore security. In any case, this will be a dangerous precedent.' To demonstrate this point, he provided a list of all the local rulers who had been disposed of by the French, whose men had been killed, whose territories had been conquered, and whose treasures had been seized. The continuation of the affair could create the inconceivable situation whereby all these rulers would be able to turn to the courts and sue the administrators who had harmed them. This, remarked Tautin, would mean anarchy and revolt. For him, all these actions were not crimes to be brought to trial, but rather legitimate political actions aimed at ensuring French colonial rule. Indeed, the actions Tautin described were what made French colonization of West Africa possible in the first place. Tautin therefore saw the acceptance of Ba's lawsuit as a threat to the entire colonial project.[15]

De Lamothe recognized the illegality of the executions. The final sentence of a letter he sent the colonial under-secretary in early November proves this point, as well as the governor's anger and frustration at the administrators' conduct: 'And to think that none of this could have happened if, while delivering summary justice, there had been some concern to make it less extra-legal!'[16] The governor was not upset by the decision to execute summary justice, as he called it, but rather by the grave mistake of performing it in the wrong place, thereby generating the opportunity for a legal scandal. His position, though, was that French law could not be applied to the people the French were in the process of subjugating. As he also tried to limit the democratic institutions in Saint

Louis, his objection to extending the protection of French law to the inhabitants of the newly conquered territories is not surprising. Nevertheless, aware of the Saint Louis judiciary's strong stance in favour of Ba's legal struggle, de Lamothe tried to beat the judges at their own game by manipulating the law to fit his own aims.

Manipulating the law

In its first session, the Advisory Council discussed the question of who had given the order to carry out the executions. De Lamothe said that initially this was not clear, but he checked this point with Clément-Thomas who assured him that it was indeed he who had given the order. It is most likely that this was a lie. Clément-Thomas had been absent from Saint Louis when the executions took place. His replacement, until de Lamothe's arrival, was Fawtier. While in principle, Clément-Thomas could have given the order from Dakar, no documentary order could be found. The only document was the telegram that was sent by Fawtier to Podor ordering no further executions and for the suspects to be brought to Saint Louis for trial.

In fact, de Lamothe had sent a letter to Etienne on 5 November, just after he had heard the rumours that Devès intended to revive the scandal, expressing his astonishment at the lack of written evidence for Clément-Thomas's order to carry out the executions. He wrote:

> Bayedi Catié [sic] was executed on September 10. The other executions were the subject of numerous telegrams exchanged from the 11th to the 14th. They took place on the morning of the 15th, and on the same day, Mr. Tautain telegraphed from St. Louis to Mr. Aubry-Lecomte, who was seeking instructions on various points left pending, telling him that he could no longer respond—given the Governor's departure. How is it that Mr. Clément Thomas did not see fit to personally sign orders that raised such serious questions of responsibility? He must have said it, and it is not for me to investigate.[17]

In view of this letter, it is unclear whether de Lamothe indeed asked Clément-Thomas about his responsibility for the executions. While de Lamothe might have spoken with his predecessor between 5 and 20 November, the words 'Il a dû le dire' (he must have said it) and 'il ne m'appartient pas de le rechercher ' (it is not for me to investigate) seem to suggest that he did not. Why then would he insist that Clément-Thomas had given the order?

The main reason for de Lamothe's insistence was a clause of an 1840 law that prohibited taking legal action against a serving governor. De Lamothe thought that, if Clément-Thomas took responsibility for the illegal executions, then the complaint was in fact against him and therefore legally void. When de Lamothe opened the first council meeting on 20 November, he suggested that the legal procedures should be stopped immediately as they contravened article 61 of the organic ordinance of Senegal. According to this clause: 'The governor cannot be sued or prosecuted within the colony during the exercise of his functions.'[18]

The governor had two difficulties in relying upon this law dated from 1840. One was that the complaint had not been made against the governor, but against his subordinates, and there was no proof the order had come from Clément-Thomas. The other was that the governor was no longer present in the colony. Nevertheless, de Lamothe and his supporters in the council found creative ways to overcome these difficulties. De Lamothe first insisted that Clément-Thomas had given the order to execute the suspects. When Fawtier raised doubts about that and asked for written proof, the governor apologized for not being able to present the documents attesting to it. He offered no explanation, probably because no such documents ever existed. He then declared that Clément-Thomas had confided to him that it was indeed he who had given the order. He concluded that the complaint was therefore ultimately against the governor and should duly be rejected. This argument was dubious, as the complaint was specifically aimed at the administrators and not at the governor. As for the absence of Clément-Thomas from the colony, de Lamothe was even less persuasive and very vague saying:

> It is true that Mr. Clément-Thomas is no longer in the Colony, but is there no reason to consider that, even though he is no longer in office, he remains covered by article 61, which may also have intended to state that a governor cannot be pursued within the colony 'during the exercise of this functions' as well as on the occasion of the exercise of his functions.[19]

The blundering formulation of this argument reflects the governor's state of mind. The desperate urgency he felt to stop the legal proceedings against his subordinates led him to rely upon a law that had little to do with the case before him. This law, according to him, 'may have also intended to state' something that would save the colony from a scandal. But as Larrouy calmly argued, it had not. 'There was no point in searching in the law from 1840 something that simply is not there,' Larrouy explained to the agitated governor. He continued to cite a different article from the same law, which the governor conveniently forgot to mention, and which forbade the governor from interfering with the course of justice in the colony. Larrouy also rejected the governor's claim that the complaint was in fact ultimately against Clément-Thomas. First, it was not against Clément-Thomas and, in any event, the civil party had the right to choose the target of the complaint. Second, because there was no proof that Clément-Thomas had indeed given the order, he may have taken responsibly later in order to protect his subordinates. Third, even if he had given the order, such an order was illegal, and the administrators should not have followed it.[20]

After failing to convince Larrouy to cite article 61 to stop the procedures, de Lamothe tried a different strategy. He raised the question of formality, arguing that this was the only problem with the executions. The murder was committed by a foreigner, on foreign soil. Had the ruler of that territory punished the murderer, it would have been done in exactly the same way and the justice system in Saint Louis would have nothing to say about it. The formalities were not observed, there was no debate about that, but that was all that had been wrongly done. Had the executions taken place a few steps outside of Podor, the scandal would never have arisen.[21] By means of this strategy, the governor tried to create the impression that the issue was not as grave as had been suggested by Larrouy.

But Larrouy refused to accept these arguments as well. When the superior commander of the army supported the governor's position and said he would be happy to know if the '*femme*' (woman) Ndiereby Ba, came to Saint Louis alone out of her own free will, Larrouy could not contain himself any longer and responded in what seems to be an angry and accusatory manner:

> Mr. Head of the Judicial Service responds that he is not tasked with playing the role of the police; he has no spies under his command and does not concern himself with matters that do not fall under his jurisdiction. We are faced with a fact. The complaint from the civil party, the requisitions are recorded, and the Examining Magistrate is obligated, under penalty of denial of justice, to investigate the case. If it were only a matter of the sole person of Mr. Jeandet's murderer, even though the protective forms of justice owed to any accused were lacking, the justice system would have contented itself with protesting without attaching any further interest to this case. However, two alleged accomplices were executed, whose guilt was so doubtful that the commission, which had just carried out the execution of the [main person], did not dare to take it upon itself to execute the accomplices. Instead, it limited itself to referring them to Saint Louis at the disposal of the Governor.[22]

Larrouy's words convey his frustration with the entire debate. The statement that he did not have spies at his disposal could be an allusion to the spies hired by Tautin to follow Ba and her supporters all over Saint Louis. While remaining polite for most of the discussion, Larrouy here criticized the administration in very clear terms. He rejected the efforts to find a legal way to stop the proceedings, and even argued that the examining magistrate would be denying justice were he to do so. Larrouy, interestingly, separated Kaccé's execution, which was also illegal but would not have called for an investigation against the administrators, from that of Sall and Yoro. He suggested that they were not executed along with Kaccé because the local commission had found their guilt to be very dubious and had wanted to send them to Saint Louis to face trial. This is the first time anyone had clearly stated that some of the participants in this delegation were opposed to the second execution. This allegation also raises doubts about the claim that Clément-Thomas had taken responsibility for the order to execute Sall and Yoro.

De Lamothe then suggested another legal mechanism—a challenge to the jurisdiction of the Saint Louis court by employing the decree of conflict (*arreté de conflit*) available in French law.[23] Unfortunately for the frustrated governor, article 1 of the original decree raised an obstacle against its use. It made it very clear that, 'In the future, the conflict of jurisdiction between courts and administrative authority will never be raised in criminal matters.'[24] Larrouy emphasized that, as Ba's complaint was a criminal matter, the conflict decree was not legally valid and could not be used in this case.

Another legal device the governor proposed to use during the debate in the Advisory Council and that was related to the previous one he had suggested was the *déclinatoire de compétence* (plea for jurisdiction), which he occasionally mistakenly referred to as '*déclinatoire de incompétence*.' It seems that de Lamothe used these two terms, the other being the decree of conflict, as alternatives, while in fact they refer to the same legal device. Legally, Larrouy was right to reject the idea of a plea for jurisdiction, as it was part of the same 1828 law, which was irrelevant in criminal cases.[25] Larrouy thus blocked the way for a supposedly legal conclusion of the affair. The governor now had to resort to another more aggressive mechanism to prevent his administrators from being arrested—the removal of the people who stood in the way of the so-called legal termination of the affair.

Eliminating rivals

To clear the way to silencing the affair, the governor had to dispose of a raft of opponents. All barring one, Paul Fawtier, were members of the Saint Louis judiciary. What followed in the next months was a real purge of the judicial service of the colony's capital. Before we examine this purge, a few words are needed about the judicial corpus.

While metropolitan judges had been elected by means of an examination since 1890, this was only applied to judges serving in the colonies from 1924. At the time of the affair, then, colonial judges were appointed by means of discretionary choice and were not elected via a fixed set of rules or professional standards. Most of the judges were probably relatively young. In a census carried out of colonial judges under the Fourth Republic (1944–1958), only 10 percent were above the age of 32. There is no reason to believe that the figures were much different earlier, when conditions in the colonies were much more challenging. The status of overseas judges was first set by a decree on 28 July 1828. A second decree of 1 December 1858 established that they would be under the authority of two ministries—the Justice and the Colonies, or as the latter was known at the time, Algérie et colonies (Algeria and the Colonies). Unlike metropolitan judges who could not be moved from place to place, colonial judges could be transferred to any other location by the governor and the procureur général. This turned the judiciary in the colonies into a service under tutelage. Judges were thus always under threat of transfer at the whim of these two functionaries without any recourse. Transfers were common. Among 680 judges who served in the colonies under the Fourth Republic, only 30 per cent served in the same place for their entire careers.[26]

De Lamothe took advantage of his authority to transfer judges. First, to prevent the immediate arrest of his subordinates de Lamothe had to get rid of Larrouy. He first tried to appoint him as the chief of the Dakar tribunal, but Larrouy refused, claiming this post was inferior to the one he then held. So the governor asked the colonial under-secretary to summon Larrouy back to Paris. His interim replacement, Crayssac, who served as an examining magistrate in Saint Louis at the time, had no objection to the legal measure proposed by the governor. A few days later, the position was given to Chambaud, who also replaced de Montplanqua, the tribunal's president who had supported Larrouy. With Larrouy removed, the governor was now free to ask the ministry in Paris to issue a plea for jurisdiction, which immediately stopped the legal procedures against his administrators.[27] But with the encouragement of his new recruit, Chambaud, de Lamothe was not satisfied merely with Larrouy's removal, and he continued to distance judges who supported Larrouy's position.

Like Ursleur, Chambaud originated from Cayenne, Guiana. Nevertheless, he was very different in his views from Ursleur and other creole judges. His decision to support the governor at the price of his colleagues' hostility and contempt is somewhat unusual for an Antillean serving in the colonies. The governor was very happy with Chambaud, whom he viewed as crucial to his position in the affair. According to his own testimony, Chambaud was isolated from all his colleagues and, in a report he sent the governor on 30 November, only one day after he had confirmed the plea for jurisdiction that stopped the procedures, he denigrated several judicial colleagues, accusing them of acting maliciously against the governor based on political motives while using the term 'justice' as a pretext for their political actions. While he supposedly left to the governor the decision of which measures should be implemented against these judges, he called for a thorough purge of the judicial service, which he now oversaw. Chambaud's fierce stand against his colleagues and the accusations he threw at them may have been borne of their hostility towards him about which he had complained bitterly. It should be stressed, though, that Chambaud had earned this hostility. According to an article published several years after these events in the metropolitan daily *Le Petit Moniteur Universelle* 'as soon as he [Chambaud] took up his position as head of the judiciary, he adopted a tone and demeanour with his colleagues that were hardly in line with the traditions that had prevailed until then.' Chambaud's first action in the colony was to humiliate Larrouy by demanding that the latter administer the oath for him, the same one Larrouy himself had taken when he took up the position. Chambaud was so blinded by his animus that he failed to realize that Larrouy had been dismissed from his position as procureur de la république, and therefore lacked the authority to perform this ceremony designed to humiliate him.[28]

Chambaud accused Larrouy, his deputy Simoneau, the juge d'instruction (examining judge), Raymondon, the tribunal president, de Monplanqua, and other judges of deceiving the governor and of trying to prevent him from blocking the scandal. He refused to accept their claims that they were defending the independence of the court and were acting in the name of justice. He wrote:

> No, the judiciary cannot be a refuge for zealots, imbued with ideas from another era, unwilling to back down from any conflict, no matter how serious, for the sake of mere self-esteem. It is not a class of privileged individuals, as some would claim; it is enough for it to be the elite body that it truly is. Since it is called upon to wield the formidable right to punish others or decide on their interests, it is important for it to show respect and submission to the higher interests of government policy with which it may come into contact.[29]

Chambaud ended this 15-page report specifying all the infractions that his colleagues had supposedly committed by declaring: 'Perhaps ruthless and eternal grudges will follow me in my career. I care not, conscious of having fulfilled the high mission entrusted to me.'[30] The governor took this report very seriously and it apparently convinced him that, in order to prevent the scandal from being resurrected, a thorough purge of the judiciary service should take place. It also convinced him that Chambaud was the right man in the right place at the right moment. Less than a week later, he wrote to the under-secretary of the colonies to ask whether he could make Chambaud's interim position permanent. He expressed his conviction that Chambaud would restore tranquillity and order in the colony, and that he was the right person to oversee a rejuvenated judiciary service after all the disobedient and undisciplined judges had been replaced. The only reservation de Lamothe had regarding Chambaud was his marriage to a local woman *à la mode du pays*. But this was apparently a small price to pay for absolute loyalty in a time of crisis.[31]

Despite the governor's enthusiasm for keeping Chambaud in his post, three months later he was forced to allow him to leave the colony and to move to Cochin-China, where he had served before for a period of ten years, to take up the position of president of the tribunal in Vinh-Long.[32] The reason for Chambaud's decision to move is unclear, but it could be related to the hostility his colleagues felt towards him after he had taken the governor's side.

A long letter the governor sent the colonial under-secretary around the time of Chambaud's departure demonstrates the resentment of the Saint Louis judiciary following Larrouy's dismissal and the suspension of the legal proceedings against the administrators as well as their continued efforts to revive the scandal. The governor opened his letter with an apology for disturbing the under-secretary again concerning the judiciary of Senegal, but suggested that it would be useful for him to hear about even the smallest incident with this body that seemed to have lost all sense of duty:

> Severely judged by the vast majority of the population and almost unanimously by other officials, they had come to form among themselves a kind of circle of admiration and mutual support where all grievances were shared, and a decision was made to overlook all professional shortcomings and other failings of those who were part of it.[33]

He then added that the under-secretary should agree that it was about time all this should end. The governor named three judges who he considered problematic in various degrees. Finally, de Lamothe mentioned Chambaud's report about the behaviour of the remaining judges who remained loyal to Larrouy, and reminded the under-secretary that the resistance of these judges to Chambaud was in fact a challenge to the administrative authority of both himself and of the under-secretary.[34]

After de Lamothe had eliminated all his rivals from the judiciary, there was still one administrator who remained for him to deal with. This was Paul Fawtier, the head of interior affairs, who had briefly replaced Clément-Thomas before de Lamothe's arrival. Fawtier is an interesting figure, as he was the only French administrator who backed Larrouy in the two Advisory Council meetings in November. He opposed the illegal executions from the start, and even tried to prevent the second execution from taking place by sending a telegram, but it was either ignored or did not arrive in time.

Unlike some of his judicial colleagues who were summarily dismissed from their posts in November, Fawtier managed to retain his position until early 1891. On the first day of that year, de Lamothe wrote to Paris that he had managed to smooth out a dispute that erupted between Colonel Dodds and Fawtier involving some insults the administrator had directed at the colonel. While Fawtier eventually withdrew his harsh words, the governor still insisted that he should be sent away from Senegal in the interests of the service of interior affairs and for Fawtier's own personal sake.[35] The telegram does not mention the nature of the unpleasant exchange between the director and the colonel, but it is quite likely that the dispute related to Fawtier's stance in relation to Ba's complaint and his insistence that justice had not been upheld.

Unlike de Lamothe's obvious hostility and personal animosity towards the judges he wanted to remove from Saint Louis, the governor seems to have felt some guilt in complaining about Fawtier to the under-secretary of state. Less than a week after his initial request to remove his subordinate from Senegal, de Lamothe wrote a more detailed letter in which he tried to explain his position. He was aware of Fawtier's administrative career before arriving in Senegal—in Algeria, India, and New Caledonia. He recognized that he was a gifted and intelligent official, but unfortunately, according to the governor, Fawtier 'has everywhere lost himself due to his messy nature and acrimonious turn of his mind.' In an almost psychological analysis, the governor identified a paradox or contradiction within Fawtier that made him 'throw himself into the arms of agitators with restless temperaments and sometimes questionable reputations.'[36] De Lamothe then emphasized that he had no personal grudges against Fawtier and was aware of his difficult circumstances in Senegal and his family situation, about which he did not elaborate. Nevertheless, he could not keep him in his position as he needed loyal people around him to manage the difficult political and financial situation in the colony.[37]

But Fawtier was not willing to leave Senegal without a fight. He kept postponing his departure by citing the cold in Europe and his concern for his family's health. After the governor complained about these delays to the under-secretary the latter forced Fawtier to leave on 6 February. Just before leaving, though, Fawtier managed to infuriate the governor one last time. He wrote a report on the revenues of the colony during his six-month term to be published in the *Journal Officiel de la République*. According to de Lamothe, Fawtier had arranged with the printing house to send the report to the governor on the day the post left for Paris, knowing that the governor would not have time to read it. Thus, the members of the General Council only received the report when it had already been published. Descemet, the president of the General Council, and Devès's main rival in Saint Louis, responded with rage, as, according to him, Fawtier had used the journal to advance his position. Descemet received the governor's permission to publish a protest letter in the journal a week later, in which he asserted that Fawtier praised himself for his predecessors' achievements and, while doing so, wrongly denigrated them. He emphasized that this conduct reflected his ongoing hostility towards his colleagues in Senegal.[38]

It is not stated in any of the governor's letters complaining about Fawtier, nor in Fawtier's report, nor Descemet's letter of protest whether this incident was related to the Jeandet Affair and the legal struggle around it. It is likely that Fawtier's hostility towards his colleagues, as well as their obvious dislike of him, was a result of his alignment with the judges who supported Ba's right for justice. The governor did not hide his resentment of Fawtier's stand on this matter and was anxious to get rid of him as quickly as possible. Dodds and Descemet, who did not hide their contempt for the director of interior affairs, both supported the governor's efforts to silence the affair.

The foreignness of Ndiereby Ba

The combination of the manipulation of the law with the dismissal of those who supported the legal proceedings stemming from Ba's complaint managed to prevent the legal scandal and the arrest of the administrators who had ordered and supervised the executions. With Fawtier's departure, the purge was complete, and all resistance to the dubious legal measures used to bury the affair was stifled. Nevertheless, the game was not yet over as long as a young Fulbe woman, supported by her devoted attorney, still resided in Saint Louis. Even though the governor and his supporters tried to minimize her importance, Ba's presence in the city was a constant alert that the affair might explode again at any moment. It is not surprising, then, that one of the measures de Lamothe used to try and put an end to the affair once and for all was to highlight Ba as a foreigner and, as such, was not entitled to the protection of the French legal system she could not even understand. Behind the governor's attempts to manipulate the law and stop the legal procedures against the administrators lay a deeper notion that the legal debate was irrelevant, because the scandal was, in reality, a wicked game played by the enemies of the administration to embarrass the governor and to gain African supporters. All the Advisory Council's members, except for Larrouy and Fawtier, thought this was the case. As we have seen, the argument of de Lamothe and his supporters was that the only reason the judicial authority could open the investigation was the location of the execution. Jeandet's murder was performed by a foreigner, on foreign land. If only the administrators had executed him and his accomplices at that same geographic location, or even '*deux pas*' (two steps) away from Podor, the affair would never have arisen. Furthermore, they claimed, the person who had submitted the complaint, the so-called '*partie civile*' (civil party), was a foreign woman, who, so the governor's supporters asserted, had no understanding of French law and was only a puppet in the hands of the métis men who used her for their malicious ends.

The term '*étranger*' (foreign) used during the debates mentioned above, should not mislead us. When the members of the Advisory Council referred to the foreignness of the culprits, their land and that of Ndiereby Ba, they did not mean that they were simply strangers, to whom French law did not apply. This 'foreignness' implied inferiority. At the beginning of this chapter, we discussed the way in which the French perceived the populations that were added to their territories in West Africa during the second half of the nineteenth century. Influenced by the racial theories of the time, and convinced of the superiority of their culture and laws, they simply did not believe that these populations could be subject to the same laws as Europeans. It is true that métis and Africans living in Saint Louis and the other three communes of Senegal were allowed into the metropolitan legal system, but this was seen as an exception, and was not accepted with much delight by the colonial administration. In any case, it was never meant for the French legal system to be applicable to the newly conquered territories. The system of protectorates was supposed to solve this problem. However, the Jeandet Affair proved that it was possible for a person living in a protectorate to put the colony in turmoil, by using French law as a weapon against administrators in a manner that could upset colonial stability. The governor's supporters in the Advisory Council could not argue with the fact that the executions should not have taken place on French soil. But they tried to mitigate this fact and to claim that, in essence, the people who were executed and the woman who had submitted the complaint were not worthy of the protection of French law, as they were not advanced enough even to understand them.

The real problem the governor and his supporters now had to face was not the executed men, but the woman who fought on behalf of one of them. Unlike them, she was alive and active. Even after the governor issued the plea for jurisdiction, which stopped the procedures and in fact put an end to Ba's struggle in Saint Louis, she refused to leave the city. This young Fulbe woman constituted a real threat to the colonial administration. From the moment she set foot in Saint Louis, she was seen as a menace and, as long as she remained in the city, there was a risk the affair could be rekindled. The administration chose to define Ba as a stranger to French law, not only because she originated from outside the territory under direct French law, but also because it saw her as foreign to the basic principles of this law. Ba, so these administrators claimed, was not advanced enough to understand what she was doing. She was only a puppet at the hands of Devès and his strawmen. In a way, they claimed she was not a legal entity and therefore her complaint was not valid.

The attempt to claim that Ba's complaint should not be taken seriously and could be summarily dismissed included actions by different administrators aiming not only to deny her agency and belittle her, but also to chase her away from Saint Louis. These two lines of action were, in a way, contradictory. If Ba was so unimportant, why was so much effort invested in getting rid of her? The administration's actions against Ndiereby are not only interesting in that they help us understand the measures taken to end the affair. They also demonstrate that she was in fact the person who made the affair. Without her the entire case could not have existed. She is therefore crucial to the story. Chapter 5 attempts to look at the affair from Ndiereby Ba's perspective.

Notes

1 On the activities of the Hungarian Legion in Italy following its unification see: Andrea Carteny, 'Volunteers' Employment and Counterinsurgency in Italy: The Case the Hungarian Legion (1861–1862),' *Mediterranean Journal of Social Sciences* 3, no. 11 (2012), 397–403.

2 Henri de Lamothe, 'Excursion au Canada et à la rivière Rouge du Nord,' *Le Tour du monde* 30, no. 5 (1875).

3 Hilary Jones, The Metis of Senegal: *Urban Life* and *Politics* in French West Africa (Bloomington: Indiana University Press, 2013), 116; 162–167.

4 Interview with Xavier Ricou (Crespin's great grandson), 14 March 2024.

5 François Manchuelle, 'Métis et colons: la famille Devès et L'émergence politique des africains au Sénégal, 1881–1897,' *Cahiers d'études africaines* (1984), 493.

6 Henry Dahl, 'Assassinat,' in *Dahl's Law Dictionary—Dictionnaire Juridique Dahl* (Paris: Dalloz, 2007).

7 CAOM Sénégal IV 66a, 19 November 1890.

8 *Ibid*, 20 November 1890.

9 *Ibid*, 22 November 1890.

10 *Ibid*, 4 December 1890.

11 Or la justice qui n'est d'ailleurs pas préparée à cette catégorie d'affaires par une étude constante, serait aveugle et elle est toujours boiteuse. *Ibid*, 4 December 1890.

12 Abdoul Bokar was not a Tijjani, and nor were many of the Muslims living in Fouta Toro. Tautin probably used this term because al-Hajj

Umar was indeed Tijjani, and this term soon became a synonym in the French colonial vocabulary for fanatical Islam. On the French policy towards Islam in this period see: Christopher Harrison, *France and Islam in West Africa, 1860–1960* (Cambridge: Cambridge University Press, 2003), 11–24.

13 CAOM, Sénégal IV 66a, 4 December 1890.

14 CAOM, Sénégal I 90, 20 November and 22 November 1890.

15 CAOM, Sénégal IV 66a, 4 December 1890.

16 Et penser que rien de tout cela n'aurait pu se produire si, tout en faisant justice sommaire on s'était quelque peu préoccupé de la rendre moins extralégale! CAOM, Sénégal I 90, 5 November 1890. Letter from de Lamothe to the Under-Secretary of State in the Ministry of the Colonies.

17 CAOM, Sénégal I 90, 5 November 1890. Letter from de Lamothe to the Under-Secretary of State in the Ministry of the Colonies.

18 Le gouverneur ne peut être poursuivi dans la colonie pendant l'exercice de ses fonctions. CAOM, Sénégal IV 66a, 20 November 1890.

19 CAOM, Sénégal IV 66a, 20 November 1890.

20 *Ibid*, 20 November 1890.

21 *Ibid*, 20 November 1890.

22 *Ibid*, 22 November 1890.

23 The decree of conflict, published on 1 June 1828, was a tool conceived during the Second Empire to regulate conflicts between the judiciary and the administrative authorities regarding the jurisdiction of a specific court. This decree could be issued by a prefect in cases in which the judicial court rejected a jurisdictional challenge, also referred to as a declination of competence (*déclinatoire de compétence*). In such a case, the tribunal of conflicts could intervene and remove the case from the judicial court. See: Bernard Pacteau, 'Les conflits entre l'ordre administratif et l'ordre judiciaire, avant et donc sans le tribunal des conflits,' in *Les Désunions de la magistrature*, ed. Jacques Gaven and Jean-Christophe Krynen (Toulouse: Press de l'université Toulouse Capitol, 2012), 355–359.

24 A l'avenir, le conflit d'attribution entre les tribunaux et l'autorité administrative ne sera jamais élevé en matière criminelle. Jean-Louis Gallet, 'La Procédure D'élévation De Conflit Le Conflit Positif,' www.tribunal-conflits.fr/documents/Actualites/La_procedure_de_conflit.pdf, 16 (Accessed 23 January 2024). The term 'conflict of attribution' means a conflict over the jurisdiction of a certain court to judge a case.

25 CAOM, Sénégal I 90, 23 November 1890.

26 Martine Fabre, 'Le magistrat d'Outre-mer: L'aventure de la justice,' in *Le juge et l'Outre-mer: Les roches bleues de l'Empire colonial*, ed. Bernard Durand and Martine Fabre (Lille: Centre d'histoire judiciaire, 2004), 72–79.
27 CAOM, IV 66, 29 November 1890.
28 'L'Affaire de Podor,' *Le Petit Moniteur Universelle*, 2 November 1899.
29 CAOM, Sénégal IV, 66a, 30 November 1890.
30 *Ibid.*
31 CAOM, Sénégal I 90, 6 December 1890.
32 *Ibid*, 6 March 1891.
33 *Ibid.*
34 *Ibid.*
35 CAOM, Sénégal I 90, 1 January 1891.
36 *Ibid*, 7 January 1891.
37 *Ibid*, 7 January 1891.
38 *Ibid*, 16 February 1891; *Journal officiel de la République*, 5 February 1891, 12 February 1891.

5

The affair from Ndiereby Ba's perspective

In some respects, the Jeandet Affair, also referred to as the Podor Affair, or, more recently, as we shall see in Chapter 7, the Baidy Kaccé Affair, should have been named after the woman who made it happen—Ndiereby Ba. Simply put, without Ba there would have been no affair. By September, when Ursleur was sent to Paris, the governor might have been able to put the entire unpleasant incident behind him and calmly resume his administrative duties. It was the entrance of Ba onto the scene, when she stepped off the boat from Podor, that revived the scandal, much to de Lamothe's horror.

And yet, perhaps unsurprisingly, Ba remained at the margins of the story, both as told by the colonizer as well as by her own society. The colonial documents highlight Ba's lack of agency. For the administration, she was no more than a puppet, exploited by France's enemies in the colony. She had no legal understanding, no idea what she was doing, no concept of the scandal she was creating—an ignorant African woman, who should have remained at home mourning her husband rather than being tempted to embark on a dangerous journey that would only cause her harm. Local traditions treat Ndiereby much more respectfully when she is mentioned at all. She is royalty, an intelligent woman who sought justice. But Ba is mostly absent from these narratives and, when mentioned, very little is said about her. As we shall see in Chapter 7, the heroes of the story are her husband, Sidick, and, even more so, Jeandet's killer, Baidy Kaccé.

This chapter focuses on Ndiereby's crucial role in the affair. Despite the massive challenges the existing sources present, I will attempt to describe the affair from the illegal executions until it failed in Saint Louis from this young woman's perspective. Jeandet's detailed and vivid letters to his parents highlight the enormous gap between our ability to understand his motives, inner thoughts, and emotions and, much more so, the difficulty of getting even a glimpse into Ndiereby Ba's mind. Unlike Jeandet and the other main characters in this affair, Ndiereby left no written records. We cannot know what went on in her mind during the long and difficult months she stayed in Saint Louis. What we know about her is derived solely from reports, letters written by French administrators and her lawyer, and some reports in the metropolitan press. Of these, Chadelle's letters to the governor are the only sources that seem to tell us anything substantial about Ba's feelings and thoughts. All the other sources can reveal only what their authors thought about her. Even the interviews I conducted cannot tell us much about Ba, and this is not only because of the distant time of the events in question. Most of my informants did not speak about Ba at all and, when asked about her, could not say much. The reason for this silence was quite simple. They had no knowledge whatsoever about Ba's important role in the affair. Most knew she had existed, but not much more than that. I will discuss this lacuna in local memory in Chapter 7. Unlike the other informants, Ba's direct descendants were very much interested in her, but their knowledge stemmed from colonial records and not from any oral traditions, so they could not add much to what I already knew.

I will rely on the available sources to gather at least partial information about Ba, while regarding administrative reports with great caution. The French administrators did their best to prove that Ba had no real agency in the affair, so the information they offer about her is obviously biased. The transcript of Ba's interrogation during the second meeting of the Advisory Committee, read carefully, can offer some interesting insights about her character and mode of operation in Saint Louis. Finally, I will try to complete the picture by relying on sources dealing with Fulbe society of the time and customs related to marriage and widowhood.

In her article about the disappearance of an important female political leader in Ghana from the national narrative, Jean Allman argues that reconstructing the lives of forgotten women in African historical narratives is not enough. Moreover, the partial reconstruction of bits and pieces of these stories only amplifies the silences regarding the role of African women in history. She contends that we must try to learn from the marginalization of women in historical narratives to understand what they say about the historical discipline, about nationalism, and the power of states in the post-colonial world.[1] I agree with this statement and will indeed discuss the deeper meaning of Ba's erasure from the story in Chapter 7. I still think it is crucial to try and reconstruct her perspective because, as Helen Bradford demonstrated in an article on the Xhosa cattle killing in the British cape colony, without considering women and aspects of gender, colonial history is not only incomplete but could also be totally distorted.[2] So I will now try to trace the events told so far from the perspective of a young African woman called Ndiereby Ba.

Ba's life before Jeandet's murder

We possess no written sources about Ba's life before she became the main character in a French legal scandal. According to Haruna Diop, the griot of Guédé, Ba came from a respected family and was carefully chosen as the Lam Toro's first wife. She would probably have been in her teens, perhaps 14 or 15 years old, at the time of her marriage, as was the custom at the time. She married Sidick about seven or eight years before he was executed. This means that, when she boarded the boat to Saint Louis, she was between the ages of 21 and 23. According to Diop, Ba moved to her husband's compound with her enslaved people, but her sisters came to visit her often. Her native village, Bantou, was only 5 kilometres away from Guédé, so she could stay in close touch with her family.[3]

We can learn more about her marriage from a comparative ethnographic study on the Fulbe conducted in the late 1960s. According to Marguerite Dupire, the process of marriage among the Fulbe was complex. It was accompanied by much consideration and thought, especially at the highest echelons of society, and involved rituals and a series of payments. The father of the proposed husband would consult with his sisters, daughters, and nieces before transmitting their final decision to the elders of his lineage.[4] We can assume that in the case of royal marriages this process would have been even more complex. Ba bore two children before her husband's

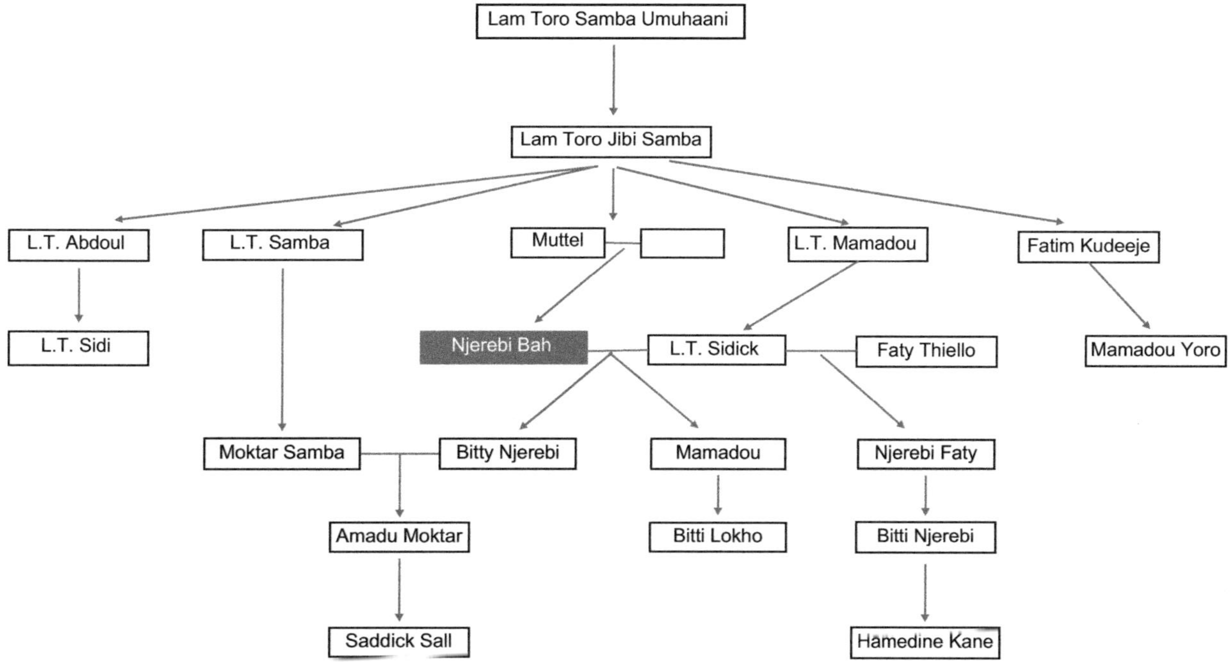

Figure 5.1 Genealogy of Ndiereby Ba (Saddick Sall)

execution, an older daughter, Bitti, and a younger son, Mamadou. Her husband married a second wife sometime after their marriage.[5]

The family tree made by Saddick Sall, Ndiereby Ba, and Lam Toro Sidick's great grandson (Figure 5.1), sheds some light on Ba's position within the extended family.

We can learn from this chart that Ndiereby and Sidick were first cousins, and that Sidick had a second wife, who bore him a third child (Ndierebi Faty). We can also see that the name Ndiereby is often used in the family, as well as the name Bitti. Ndiereby's daughter's first name, for example, is the same as Bitti Lokho, who assisted Ndiereby during her time in Saint Louis.

Diop explained that the role of the first wife in a royal marriage was very important and could also explain her decision to go to Saint Louis to submit a complaint after her husband's illegal execution:

> What drove her to go to Saint-Louis to support the complaint was also her sense of responsibility. The queens are responsible within the royal palace. Sometimes, they are even the ones who hold their husbands' secrets [...] Generally, the last person you see before going to sleep, when you are a woman, is your husband. She is in the palace; she can also hear things that the king did not hear. She could positively assist her husband as a special advisor.[6]

Figure 5.2 The mosque in Guédé (photo: Eyal Ginio)

So, we can gather that, despite her young age, Ndiereby had some political power. The brutal execution of her husband must have shocked her and undermined her world. It certainly left her with much less power. But Ba was used to playing a role in the running of political affairs, and therefore did not remain helpless under the new horrifying circumstances and the dramatic change in her life

A widow determined to act

The possibility of becoming a widow was probably a constant in Ndiereby's mind. After all, her husband was involved in battles with the French, in political conspiracies against other local leaders and among his own family members. He was also a target of similar conspiracies. Jeandet, who was a powerful administrator, saw Sidick as France's main enemy in the region, and that perception alone was enough to put Ba's husband's life in constant danger. But the way Sidick died must have been a shock for his young wife. The public execution, in which one of his enslaved people was ordered to decapitate him, after which his body was thrown into the river and his head presented on a spike for a long period of time, was an especially horrifying and humiliating way for a royal to die. Many of the inhabitants of Podor and its surroundings witnessed this horrific spectacle. We do not know if Ba was present—we can assume that she remained at her compound beginning to mourn her husband. But, even if she was not there, she could not have avoided hearing vivid descriptions of the event.

Ndiereby was now in a new position; no longer the first wife of a distinguished ruler, but rather his widow. According to Fulbe custom, when a first wife becomes a widow, she must observe a mourning period at her husband's compound. She is then free to choose whether to remarry or not. Her late husband's younger brother might have been encouraged to propose marriage but, unlike in other ethnic groups, the widow is not obliged to accept such a proposal. She could marry someone else or remain a widow. Her children, however, would remain under the responsibility of her late husband's family. The widow herself does not have to remain at her late husband's house, but she had to do so to remain with her children.[7]

At first, Ndiereby acted accordingly. She remained at her late husband's house to mourn him and did not venture out. But when only half of the mourning period had elapsed, a delegation from Saint Louis arrived at her doorstep. Ndiereby received an interesting but dangerous offer. She would board a boat in Podor to Saint Louis. There she would be hosted at Lokho's house and would receive legal advice for free. With the help of a local attorney and an interpreter who would tutor her for a few days, she would sue the people responsible for the brutal murder of her husband. We know from the correspondence between Podor and Saint Louis that Ndiereby hesitated. This is hardly surprising. She was a young grieving widow whose period of mourning had not yet ended, and she had two young children to take care of. She had never travelled to Saint Louis before, and she could not speak French. She was to renounce the protection of her husband's family and rely on several relatives from Saint Louis and an attorney she had never met. She had no idea whether she would succeed and how much time she would have to spend in Saint Louis. She could not have anticipated the reaction of the French administration to her arrival in the capital, but she must have been concerned about that as well.

Finally, Ndiereby accepted the challenge. In addition to the anxiety she must have felt, it is highly probable that Ba's relatives, mainly the male ones, were not happy about her agreement to take part in the legal struggle in Saint Louis and found it highly inappropriate for any woman—even more so for a young woman, newly-widowed with two children. And yet Ba agreed and ventured into the scary unknown. We have no way, unfortunately, of knowing why she chose this dangerous course of action. It is certain, though, that she was not coerced into agreeing to travel to Saint Louis. There are two reasons for this certainty. First, as we have seen, another female relative of Sidick Sall was approached before Ba, and she had had no problem to refuse. Second, as we shall see, several of her Fulbe relatives assisted the administration in its attempt to drive Ba out of Saint Louis. It is therefore obvious that the more difficult option was to follow Devès's messengers. Refusing to follow them would have been much simpler.

It is also difficult to ascertain Ba's motives for this unusual decision. While the administration claimed that she was tempted into believing that the lawsuit would result in her receiving a large sum of money as recompense, it is hard to believe that this would have been sufficient to convince her. It is more likely that Ba indeed sought justice for her savagely executed husband. Perhaps, also, this was a chance to escape the harsh circumstances that widowhood imposed upon her.

Accompanied by her enslaved person, Lamine, Ndiereby arrived in Podor on 6 November. As we have seen, it took several more days to convince her to board the *Germaine*. Taking this perilous journey was certainly not an easy decision for her. She finally agreed to take this step on 10 November.

The journey to the colony's capital and the preparation for the legal struggle

We have no information about Ba's voyage to Saint Louis and we can only imagine her trepidation during the trip on a crowded steamboat to an unknown city. Steamboats at the time were the only means to reach Saint Louis from the hinterland. Until they were introduced, the French were confined to Saint Louis and could not even attempt to expand their rule into the continent. Robert Kubicek has tried to understand the specific impact of the steamboat on the colonial administration of British West Africa, and the ways in which administrators perceived these vessels and used them. While focusing on the British, Kubicek mentioned the impact French deployment of the steamboat in Senegal had on administrators in the Gambia and in Lagos. In 1840, for example, the Gambia's administrator mentioned Senegal as proof of the British need to invest in steamboats. He noted that the French easily controlled Senegal by patrolling it with a war steamboat. The British were also motivated by the large number of steamboats the French owned and the superior quality of the French vessels to their own.[8]

Kubicek does not provide any details about the French boats apart from mentioning their superiority over those of the British. However, travelling on the 1950 renovated boat, *Bou el-Mogdad*, which nowadays carries tourists from Saint Louis to Podor, can shed some light on the experience of journeying in such boats in the late nineteenth century, although one must assume that some improvements were implemented between 1890 and 1950. *Bou el-Mogdad* sailed the Senegal River from 1950 to 1970. It was named after a celebrated interpreter who worked for the French administration. His son, who also served as an interpreter, would later play a dubious role in the final stage of the affair.

According to the ship's captain, the *Bou el-Mogdad*'s maximum speed in 1950 was 8 kilometres per hour in the direction of Podor and 15 kilometres per hour on the way back. As a luxurious tourist boat, the *Bou el-Mogdad* nowadays carries 50 passengers and 20 crew members, but while functioning as a trading boat it carried around 200 passengers and had no private cabins—everyone stayed in the same shared space.[9] It is unlikely that the voyage was any more convenient when Ndiereby Ba boarded the *Germaine* on 11 September 1890. One can only try to imagine what Ba must have felt while she was on board, along with another 200 passengers, travelling for at least 17 hours, probably more, as the boat stopped several times on its way via other commercial posts, to an unknown city so far from her home village, Guédé.

When Ba alighted from the *Germaine* in Saint Louis on 14 September 1890, spies were already waiting for her, ready to report her movements to Tautin, their superior. One of these spies reported to Tautin that the widow was alone at first but on 17 September was joined by several people when she went to the notary's office to submit her complaint. When Tautin first reported on Ba's activities to the governor, he referred to her as '*femme Sidick*' (the wife of Sidick), rather than using her name, which perhaps he still did not know.[10]

As we have seen, Rivet was summoned to the meeting of the Advisory Council to testify about his encounter with Ba on 17 November, three days after her arrival in Saint Louis. The object of questioning him was to prove to the council's members that Ba was not a free agent in this affair and, therefore, that the legal procedures she had opened were not valid. His testimony could shed some light on Ba's initial movements in Saint Louis. When asked whether he believed that she had acted out of her own free will or suspected that she was forced to file the complaint, Rivet responded that, at first, he did not pay much attention to this point. He then continued:

> But when she started telling me what she wanted, she struck me as someone repeating a hard-learned lesson and looking for some detail; also she could not designate the people she intended to prosecute and

it was with the help of the interpreter that she ended up making it clear that it was the Director of Political Affairs, without being able to give his name.[11]

The interpreter Rivet mentioned was Samba Fall. Fall was an appointee of the colonial administration. According to a report that Tautin wrote after the Saint Louis tribunal was declared incompetent to judge the case, Fall was working in the service of Crespin. Fall's role was to visit Ba, who was living in Bitti Lokho's house in Saint Louis, to explain to her how she should communicate with the authorities.[12]

Indeed, the role of Samba Fall as a tutor was also alluded to during Ba's questioning in the second meeting of the governor's council on 22 November 1890. She was asked where she found Samba Fall, and replied that she had only met him in court. The next question was: 'Is it not true that he came to you?' Ba replied again that she had only met Fall in court. Ba was probably not entirely honest in her answers. Although, as I will later show, she was certainly not a puppet in the hands of others and knew what she was doing, she had no way of mastering the French legal language without help. Samba Fall therefore served not only as a translator from French to Pulaar for Ba, but also as a tutor. He had to teach her complicated legal terms with only a few days at his disposal. To do that successfully he had to know the legal system well. The fact that Ba managed to file the claim meant that he was a talented teacher, and that she was a quick learner.

Ba's questioning before the Advisory Council is our only opportunity to hear her voice directly; otherwise it was mediated variously by hostile and supportive French and métis men. But we do have to bear in mind that this interview, unlike the two others that were held during that meeting, was conducted with the help of an interpreter. Rivet obviously did not require one and the summoned interpreter, Boubakar Abdoul, could speak French well enough. The interpreter employed for Ba's questioning was Hamet Fall (who was probably unrelated to Samba Fall).

Fall became an interpreter with Jeandet's help. The two first met when Jeandet was the guest of Diambour's ruler. During his visit, Fall was caught stealing the ruler's jewellery and was severely punished. Jeandet felt compassion towards Fall and brought him wine so that he could endure his punishment more easily. After that, Fall became his protégé and, with his assistance, learned French and worked as an interpreter. It is hard to know how Fall's relationship with Jeandet might have influenced his translations of Ba's words if at all, but his connection to the affair should, perhaps, have undermined his credibility.[13]

As we have already seen, the committee invited Ba for one purpose only. Most of its members wanted to prove that she had no agency nor legal understanding. They claimed that she was only a puppet serving the interests of manipulative métis men. Therefore, the line of questioning did not concern Ba's complaint at all. Her husband and his relationship with Jeandet were only mentioned once briefly. The entire interrogation concentrated on her ostensibly insignificant role in the lawsuit.

The text of this interview is, of course, available to us only in the French translation of Ba's words. This text includes terms that did not exist in Pulaar, Ba's native language, such as 'governor,' 'attorney,' and 'tribunal.' We have no way of knowing how these terms were transmitted to her. It seems that the constant use of legal terms was intended to demonstrate Ba's total ignorance and lack of understanding of the legal process she was supposedly leading.

The following segment of the interview demonstrates this point well:

> **Q.** Are you [the term used was the familiar *tu*] the *legitimate wife* of the former Lam Sidick?
> **A.** Yes.
> **Q.** Have you been intending to go *to court* for a long time?
> **A.** Perfectly. I had thought for a long time to come to St Louis to find the Governor to tell him of my agonies.
> [...]
> **Q.** Who told you that you had to go find *the notary*?
> **A.** Since my arrival in St Louis I have not moved from my place, since I wanted to see the Governor and he was absent. I went to find the notary, they told me to file my words, they would show them to the Governor.
> [...]
> **Q.** Are you persevering with *the complaint* you filed?
> **A.** Yes, I persist, I am a widow for that.

Q. Didn't you confuse the '*Governor*' with the '*Government*'?
A. I only know the Governor, he is the master of the land.
Q. Who introduced you to *an attorney*?
A. No one. I persist in saying that I only came to see the Governor.
Q. Who told you to choose one attorney rather than another?
A. No one. It's true, I submitted my words to *the Tribunal*, but that was not my intention.
Q. But now that the Governor has arrived you are thinking of addressing him.
A. I came to *lodge a complaint* against Martin, Aubrey and Riquetty.[14] [italics are mine]

We have no way of knowing exactly what the actual words were that Ba used during this stressful interrogation. We can only rely on the transcribed text in French that went through two mediators—the interpreter and the court secretary. Yet, this text is still useful. If we look at it closely, we may note certain terms that would not have been easy to transmit from French to Pulaar. The committee representative who questioned Ba first asked if she was the '*femme légitime*' (legitimate wife) of Sidick Sall. This term would not have made much sense to Ba, as all wives would be legitimate. The term probably stemmed from a French perception that only the first wife was legitimate and all the others were in fact concubines.[15] We can thus assume that Hamet Fall used a different term when he posed this question to Ba. As Ba was Sall's first wife, Fall could have used the term 'first wife' instead of 'legitimate wife.' Had she not been his first wife, the translation would have been more problematic.[16]

The existence of so many legal and administrative terms in the questions posed to Ba are related to the administration's resolve to prove that she was not a free agent and, consequently, to reject her complaint. The idea was probably to bombard her with difficult terms to expose her total ignorance. This strategy failed. Ba demonstrated a good understanding of these terms and even used some of them correctly. Her confidence was not even undermined when the person who interviewed her doubted her ability to distinguish between the term 'governor' and 'government.' Ba knew exactly how powerful the governor was when she described him as the master of the land.

The person who interrogated Ba was probably the one who demanded that she, Rivet and Abdoul appear before the council. After trying to undermine her credibility by bombarding her with legal terms, he then moved to another strategy suggesting that, by coming to Saint Louis Ba, she had violated local mourning customs:

> **Q.** Why did you wait so long to file a complaint?
> **A.** Because I was in mourning, I wanted to wait until it was over.
> **Q.** Haven't you received any dispatch or document from Saint Louis? Your mourning doesn't seem to be over since it's supposed to last for four months.
> **A.** I haven't received anything from anyone. I admit that my mourning is not yet over.
> [He then inquired into Ba's movements in Saint Louis, suggesting again that she only followed instructions and had no free will in this affair]:
> **Q.** How come you didn't come to see the governor's representative during his absence?
> **A.** I don't know his representative.
> **Q.** What did you do then?
> **A.** I did nothing; I went to see the Governor. I swear to God that I came only to see the Governor.
> **Q.** Have you been to Saint Louis before? Is this your first time?
> **A.** Yes, it's the first time. I don't know anyone.
> **Q.** Where do you live?
> **A.** At a woman's named Bitty-Löghö [refers to Bitti Lokho, her relative].
> [...]
> **Q.** Can't you remember who brought you to the Court? Were they white? Were they black?
> **A.** No.

Finally, the chief of the judicial service asked Ba the following question: 'Do you persist in the mandate you gave to Mr. Chadelle?' Ba answers affirmatively.

An article published in a metropolitan newspaper offered the following interpretation of Ba's summoning before the Advisory Council:

> The plaintiff herself was made to appear. Unfortunate example, the supporters of her husband's murderers made her appear as a guilty party! She, who came seeking protection from the laws and justice! 'Why did you address the judiciary and not the governor?' they asked her. 'It's because,' she replied, 'it's the judiciary that dispenses justice!' An admirable response in its simplicity! Alas, the poor woman was mistaken. Countless obstacles arose that prevented the judiciary from relying on the legal code. The law, thanks to the friends of the murderers, was no longer enforced.[17]

This description highlights the difficult situation in which Ba found herself and the aggressiveness of the questions posed to her. Her answer, which the reporter admired, was probably less dramatic and more like the one noted in the transcript. Nevertheless, there is no doubt that this interrogation's aim was indeed to present Ba as a guilty party, deny her agency and intimidate her into dropping her complaint. This aim failed. Ba, a young woman who did not speak French, was summoned to the council without informing her lawyer, who therefore did not accompany her. It is not difficult to imagine what her state of mind must have been. She was probably confused and terrified—a young Fulbe woman, standing alone in a room full mostly of French men and one métis military officer who were mostly hostile towards her. She was presented with difficult and persistent questions, asked in a condescending and belittling manner. Of the three people interviewed, she was the only one for whom the familiar term *tu* rather than the respectful *vous* was used. This was not a question of her being African, as the interviewer used the term *vous* for the interpreter Boubakar Abdoul. This pronoun is used for children or close friends. In this case it is obvious that Ba was not considered a friend of anyone in the room. She was, though, considered a child, manipulated by others, with no understanding of the legal scandal she was about to cause. Although she could not have known that the term *tu* was used, she probably could sense the belittling manner with which she was treated.

Nevertheless, despite this stressful situation, Ba did not admit at any point that the version put to her was true. She denied being asked by anyone to come to Saint Louis and lodge the complaint. She also denied meeting with the interpreter Samba Fall before arriving in court. She claimed that no one had hired Chadelle for her and insisted that she had only wanted to speak to the governor about the injustice perpetrated on her late husband. While doing so she described her aim clearly, remembering the names of the three administrators against whom her complaint had been filed. Finally, she insisted, following Larrouy's question, that she intended to keep the mandate of her attorney, Chadelle, thus persisting with her complaint.

Intimidation and harassment in Saint Louis

The interview, or rather interrogation, Ba had to endure without any kind of support was no doubt an ordeal for her. We know this because, immediately after leaving the council hall, she went directly to her lawyer's house. Chadelle was extremely worried about her as he had heard about his client's summoning to the council, thinking that she had been arrested. He wrote to the governor saying that he had heard a rumour that Ba was arrested and hoped that this was false. He then pleaded with the governor to leave his client in peace, saying:

> This woman is not and has never been a source of trouble. She herself seeks justice from the French judiciary, invoking laws to which we are all subject. In the name of law and justice, Mr. Governor, I implore and beg you, if this woman is arrested, to release her back to freedom.[18]

When Ba appeared later that day at his door, Chadelle was probably relieved that she had not been arrested. Yet, after talking to her and hearing about her unpleasant experience, he wrote another letter to the governor in which he protested, albeit in a very polite way, about the summoning of his client without notifying him and thus allowing him to accompany her. Chadelle told the governor that Ba came to him after being interviewed before the council and asked to move into his house. She was terrified that she might be summoned again without him, and therefore did not wish to return to her relative's house; but he had convinced her that she would be safe at Lokho's house. He assured the governor that, if his client was summoned again, she would present herself; but he suggested that he should accompany her as otherwise her thoughts might not be well comprehended. Chadelle also offered to clarify for the governor what she had told the council in case she had not been clear enough. He then reminded the governor again that his client only sought justice and was protected by French law: 'Placing herself under the protection of French laws, she has and will always show absolute respect towards the highest magistrate of Senegal.'[19]

But Ba was not left alone. Shortly after her summoning to the Advisory Council, she received another order directly from the governor's office. She was to leave her relative's house and move into the house of the governor's interpreter, a man by the name of Hamet Khorissel. Ba was alarmed by this order and went again to Chadelle. She arrived at his house while he was out dining at a local restaurant; when he returned, she again implored him to let her stay. Chadelle was probably concerned that, by letting Ba live at his house, he might create a new kind of scandal, which is why he hesitated so much. Finally, though, he agreed.

About two weeks later, while Chadelle again was away, a police commissioner, Beval, arrived at his house, probably with the aim of intimidating Ba. He threatened Chadelle's interpreter, who had refused to let him in and sent him away. Beval then posted two policemen across from Chadelle's house, probably to watch Ba's movements or approach her when she ventured out of the house. On 19 December, Chadelle wrote to protest about this intrusion on his privacy: 'I cannot believe that you gave these orders to the Police Commissioner. I protest this official and his behaviour; I respectfully protest this initial violation of my home, which was only prevented from being fully carried out thanks to the courageous stance of my interpreter.'[20]

Around the same time, Chadelle heard rumours about the governor's intention to send his client back to her village. He met with de Lamothe and explained to him that Ba would not be safe in Fouta Toro. He then wrote again to the governor, noting that, although he was not enthusiastic about letting Ba stay at his house, she was frightened and refused to leave. As her lawyer, he could not send her away in such a state. He expressed his hope that the explanations he had given the governor about the danger that awaited Ba in Toro had convinced the governor, and ended his letter with a desperate plea:

> I implore you, please let this woman stay at my place; she asks for nothing, and she never goes out. Her relatives visit her whenever she desires. Her meals are regularly brought from her relatives' home. She causes no trouble; she came seeking justice, and she is a widow. I am certain that my plea would be heard.[21]

Chadelle's description of Ba's routine allows us a glimpse into the difficult conditions under which she lived in Saint Louis. She was in an unfamiliar city, under constant surveillance by the colonial authorities. At any moment she could have been summoned to interrogation or harassed by one of the governor's henchmen. It is no wonder under such circumstances that she would confine herself to Chadelle's house, never venturing out. Luckily for her, she had relatives in the city who could supply her with food she was accustomed to, but still it seems that she lived like a prisoner.[22]

An article in the metropolitan daily *Le petit moniteur universelle*, published eight years after these events, sheds some more light on Ba's living conditions in Saint Louis. According to this article, Chadelle offered Ba a room in his house following rumours spread in town that she was about to be abducted and sent into exile in Gabon (this possibility is not mentioned in the colonial documents). Ba refused to live inside Chadelle's house because she did not want to disturb him, so she stayed in a wooden shack at the back of his courtyard. 'There she remained, never venturing out, calm with her memories, mourning her husband, and nursing her youngest child.'[23] According to her great grandson, Saddick Sall, this baby was Mamadou, Ba's youngest son and his father's uncle. Some years later, after Ba had returned to Guédé, she would send this child to her late husband's relatives in Saint Louis, where he would study in a French school, later to be appointed as canton chief in Guédé.[24] The fact that Ndiereby brought her child with her was never mentioned anywhere else but, if it was a child that young, it is indeed plausible that she took him with her to Saint Louis.

Saddick Sall sheds some light on another question, namely the nature of the danger that awaited Ba in Fouta Toro. According to him, certain people who had collaborated with the administration in implicating the ex-Lam Toro Sidick in Jeandet's murder saw Ba as a threat.[25] Another possibility is that Ba had acted against the social norms of her gender and status by leaving her home and going to Saint Louis even before the end of her period of mourning. Staying at her attorney's house was another serious breach of social norms, which was probably viewed negatively in her home village. These are all speculations, of course, but it is certain that Ba was frightened to return to Guédé despite feeling harassed in Saint Louis.

Sometime in February 1891, Ba was approached again, this time by her late husband's uncle, Ahmet N'Diack, who was working at the governor's request. De Lamothe, who was concerned by Chadelle's plans to appeal the decision declaring the court in Saint Louis incompetent to consider her complaint, tried to get rid of Ndiereby in a more subtle way than by intimidation by his police officers.[26] This time, he chose a person he believed Ba would trust. N'Diack was also a minister of Sidi Ely, the emir of Brakna. The region of Brakna, which the French had termed '*royaume*' (kingdom), lies in today's south-western Mauritania along the Senegal River. During the nineteenth century, the French offered the people of Brakna gifts to maintain their loyalty and to disincentivize them from robbing their commercial posts along the river. The Brakna Moors were often able to influence political life in Fouta Toro and therefore played an important role in the events that preceded Jeandet's murder. In one of his letters, Jeandet mentioned Sidi Ely, whom he referred to as the '*le roi des Maures Bracknas*' (King of Brakna Moors) but who was in fact the emir of the Hasani warriors in the region of Brakna. Sidi Ely's son offered Jeandet a young tiger and a gazelle, promising to bring him also a young lion, a promise that he later kept.[27]

The governor set up a meeting between N'Diack and a creditor of Sidi Ely, who persuaded him to try and convince Ba to return to Guédé, probably in return for cancelling the emir's debt. N'Diack agreed and travelled to Saint Louis, where he met with Ba in what seemed to be a successful meeting as far as the governor was concerned. Ba seemed persuaded and even promised to leave Saint Louis quickly. However, the next day, according to the governor, she shared her plan to return to Toro with her 'champions,' who promised her that it would be safer for her to stay in Saint Louis and that she would be able to sue for damages in the sum of 50,000 francs. Consequently, when N'Diack came back to meet her, she categorically refused to leave. The governor then wrote to Etienne, the colonial under-secretary, that after this failure, he saw no further way of resuming the efforts to drive Ba away from Saint Louis that would have the slightest chance of success.[28]

De Lamothe blamed Chadelle for this failure. He was certain that the attorney controlled his young client. He therefore suspended him for a period of three months. Chadelle complained to Etienne about the illegality of his suspension as, according to an organic decree from 1840, the governor had no authority to suspend him without first consulting the Saint Louis court. De Lamothe had to retract, but not before complaining bitterly to the under-secretary about Chadelle, and expressing his suspicions regarding the attorney's relationship with his widowed client:

> Since then, he has appointed himself as the guardian of Ndiereby Ba, the alleged widow of one of Jeandet's assassins: holding her at his house, to the great scandal of all, as a threat that he believes to have suspended over the Government until the Court of Cassation has ruled on the appeal that he made her sign.[29]

De Lamothe refers to her as '*la prétendue veuve*' (the alleged widow) of Sidick Sall, a term he had never used before in his correspondence about the affair. This paragraph also reveals that Ba was about to appeal the decision to close her case. The governor's claim that Chadelle was forcing her to do so, along with the insinuation that Ba was not necessarily who she had claimed to be, was meant to present Chadelle as a scoundrel who was prepared to go to great lengths to embarrass the administration for the sake of his patrons, even so far as to lodge an African woman in his house 'to the great scandal of all.' The relationship between Chadelle and Ba is indeed intriguing. There is no reason to believe the governor's insinuations, as his main aim was to convince Etienne that Chadelle was a dubious character. Ba's insistence to stay at her attorney's house was probably a result of the fear and insecurity she felt, as every one of her movements had been monitored, and due to the harassment and pressure she had been subjected to. Chadelle's letters express his compassion for his client and seem candid in their plea to the governor to stop harassing a widow who was only seeking justice. Chadelle was the only person in Saint Louis Ba trusted to protect her.

Nevertheless, the sources at hand suggest that, although Ba was heavily dependent on her métis supporters, and especially on Chadelle, she was also to some extent a free agent. As noted, she could have refused to board the boat in Podor. We know that another candidate refused to do so. There was no way in which Devès, despite all his power and influence, could have forced Ndiereby to leave Guédé halfway through her period of mourning and come to Saint Louis. And yet, she agreed to do so. We can easily imagine what a difficult decision this must have been for her. A young widow of a husband who had enemies, going to the capital of the colony, which was a foreign world for her, without any knowledge of French and with only one person she knew in the city—her relative, Bitti Lokho. She must have been horrified by the brutal way in which her husband had been executed. The public spectacle of death had probably been on everyone's lips and many people around her would have witnessed and discussed it. In this unbearable state of mind, she had to board the *Germaine* and sail to an unfamiliar destination, putting her fate in the hands of people she did not know. After a long journey on the crowded boat, she had three days to learn about the legal process and its peculiar language. That must have been challenging as well. She then had to stand before French men and explain her case, while constantly being ridiculed and dismissed. The questions posed to her during the first meeting of the Advisory Council did not aim to understand her position, but rather to assert that this position was irrelevant as she was just a puppet of powerful men with political motives. When the legal procedures were halted, Ba could have gone back home, but she did not. Here it could be claimed that she stayed in Saint Louis because she was afraid of the administration's supporters in Fouta Toro, and not because she wanted to continue the legal process. Nevertheless, it seems that staying in Saint Louis could not have been an easy choice, as Ndiereby kept being harassed by de Lamothe's various emissaries and she could not leave Chadelle's house. She stayed there until another opportunity to continue the legal struggle materialized, when Devès found a celebrated attorney in Paris who agreed to represent her case there. Let us now follow her legal struggle all the way to the metropole, where she was represented by one of the best criminal lawyers of the late nineteenth century, Félix Decori.

Notes

1 Jean Allman, 'The Disappearing of Hannah Kudjoe: Nationalism, Feminism, and the Tyrannies of History,' *Journal of Women's History* 21, no. 3 (2009), 24.
2 Helen Bradford, 'Women, Gender and Colonialism: Rethinking the History of the British Cape Colony and its Frontier Zones, c. 1806–70,' *The Journal of African History* 37, no. 3 (1996).
3 Interview with Haruna Diop, Dakar, 13 February 2020.
4 Marguerite Dupire, *Organisation sociale des Peul: étude d'ethnographie comparée* (Paris: Plon, 1970), 48–50.
5 Interview with Saddick Sall, Dakar, 14 March 2024.
6 Interview with Haruna Diop, Dakar, 13 February 2020.
7 Dupire, *Organisation sociale des Peul*, 54–55.
8 Robert V. Kubicek, 'The Colonial Steamer and the Occupation of West Africa by the Victorian State, 1840–1900,' *The Journal of Imperial and Commonwealth History* 18, no. 1 (1990), 12, 18.
9 Interview with the captain of the *Bou el-Mogdad*, Mamadou Goudiaby, on the Senegal River between Saint Louis and Podor, 4 February 2020.
10 CAOM, Sénégal IV 66a, 18 November 1890.
11 FR ANOM Sénégal IV 66, 20 September 1890.
12 *Ibid*, undated (probably after the end of November 1890).
13 Gausseron, *Un Français*, 38–41. Letter dated 23 April 1887. This story also appears in a catalogue Jeandet's father prepared for a future Senegalese museum he planned to open in Mâcon, and which was based on documents his son had written: Académie de Mâcon, Fonds Jeandet, Catalogue du musée sénégalais, 2 May 1891.
14 CAOM, Sénégal IV, 66 a, the Advisory Council session of 20 November 1890.
15 This perception was apparent when the French compensated only the first wife of African soldiers who fell into captivity during the two world wars. They used the term 'legitimate wife,' which was offensive to the soldiers and therefore was later changed to 'first wife'. See:Ruth Ginio, *The French Army and Its African Soldiers: The Years of Decolonization* (Lincoln: University of Nebraska Press, 2017), 123.
16 WhatsApp communication with Saddick Sall, 27 September 2022.
17 'L'affaire de Podor', *Le Petit Moniteur Universelle*, 2 November 1899.
18 CAOM, Fond ancien AOF 13G 135, 20 November 1890.

19 Se plaçant sous la protection des lois françaises, elle fait et fera toujours acte de respect absolu devant le premier magistrat du Sénégal. CAOM, Fond ancien AOF 13G 135, 20 November 1890.
20 CAOM, Fond ancien, 13G 135, 19 December 1890.
21 *Ibid*, 20 December 1890.
22 WhatsApp communication with Saddick Sall, 26 January 2024.
23 'L'affaire de Podor', *Le Petit Moniteur Universelle*, 2 November 1899.
24 Email communication with Saddick Sall, 20 February 2024.
25 WhatsApp communication with Saddick Sall, 26 January 2024.
26 CAOM, Sénégal I 90, 6 March 1891.
27 Archives de Saône-et-Loire, François Joseph Etienne Abel Jeandet, F 1412, 13 January 1888.
28 CAOM, Fond ancien Série G 13G 135, Undated, probably June 1891.
29 CAOM, Sénégal I 90, 6 March 1891.

6

The affair in Paris

The harassment Ndiereby Ba endured in Saint Louis had one main objective—to chase her away from the city to prevent the affair from being reawakened. Indeed, by June 1891, while the persistent widow was still living under Chadelle's roof, or more accurately in his back yard, de Lamothe's fears became reality. On 15 June the tribunal de première instance de la Seine (court of first instance of the Seine) in Paris convened a hearing to discuss a new lawsuit that Ba had submitted. This time, she had aimed higher. Clément Thomas, who was the governor of Senegal up until early September 1890, was accused of being responsible for the illegal executions. De Lamothe, his successor, was accused of obstructing the course of justice.

The idea of submitting a lawsuit against the governors was inspired by a trial that took place in 1888, when Jeandet was still alive. In that trial, the ex-governor of Senegal, Alfred Genouille, was convicted of manslaughter. Genouille had sent four African soldiers to a small island, Alcatraz, off the coast of Senegal. The soldiers were posted there for three months without sufficient supplies of food and water. The governor forgot all about them and was reminded of their existence only when a delegation arrived on the island and was horrified to discover the soldiers' bodies. It was obvious that their deaths had been slow and torturous.[1]

In an article ironically titled 'The Beauty of Colonization' ('Les Beautés de la colonisation'), the horrific deaths of the four soldiers' were described in these words:

> 40 miles south of the Senegalese coast, scorched by the sun [...] are the Alcatraz islands. In October four blacks were thrown there with a tent and 1300 litres of water. Then the boat that had brought

> them there departed, leaving them insufficiently equipped on the arid rocks. Six months later, on 17 May, a vessel by the name of *Dakar* stopped there by chance and found four dead bodies twisted in front of empty barrels—they had died of thirst. Who brought them there? Who imposed upon them this horrible torture, this horrifying death? Some savage king, no doubt, wanting to take revenge on them. No, it was a vessel of our own navy that had brought them to these rocks. It was the governor of Senegal, monsieur Genouille who asked king Dina-Salefou [sovereign of the region of Rio Nunez] for these soldiers so that the French might protect these islands under the tricolour of the French Republic that was to be raised on the islands. It was France that was supposed to feed them, pay them, that had brought these miserable people to this reef; it was our administration—that the black king had no reason to envy [those] who let them perish, forgetting or neglecting to supply them with food and water.[2]

This short description embodies the main anti-colonial arguments of the time: France regarded Africans as savages, but it was France that was committing acts of savagery in its newly acquired African territories. As we shall see, this will also be the main argument of some of the journalists who reported on Ba's lawsuit. Genouille's eventual punishment was rather light considering the horrible consequences of his criminal neglect. He was fined 600 francs. But it demonstrated that a governor could be convicted in court for causing the death of colonial subjects.[3] It was this conviction that led Devès to take Ba's lawsuit to Paris and target the two governors who served at the time of the affair. He hoped that the fact that a governor had already been convicted in a Parisian court after causing the death of colonial subjects might encourage the court to take a similar stand while deliberating Ba's case.

Ba's lawsuit was represented by Félix Decori, one of the best criminal lawyers in France at the time. In an article describing his appearance in another case earlier that year, Décori's final remarks were described in these words: 'After a very vibrant peroration, the eloquent defender called for the jury to acquit speaking from the heart and inspired by reason. The effect produced was enormous; I have rarely heard more skilful pleading.'[4] Ba's lawsuit could not have been entrusted to better hands. Unfortunately, even Décori's remarkable rhetorical skills were not sufficient to win her case.

Relying on legal article 31 of the Civil Procedure Act, the plaintiff demanded that the governors be punished. She also asked for compensatory damages of 50,000 francs. In a hearing convened on 15 June 1891, the judge decided to summon the two governors, according to article 69 of the Civil Procedure Act, to appear on 19 November 1891 at 10 a.m. before the court of first instance of the Seine in Chamber 10.[5] Decori presented himself to the court at the specified time that day, but the two governors did not. Instead, a letter from Etienne, the colonial under-secretary, informed the court that it was impossible to deliver the summons to them without risking legal consequences. Etienne quoted article 121 of the penal code, which imposed punishment on anyone who 'gave or signed mandates, orders, or judgments against the governor, or who had authorized such an act against him, without the requisite authorization prescribed by the laws of the State.'[6]

Decori was furious. He protested vehemently against the under-secretary's interference in the legal proceedings and raised two objections to Etienne's position. First, he claimed that the summons did in fact reach the two governors, and that he could provide evidence for that. He then added that the gouvernement de la défense nationale (government of National Defence), established in 1870 following the defeat to Prussia, and which was in fact the first government of the Third Republic, issued on 29 September 1870 a decree repealing all provisions that hindered proceedings against officials of all ranks. Decori asked the court for a week's extension so that he could prove that the governors had received the summons, but his request was declined. The judge then declared that there was no cause for further legal action or judgement. He dismissed the motion, leaving the plaintiff to take whatever action she saw fit regarding the matter.[7] This decision blocked any further legal action and, while Decori declared that he would appeal, the chances for success seemed low.

From the way the affair turned out in Paris, we can see that legal manipulation was not only a colonial speciality. In the metropole too such dubious measures were used to prevent the case from reaching trial. It seems that the claim that the governors did not receive the summons was indeed a lie. The court's refusal to allow Decori to present evidence to the contrary supports this view. But, beyond this lie, as we shall soon see, lay a more sophisticated legal manipulation.

The colonial authorities, this time at the highest level, succeeded again in blocking Ndiereby's road to justice. Devès's hope that the precedent set by the conviction of a colonial governor in 1888 could lead to victory proved unfounded. There were two main reasons the Genoille Affair had no influence on the court's decision regarding Ba's lawsuit. First, unlike the common law system, the continental system did not regard judges' decisions as establishing a legal precedent. It was nearly always a statutory provision found in the codes, such as article 121, that served as the legal basis—this is what occurred in the judge's decision in Ba's case.[8] No binding rule of precedent exists in French Law, therefore Genouille's conviction could not have helped Decori, who indeed did not mention it in his response to the court. Second, and perhaps more importantly, Genouille's victims were not 'enemies of France.' They were soldiers recruited to guard a French possession against its colonial rivals. It was perhaps easier for the court to find Genouille guilty and inflict a symbolic punishment on him. The lawsuit against Clément Thomas and de Lamothe was different, as it targeted governors who had supposedly only intended to protect France's colonial interests in Senegal. A trial against these governors and, even worse, a conviction, could have damaged the already unstable situation in this colony. It is no wonder, then, that the colonial under-secretary chose to intervene and prevent the case from reaching trial. He could not, however, prevent the animated debate around the affair when it reached Paris. Let us now examine this debate, relying mainly on reporting by the French press at the time, and on a long deliberation in the Chambre des députés (Chamber of Deputies, the legislative body of the French parliament at that time) in which the affair was described as a demonstration of the immorality and uselessness of French colonial expansion into West Africa.

Debating the Jeandet Affair in Paris

The two very short hearings conducted in the Seine courthouse five months apart in 1891 might have been expected to remain unnoticed. Unlike the many other legal scandals that abounded in *fin de siècle* France, the Jeandet Affair did not result in a long and sensational trial that was bound to draw attention. Etienne's letter had meant to prevent any public debate around the affair by preventing it from ever reaching trial. While, indeed, public opinion was not deeply moved by the Jeandet Affair as it had been by previous and subsequent scandals, it still drew some attention, especially in the French press. Around the two hearings on 15 June and 19 November, a substantial number of articles were published in many of the metropolitan newspapers. Some only reported about the legal procedures; others interpretated them and, occasionally, harshly criticized them.

To better understand the discussion of the affair in the French press, some attention should be given to the characteristics of the rise of the media in late nineteenth-century France. The Jeandet Affair found its way into the French press at a crucial moment in its expansion. While it had existed since the seventeenth century, the French press began to transform in the later nineteenth century, becoming more professional. Up until then the history of the French press had two recurring features, politics and literature—those who wrote in French newspapers were either politicians or men of letters. Journalism only became a professional occupation in the last decade of the nineteenth century, and a professional school of journalism was established at the end of the century. This was the period when the French press became an autonomous force, becoming very powerful during the following century.[9]

The *belle époque* is often regarded as the 'golden age' of the French press, as it was an era characterized by political liberalization and economic growth, which allowed more people to buy newspapers. The liberation of the press from governmental tutelage was confirmed by a decree in 1881, but this decree did not put an end to the close ties between the world of journalism and the political sphere.[10]

According to Thomas Ferenczi, even as the French press was being influenced by American journalism and becoming more professional, it still preserved some of its cultural heritage—its political affiliations and literary writing. The French press became an original blend of information and opinion journalism, both political and literary. This configuration took shape during the last decade of the nineteenth century, and it had a place for writers of different values and political convictions, such as Jean Jaurès, Maurice Barrès, Émile Zola, and George Clemenceau.[11]

The revolution within journalism started with the establishment of the tabloids (*petits journaux*) aimed at the 'masses'—such as *Le Petit Journal* (1863), *Le Petit Parisien* (1878), and *Le Matin* (1884), which were much cheaper than the broadsheets (*grands journaux*) and therefore reached many more readers. During the 1890s they sold altogether about a million copies a day. This was also the time that preceded new and competing communication media, such as radio and cinema newsreels, which meant that the only way to be exposed to news was through print.[12]

At the time the Jeandet Affair reached the French press, it was therefore just beginning to be more professional, free, and widespread. With the advances in technology that enabled printing more copies and the growing literacy of the French public, the press had the means to control public opinion. At this time the press entered a period of intense activity and immense upheaval. Later, during the final years of the nineteenth century, it would play a critical role in two major scandals—the Panama Canal Affair and the Dreyfus Affair.[13] While the Jeandet Affair did not generate nearly the same degree of public debate or political ramifications as these two scandals, it was still present in the French press, and the debates around it sowed the seeds for the bigger ones to come.

The affair gained attention in the press despite its origin in a remote and unfamiliar corner of the growing French empire, and despite its anti-climactic ending, because it lay at the crossroad of two major debates occupying French public opinion at the time. One was the functioning or, more accurately, malfunctioning, of the French metropolitan justice system, and the other was the colonization of vast areas, especially in West and Equatorial Africa, the necessity of which was vigorously debated. The debate about the French colonial enterprise included the concept of the 'civilizing mission' legitimizing colonial violence. This discussion manifested not only in the press but also in the Chamber of Deputies, where certain members used the Jeandet Affair to challenge the idea that France should expand its colonial territories into areas when there were no significant benefits. In my examination of these two debates as they relate to the affair, I will also pay attention to the metropolitan perspective of the colonial 'adventure' in relatively unfamiliar areas of the globe, and how this perspective was reflected in journalists' discourse.

The affair was mentioned and discussed in about 20 newspapers, each with their different trends and characteristics. Most of the reports and articles about the affair were published during the days immediately following the court's decision on 19 November

1891 not to open a trial. Some newspapers, such as *Le Monde* and *Le Figaro*, did not discuss the affair but reported on the murder of Jeandet's cousin, Amédée in March 1891. Amédée, who worked for the French rail company in Senegal, was murdered on a train carriage on his way from Saint Louis to Dakar. The authorities investigating his murder decided that it had no relation to that of his more celebrated cousin.[14] Several of the newspapers were neutral about the affair and contented themselves with factual reports about the legal procedures that took place in Paris, first in June and then in November; however, most of the newspapers took a position regarding the affair. Out of the 12 dailies that published the facts as well as discussion about them, only three supported the administration's position. One of these newspapers was a local one, published in Saône-sur-Loire, the département of Jeandet's village, so its rejection of the widow's cause is hardly surprising. Another was *Le Temps*, whose correspondent for Saint Louis was none other than Jules Couchard, a French lawyer who was an ardent supporter of the colonial administration in the city and the one who, in February 1892, would take over from Chadelle Ba as a client in order to put an end to her legal struggle. All the other newspapers raised many objections and concerns regarding the affair, which they saw as representing much wider issues related to the two major debates mentioned above. While some concentrated on the legal implications of the affair for the French justice system, others raised doubts regarding the French colonial enterprise and the idea of the 'civilizing mission,' which served as its ultimate justification.

The affair and the metropolitan legal system

To understand the unfolding of the Jeandet Affair in Paris it is important to position it in the context of the French culture of scandals in the late nineteenth century—both metropolitan and colonial. Some of these scandals were connected. The Jeandet Affair was clearly linked to other colonial scandals, such as the Genouille Affair and the Voulet-Chanoine scandal, which shocked the French public a few years later.[15] But it was also linked to the most notorious scandal in modern French history—the Dreyfus Affair. Of those who played a role in the Jeandet Affair, the connection with the Dreyfus

Affair was via the Parisian attorney, Félix Decori, who took on Ba's case in the court of the Seine in Paris in 1891. Decori, a brilliant criminal lawyer, who took part in highly publicized cases, such as the Gouffé Affair,[16] was also a member of the Dreyfus defence team. His wife, Magdeleine, was a close friend of the wrongly accused captain. She sent him letters after his release and even invited him and his wife, Lucy, for dinner at her parents' house.[17]

The context of scandal is not only related to the individuals who participated in the Jeandet Affair, or to the encouragement that the legal victory in the Genouille Affair prompted, but also helps us understand the metropolitan legal atmosphere of the period. Discussing several metropolitan scandals, including the Dreyfus Affair, Benjamin Martin demonstrated that the civilian legal system at the end of the nineteenth century, the one that tried Ba's lawsuit in Paris, was just as corrupt as the military.[18]

Martin suggests a rather straightforward definition for the term 'justice.' According to him, justice is 'the entire process by which a crime is investigated and tried. "Fair justice" would be compliance with the written law.'[19] He maintains that during the *belle époque*, the French legal system suffered from 'hypocrisy of justice,' referring to the gap between the ideal principles of justice at the time and its practice. While examining three metropolitan scandals of the *belle époque*, all of which took place soon after the Jeandet Affair, Martin concludes that, in all three, justice departed so much from its ideal that it was no longer a strict application of the law, but rather a system of rewards and punishments that operated according to social utility.[20]

The French author Anatole France could have not agreed more with this analysis. While writing the story of an imaginary peddler in nineteenth-century Paris who had the bad luck of being arrested for an insult he had not made, France explains why the judge had to accept the testimony of police officer number 64 rather than that of a highly educated passer-by who maintained that the poor peddler had never cursed the policeman:

> Justice is the sanction of established injustices. Did we ever see it opposed to conquerors and contrary to usurpers? When an illegitimate power arises, it has only to recognize it to make it legitimate. Everything is in the form, and between crime and innocence there is only the thickness of a sheet of stamped paper.[21]

Anatole France wrote *L'Affaire Crainquebille* at the height of the Dreyfus Affair. This was his way of condemning the French justice system for its arbitrariness. The story of the poor, wrongly accused, peddler is a story of a legal conspiracy that in France's view typified not only the French military justice system but also the civilian one. This conspiracy is the affirmation of the power and legitimacy of the state. France saw the justice system as an infernal machine designed to convict selected victims in order to maintain the social order. As one of the observers at the peddler's trial notes in the book: 'Above all, do not ask justice to be just; it needs not be just precisely because it *is* justice. More, I dare say that the idea of Justice that were just can only have been born in the mind of some anarchist.'[22]

This grim definition of justice is highly relevant to the Jeandet Affair. The lawsuit against the administrators and, later, in Paris, against the governors, was an attempt to oppose conquerors, but this attempt finally failed. While Ba received support from several judges and judicial administrators, and even from one French administrator (Fawtier), her case failed twice because, as Anatole France argued, everything was in the form. Justice here too was not just; it was a machine designed to maintain the power of the colonial state and, when the law could not maintain this task, it was put aside by legal manipulations.

While such miscarriages of justice took place in the colonies, the French press barely reported on them, but when it occasionally did report, it referred to them as colonial affairs. Only *Le Temps*, a metropolitan newspaper focusing on colonial affairs, accorded the Jeandet Affair substantial attention. When the case reached Paris, it drew the attention of the metropolitan press and it began to be seen not only as a colonial scandal but also as a judicial affair, which had consequences for metropolitan France and its justice system. Some of the French newspapers saw the failure of Ba's struggle not only as a form of colonial oppression but also as a symbol of the corrupt metropolitan legal system, which also oppressed French citizens.

One of these French citizens was a young woman, Mercedes Fernandez. On 21 November 1891 the newspaper *Le XIXe siècle* reported that two policemen from the morality department brutalized Fernandez during an operation aimed at arresting sex workers, mistakenly perceiving her to be one. She was brought to prison and, despite her persistent claims that she was not a sex worker, the policeman in charge refused to verify her identity and locked her up for 15 days.[23] The young woman who had to spend 15 days in prison after being brutalized by those who were supposed to protect her had nothing to do with the African widow demanding justice for her husband executed without a trial. But according to Jean Frollo, the pen name of *Le Petit Parisien*'s editor, the two had very much in common. Both were in a position in which a public official, be it a police officer or a colonial governor, had harmed their rights. Therefore, to correct the injustice caused to them by an official figure, they had to act legally. Frollo went even further to claim that the court's decision in Ndiereby Ba's case, which was based on a legal article forbidding the prosecution of colonial governors, not only put her rights in jeopardy but also those of Fernandez.

Frollo titled his article: 'Irresponsibles!' referring to the decision not to open trial against the two governors while citing article 121, which released all officials from having to take legal responsibility for their actions. He explained that, until 1870, all persons on official duty in France were protected against all lawsuits by article 75 of the constitution of year VIII of the French Revolution. According to Frollo, this shameful protection of public officials resulted in scandals and harmed many citizens during the Second Empire (1852–1870). Article 75 became especially unpopular after several sensational trials during that period. For this reason, the new government of national defence in 1870 'was to formally repeal it by a decree whose terms are very absolute and whose validity, moreover, was never contested.' This new decree meant that, from then on, the responsibility of public officials was legally established, and they were responsible for every act they performed during their term of office, with no possibility of interference in the course of justice. Theoretically, then, Madame Ba had full rights to submit a lawsuit against the officials who had obstructed the legal procedures of the case related to her husband. Practically, however, she encountered article 121 of the Penal Code, titled 'attentats a la liberté' (offences against freedom), under which paragraph 3 forbids under punishment any bailiff from submitting a lawsuit, any prosecutor from opening legal procedures, and any judge from convicting those who had harmed her interests. The infamous article 75 had been repealed but, in practice, it was as if this had never happened.[24]

Frollo then explained to his readers that this hidden article, which was not repealed due to an oversight, and that was now exploited by the court, should worry every one of them and was not only the problem of an African woman who was searching for justice in the metropole. He used Mademoiselle Fernandez to demonstrate this claim. Unlike Ba, she supposedly should not have been concerned by the protection of colonial governors from individual lawsuits, as she lived in Paris and not in Guédé. But, in fact, while trying to sue those who had maltreated her, she might have encountered other clauses in the same law that related to other categories of public officials, such as prefects. Article 75 of the Revolutionary Constitution was indeed repealed, but it continued to survive within particular laws. Till then, these laws had been ignored but, while trying to prevent the embarrassment of the colonial authorities, the court invoked them and made them visible to other public authorities. Frollo ended his article by ironically declaring: 'It is a beautiful thing, the law!'[25]

Frollo was not alone in his concerns about the implications of the affair on the rights of French citizens. *La Loi*, a judicial journal, established in 1880 to discuss legal decisions of various courts, shared this criticism and concern. The journal described the affair, which was brought to the court of the Seine, as extremely rare. It was, according to the article that described the session on 19 November, a clear case of the administration trampling on the judicial authorities. It reported in detail on Decori's protests at the court's decision and the arguments it was based on. The attorney knew for certain that the colonial under-secretary had lied, because a certain monsieur Yon, who worked in the under-secretary's office, had told him that the summonses had been received, and had asked him for copies. That meant that the ministry had known that the summonses had reached their destination and had lied about it.[26] *Le Matin,* a journal established in 1884, and which was preoccupied with legal scandals, also agreed that the dismissal of Ba's lawsuit was outrageous. An article published on the morning of the court's decision referred to the problematic article 121, and described the illegal executions in a very critical manner. The author highlighted the administrative actions against the judicial authorities and stated that, as the affair had not reached a conclusion in court, it should reach a conclusion in parliament.[27] This statement is interesting as *Le Matin* was an anti-parliamentary and nationalistic journal, which would later collaborate with the Nazis and ultimately disappear following the Liberation. It is also intriguing that such a journal shared the same critical view of the affair as organs holding very different political views, such as the republican and anti-clerical *Le XIXe siècle*.

A common feature of all these critical reports on the court's decision is the respectful way they treated the plaintiff, Ndiereby Ba, and their perception of her as a woman entitled to the protection of French law. Unlike the references to Ba in colonial documents, which were disrespectful towards her, often avoiding mentioning her name, calling her 'the wife of Sidick' or even the 'pretended wife,' the metropolitan articles examining the legal aspects of the affair always refer to her as 'Madame Ba.' Moreover, as opposed to the administration's view of Ba as a puppet at the hands of their enemies, the authors of these articles saw Ba as an independent legal actor in the affair whose struggle for justice was perfectly understandable and justified. This perspective sometimes seems naïve or misconceived, as these articles do not take into consideration the legal status of the territory from which Ba came—a protectorate, which was not subject to French law and that therefore left her devoid of such rights. In fact, a French reader would have had no reason to suspect that Ba was not a French citizen with deep knowledge of the legal system and access to the best available attorneys in Paris. *Le XIXe siècle*, for example, tells readers that Madame Ba despaired of attaining justice in the colonies and therefore decided to look for it in Paris. She thought she would find judges in the capital. Ba then consulted the French penal code, and asked that the two governors be punished and that she receive 50,000 francs in compensation. All this is described as Ba's initiative. Only then did the author mention that she was assisted by Decori.[28] This description of Ba's actions and the respect with which she is treated stands in stark opposition to the way the colonial administration had described her. Nevertheless, it is misleading in that it totally ignored the specific circumstances of the territory from which Ba originated and her inferior status in French law.

The articles concerned with the legal aspect of the affair and its implications for the French legal system and the protection of

French citizens from unjust laws did not pay much attention to the colonial aspect of the affair. This focus on the precarious nature of the penal code and the ways it could be exploited to harm the rights of law-abiding citizens who were wrongly treated by public officials could explain the distorted perception of Ba as equal under French law. Soon, much more significant scandals would occupy the French press. But, for the time being, the Jeandet Affair drew attention to the weaknesses of the French metropolitan legal system and the lack of sufficient guaranties for justice. While the implications of the affair troubled several metropolitan journals, most were concerned with a different yet related question, namely the debate around French colonial expansion in West Africa and the validity of the notion of the 'civilizing mission' that served as its ultimate justification.

The affair and the French colonial expansion

Colonialism was never a mass movement in France. The French public was mostly indifferent to and ignorant of the French empire. The colonial policy of the Third Republic was incoherent; only in the early 1890s, exactly around the time the affair reached Paris, were some grand designs, such as the completion of French North Africa by the Moroccan protectorate, developed, which pointed in a clearer direction. Nevertheless, these plans were not a product of a French official mind, but rather of an unofficial one—a minority of devout colonialists organized in different forms and became known as 'the Colonial Party' (le parti colonial), even though they did not constitute a political party. Paradoxically, it was the weakness of the official mind that made this minority so influential. The Colonial Party orchestrated most of the military campaigns from the early 1890s. The people who belonged to it were not many, but they were determined and well organized.

The concern about the rivalry with other European nations that had colonial aspirations led, in 1890, to the establishment of the first significant colonial pressure group, the Comité de l'Afrique française. This organization's success in encouraging colonization stemmed from the correlation formed in this period between nationalism and colonial rivalry. Most of the supporters of the colonial cause were republicans from the centre of the political map. But politicians from the left and the right were soon convinced that achievements in the colonial sphere could be translated into national grandeur. And national grandeur was something French society was certainly not indifferent to.

Indeed, it is important to distinguish between the justification for colonial expansion, mainly the idea of the 'civilizing mission,' and the real motives of the politicians who advanced it, such as Jules Ferry. The motivation behind colonial expansion was often, if not always, national sentiment. The economic motive hardly existed, as most French businesses were not enthusiastic about investment in the empire. The success of the colonial idea in France was not a result of popular support but rather due to the ability of a devoted minority to present colonial issues as questions of national prestige.

The Comité de l'Afrique française, together with those of Asia and Morocco and the colonial pressure group in the French parliament, held influence over the formulation of colonial policy. The leaders of the three societies formed the inner circle that, until World War One, controlled the Colonial Party and determined its policy. Eugène Etienne, the colonial under-secretary who had supported de Lamothe in his struggle against Ba's lawsuit, and managed to prevent it from reaching trial, was at the centre of this inner circle. He was known to his supporters as the '*Notre Dame de coloniaux*' and, until his retirement in 1919, he was the unchallenged leader of the colonial movement.[29]

The Jeandet Affair reached Paris, then, at a time when official colonial policy was practically non-existent, and the unofficial pressure group was gaining power. It is no wonder, then, that it raised so much controversy in the media and even reached a heated parliamentary debate about the elevated colonial budget for 1892.

As noted, two of the most well-known and significant scandals that threatened the stability of the Third Republic were the Panama Affair and the Dreyfus Affair. Neither were connected to the colonies but, towards the end of the nineteenth century, the French public was shocked by a colonial scandal, the Voulet–Chanoine Affair, which was related to the ongoing debate regarding the French colonization of West Africa.

In January 1898 the recently promoted Captain Paul Voulet proposed to the ministry of the colonies that it put him in charge of an ambitious expedition intended to expand the French territory in the Sahel. This project gained the support of the French government, stemming from the idea that the glory colonial expansion would bring might alleviate the conflicts and divisions that characterized the Third Republic. Julian Chanoine joined Voulet in this expedition, bringing the support of his father (Jules Chanoine), who was a very close associate of the minister of war and who later gained that position himself. The two young officers personified the image of the 'colonial man,' which also served as a model for Jeandet: a fearless hero who was both daring and imaginative in his efforts to secure French possession in dangerous and unfamiliar corners of the globe.

The mission started according to plan, and the two officers adhered to their instructions; but soon the atmosphere changed. The expedition encountered some unexpected resistance on its way and the water supplies proved insufficient. Eventually, reports of excessive violence on the part of the officers began to reach Paris. Although violence was part and parcel of colonial conquest, Voulet and Chanoine's actions seemed unreasonable to officials in France. The expedition resorted to extreme violence not only when it encountered armed resistance but also when the officers perceived the slightest sign of resentment. They massacred thousands of Africans on their way, including children, who they hanged from trees.[30]

Following the reports of these horrors, Colonel Arsène Klobb was sent to stop the officers and bring them to military justice. When Voulet heard Klobb was on their trail, he felt betrayed and feared severe punishment. He therefore planned an ambush for the colonel and shot him dead upon arrival. The two officers then renounced their French citizenship and decreed themselves to be African kings who intended to establish their very own African kingdom. The Voulet–Chanoine expedition thus became yet another French scandal. As Bertrand Thaite notes in his book about the affair, the French public was much more horrified by the killing of one French officer than by the massacre of thousands of Africans. Voulet and Chanoine were now no longer heroes but mad villains. They were both eventually killed, most probably by their own men.[31]

Thaite argues that the Voulet–Chanoine Affair brought the colonial idea under scrutiny. It was certainly more horrifying than the

Jeandet Affair as the victims were more numerous, some even young children, and none of them were involved or suspected of being involved in any crime. However, the atrocities that had aroused debate in France soon came to be described as exceptions. The two officers were considered mad and therefore did not represent French military action in West Africa. The responsibility for their madness was assigned to the continent on which they committed their crimes. The African sun and the tropical climate were found guilty of causing the officers to lose their minds.[32]

The Jeandet Affair was different; no one could accuse any of the administrators involved in the illegal executions of madness. There was, ostensibly, a rational explanation for their conduct, although it had not satisfied most of the metropolitan press discussing the affair: the need for security. Many of the articles and reports about the affair, as well as the parliamentary discussion around it, reflect the debate about the colonial idea approximately a decade before the Voulet–Chanoine Affair. Because the argument of insanity brought on by the African sun could not have applied to the Jeandet Affair, the debate raised rational rather than emotional arguments for, and mainly against, French expansion in West Africa.

In a way, the affair highlighted concerns regarding the colonial project that already existed. We should make a distinction, though, between anti-colonial views, rejecting the entire colonial idea, which were extremely rare at the time, and objections to colonial conquests in areas deemed insignificant from political, strategic, or economic respects or to specific violent and unjust colonial policies or military campaigns.

One of the rare examples of a total rejection of the colonial idea and its 'civilizing mission' can be found in the radical leader George Clemenceau's response to a speech Jules Ferry gave on 28 July 1885 before the Chamber of Deputies, five years before Jeandet's murder. Ferry discussed the right of the so-called civilized people to rule the world. Clemenceau rejected Ferry's division of the world into superior and inferior races, and argued that this was an idea developed by German scholars who regarded the French as inferior. Ever since, so he wrote, he thought twice before calling a civilization or an individual 'barbaric.' Clemenceau then went on to argue against colonial conquests that were accompanied by violence and bloodshed and that therefore were barbaric acts rather than a civilizing mission. The nations who carried out these brutal conquests had therefore no right to define themselves as superior. Clemenceau also doubted the validity of the term 'civilization.' He believed that civilization, even as impressive as the French one, was only a thin coating that could be easily peeled off under various circumstances.[33]

Indeed, in *fin de siècle* France the deep belief in the idea of progress and the boasting of a superior civilization blended with various anxieties about the precarious nature of this civilization, the danger of the unconscious and the power of the crowd, and forces that might turn technological and scientific developments into a nightmare. More than other parts of the growing French empire, the African continent seemed like an irrational land that might influence Europeans badly. Gustav Le Bon, who had written about the menacing power of the irrational crowd, fiercely objected to the idea of the 'civilizing mission' and colonial conquests, but for reasons very different from those raised by Clemenceau. Le Bon believed that superior races might deteriorate by encountering inferior ones. He did not believe it was possible to elevate those inferior races, and was concerned by the degeneration they might cause Europeans who encountered them through colonization.[34]

The Voulet–Chanoine Affair brought these fears to the fore. But the Jeandet Affair raised different questions, related to the debate about empire and law. The main issue was whether it was possible to colonize vast territories while keeping to the principles of French law. And, if it were not, could such disregard of the law be justified, or would it be better to refrain from colonizing certain regions of the world even when this was practically possible?

The dilemma of supporting colonial expansion while insisting on the observation of the law is personified in one of Devès's main supporters in Paris, Alexandre Isaac, who served as a senator from 1885 until his death in 1899 as a representative of the old colony (*ancienne colonie*), Guadeloupe. In 1898 Isaac participated in the establishment of the Ligue de Droits des Hommes. Isaac intervened repeatedly in the senate sessions about Senegal, and was considered one of the most active supporters of Africans in this colony. With the encouragement of Admiral Vallon who initially took the position of the judiciary in Saint Louis and rejected the administration's claim of a political conspiracy, Isaac tried to alert the French parliament to the affair in December 1890. Luckily for the administration, the parliamentary recess prevented him from affirming his view. Unlike Vallon, who changed his position later and switched to the administration's side, Isaac remained supportive of Ba's case and continued to help Devès. In 1894 he defended one of Devès's sons as his lawyer when the latter was accused of corruption.[35]

Isaac participated as a senator in parliamentary debates, where the representatives of the old colonies, such as Guadeloupe, were doubly marginalized. They were a small minority both in the senate and in parliament, and were outnumbered by the European representatives of the colonies, including Algeria. This repartition of representatives reflected the marginalization of the old colonies and the preference for settler colonies such as Algeria.[36]

Isaac regularly intervened in debates regarding the colonies. He called for the formulation of a coherent colonial policy, and supported the ideology of assimilation, in the new colonies as well as the old. While he did not object to the colonial expansion into vast areas of Asia and Africa, and even supported the extension of the 1881 law that accorded special repressive powers to administrators in Algeria for two more years, he opposed the use of violence and disregard for the law in campaigns of colonization. In 1892, for example, he denounced the violence employed during the conquest of the Dahomey kingdom (nowadays Benin).[37]

The Jeandet Affair attracted Isaac's attention because it highlighted issues of violence and disregard for the law, which he believed should and could be avoided during colonial conquests. Many of the views expressed about the affair in the French press and in parliament saw it as proof that Isaac's position was impossible. According to some of the writers, the affair proved that colonial conquest could not be performed within French legal constraints, as colonization and the law are contradictory. Furthermore, as the justification of colonization was spreading the 'civilizing mission,' which was supposedly built upon these legal principles, the obvious conclusion was that this justification was in fact invalid. While not all newspapers reached these conclusions, and this view was also marginal in parliament, still the affair brought it to the attention of the French public and raised doubts regarding the colonial project, or at least parts of it.

Most of the media's attention was drawn to the affair only with the first court hearing in Paris on 15 June 1891. In the following days, and for some time thereafter, several articles discussed the affair in relation to French colonial expansion in West Africa. Most of the Parisienne newspapers interested in Ba's lawsuit were very critical towards the colonial administration in Senegal and the colonial under-secretary, Etienne. On the morning of the hearing, *La Cocarde*, a Boulangist newspaper, which gradually adopted a Christian Democratic line, expressed harsh criticism of the colonial administration, which accorded no value to the inhabitants of regions, who were referred to as *sauvages* (savages). The writer concluded that the real savage was France rather than the colonial subjects. He described events in Senegal while getting some basic details wrong, such as the date of Jeandet's murder. He then wrote that Ba went to Paris to seek justice (although she was not there physically). Finally, the writer raised his doubts about Ba's prospects of success. He wrote bitterly, 'We will send the widow away without paying her indemnities and tell her not to return.'[38]

It is interesting to note that many of the reports on the affair in the French press included inaccuracies regarding the events that transpired in Senegal. *Le Matin* opened its report by remarking that the administrative action against the judiciary authorities did not happen in France but 'very far away, very far away, in Senegal.' The redundant repetition served to emphasize the great distance of the colony from Paris, which perhaps explains the mistaken number of people it stated later in the report were executed (four instead of three). *Le Rappel* raised the number of the executed men to five. *La Cocarde,* mentioned above, noted 2 December rather than September as the date Jeandet was murdered. These mistakes are important, as they reflect the difficult communication with Senegal and its perception as a particularly remote and neglected region of the French empire.[39]

One of the harshest criticisms of the colonial administration, and the colonial project in general, can be found in the newspaper *L'Intransigeant*. In an article published after Ba lost her case in November, Henri Varennes referred to the executions in his title as 'massacres.' Nowhere else were they referred to in this manner. While repeating the same details as other articles, Varennes used a very literary and dramatic style:

> Listen, people of France and people of the colonies, who had the naive pretension of obtaining justice from justice, the story of Diéreby Ba [sic], the widow of Sedick [sic] Sall, the former chief of Toro, the victim of Podor's torture. Listen, meditate, and see if it is easy to obtain redress for the crimes of which one is the victim. This story, or rather the history of the massacres of Senegal, is known to our readers.

After telling his readers about the court's decision to dismiss Ba's case he ironically concluded: 'Another one [Ndiereby] who is going to appreciate the beauties of civilization.'[40]

Not all newspapers supported Ba's case or criticized French colonization. An article in *L'Événement* from 17 June 1891 quoted the one from the previous day published in *La Cocarde*. But after repeating the same description of the events it arrived at an opposite conclusion. The writer agreed that the administrators' actions were illegal and should be deplored, but then excused them by noting that the absence of civilization in certain areas that France colonized made it impossible to implement in them French legal principles:

> Undoubtedly, one can only deplore the haste with which, during the first incident, certain officials carried out summary executions. However, it should also be noted that these scarcely civilized territories are not governed like a French district, and among natives insensitive to any sense of generosity and legality, it is very difficult to consistently apply our code and laws with scrupulousness.[41]

The most ferocious attack on Ndiereby's legal struggle came, unsurprisingly, from a local newspaper, published in Saône-et-Loire the département to which Jeandet's village, Verdun-sur-le-Doubs, belonged. *Le Courrier de Saône-et-Loire* reported, somewhat belatedly, on the 15 June hearing in the court of the Seine. It lamented the emotion it caused in the Parisian press and the support some of the journals expressed for Ba's legal cause. The writer saw Ba's legal struggle as a second round in the attack on Jeandet. He mentioned several other assassinations of French representatives in northern Senegal and referred to Sidick Sall as a scoundrel (*canaille*). The article contended that, instead of rebuking the administrators for the action, the French press should commend them for protecting their countrymen so vigorously. It went on to describe the administrators on the ground as a handful of brave men surrounded by savage natives whom they needed to teach to respect France. It also attacked Ba personally, using an especially racist and derogatory term, *moricaude*, to describe her. In no other press report, even those that supported the administration, were such terms used. The writer finally accused the people acting behind Ba of holding personal grudges against the administrators.[42]

But the vicious attack on Ba and her cause in this local newspaper was certainly an exception. Most of the metropolitan newspapers raised doubts regarding the implementation of the civilizing mission in West Africa. They saw the affair as proof of the failure of this idea and as a warning sign regarding the future colonization of such areas. This debate remained not only in the press but also reached parliament.

On 30 November, soon after Decori's court defeat, French deputy Albert Alfred Martineau[43] requested an interpellation to discuss the colonial budget. The budget for 1892 increased by 1.2 million francs from the previous year, reaching the sum of 5,189,000 francs. Martineau was appalled by this huge increase and asked to speak about the budget's aims and, more generally, about the lack of a coherent colonial policy for the French conquests in West Africa. He reminded parliament that the last time anyone offered the house some information about the Sudan (West Africa) was in 1884 when the deputies heard a briefing on the railway between Kayes and Bafoulabé; since then there had been nothing.[44] Martineau also mentioned the incessant wars in this region. Every day, so he lamented, specialized journals reported that 'we waged a battle, destroyed empires, signed a peace agreement.' Martineau stressed that the government was responsible for what was happening in West Africa. Although, until then, the French had enjoyed easy victories, unexpected disasters might still happen. To prove his point, he quoted defeats that had befallen the British in Khartoum, the Italians in Ethiopia, and the Germans in East Africa. He warned that, despite the great value of French soldiers and their willingness to make sacrifices, such accidents could happen to France as well. If that indeed occurred, the public would blame the government for saying nothing and the parliament for asking no questions. Martineau therefore demanded that the government explain its plans for the colonies and the aims of certain contracts already signed, as well as report on military missions carried out in the Sudan and their results. He argued that since 1880 an average of 500 soldiers a year were sent to carry out such missions. All these wars cost money and, as the climate in the Sudan was the most murderous in the world, it also cost a lot of lives. Half of the recruited soldiers never returned.

Throughout his intervention, Martineau demonstrated a precise and detailed understanding of the various military operations in West Africa and raised significant doubts about the wisdom of the decisions made on the ground. He raised several arguments against these military missions. First, he claimed that their aim was unclear. At one point he rhetorically asked parliament where exactly the military commanders on the ground wanted to go. Did they aspire to connect Senegal to Algeria and with Chad? Martineau portrayed this objective as a utopian fantasy that France should quickly abandon. He stressed that, although West Africa contained places that had inflamed French imagination for years, such as Timbuktu, there was no real value there. While some deputies compared this region to India, the comparison was baseless. Martineau then presented proof that agriculture in the Sudan was not profitable at all. The only lucrative trade in this region was the trade in enslaved people, which was deeply immoral and shameful.

Martineau concluded that the sole purpose of colonizing West Africa was to serve as a training ground for the army. He argued that this was a purely military colonization that hindered French commerce. He warned that France was repeating the mistakes of Algeria where, for 30 years, military rule had obstructed the territory's development.

This lengthy criticism of the French colonization of West Africa ended with the Jeandet Affair. At the conclusion of his speech, Martineau asked to present Etienne with one last question. He said that he could not close his observations without asking the colonial under-secretary about the affair that had troubled public opinion as much as that of the Cadi of Milianah,[45] although it seemed to him that this affair was even more serious. He then recounted in great detail and very accurately the events of the Jeandet Affair, from the murder, through the illegal executions, the legal struggle in Saint Louis and its repression by de Lamothe, and finally the widow's lawsuit in Paris and its failure. It seemed, so he concluded, that the court in Paris was no more equitable than that of Saint Louis. Finally, he asked Etienne to provide the chamber with a satisfactory explanation of this troubling affair. Apparently, this was a rhetorical question, as Etienne did not explain. It seems that Martineau's aim was not to hear what the colonial under-secretary had to say, but rather to use the affair to prove his point: France had nothing to gain from the hinterland of its Senegalese possessions. It should not try to conquer all the corners of the world. Only Algeria and Madagascar should remain parts of its empire, as they were useful territories. Martineau recognized the impossibility of such a colonial policy, as he knew there were not enough courageous deputies who would enforce it. But he still demanded that all military missions in the Sudan be stopped and that a civilian be appointed as a governor in this region.

He also demanded the establishment of a commission of inquiry that would collect all the information about the Sudan. The contradictory information the parliament received about this region necessitated, in his view, such a measure. Another deputy, Camille Dreyfus, objected by exclaiming: 'Ask the English and the Germans if they performed any inquiries about the hinterlands of their possessions!' To that, Martineau calmly replied that he was thinking about what was good for France and that, in any case, it was impossible to continue the adventurous policy in the Sudan with its enormous expense without a proper inquiry.

After this intervention the debate about the future of French colonization continued, when deputy Pelletan Camille insisted that France should expand its colonial conquest in the Sudan as it did in Tonkin (the northern region of Vietnam). Deputy Déclassé responded that, while France should definitely support the old colonies and their economies, it should not expand its empire to other regions. Like Martineau, he expressed his resentment at the parliament's inability to control these conquests: 'We have conquered Tonkin; we are going to conquer the Sudan. We have opposed the conquest of Tonkin, and today we oppose that of the Sudan.' The conquest of Tonkin, so he asserted, did not achieve its declared aims; therefore, until parliament understood what went wrong in Tonkin, it should not approve the conquest of other regions.[46]

This parliamentary debate—a considerable part of which was dedicated to a detailed description of the affair as proof of the futility of French colonial expansion into West Africa—as well as the media reports and interpretations of the affair, reflect the gap that existed between the metropole and the expanding French possessions in West Africa. Martineau's knowledge of the reality in West Africa was an exception to the rule. In general, as he pointed out in his intervention, members of parliament and government ministers knew nothing about the military activity there. For years they had heard no reports about the army's plans, missions, and their results. They kept approving large sums of money every year for these endeavours while receiving no information about them. Successive French governments at this time had no coherent colonial policy. It was the military on the ground that planned the conquests. The great distance between Saint Louis and Paris, and that between Saint Louis and the French posts in the hinterland, created this ignorance, along with a lack of interest on the part of most ministers and deputies in these remote regions into which France was gradually penetrating. In a way, the metropole and the growing empire in West Africa were two separate worlds.

The abyss that lay between Paris and West Africa is well reflected in the media reports on the affair. The description of Ndiereby Ba as a French citizen with full rights who could decide to take a lawyer on her own, consult the complex French legal codes and articles and choose the best legal option for her, first in Saint Louis and then in Paris, demonstrates the complete ignorance of French journalists about the colonial reality in which Ba had lived. Common mistakes with regard to dates and other facts and misspelling of names, also reflect the distance and miscomprehension of the colonial scene. The shock expressed in some of these reports about French colonial brutality, which was the norm during military campaigns and even in everyday routine, shows how detached the French press was from the process of colonization in West Africa. The affair drew attention to the brutality of colonial conquest and to the ignoring of French laws, but this was mostly seen as an exception, which could have been avoided. A few years later, when the horrors of the Voulet–Chanoine campaign were revealed to the French public, they too were seen as an exception. Nevertheless, these supposed exceptions seemed, at least to some journalists and deputies, to be a warning sign for the futility and immorality of the colonization of West Africa.

The lack of understanding regarding the colonial expansion into West Africa distorted the knowledge of the French public about these military adventures and the disregard for the law and for any moral values that accompanied them. However, this same ignorance on the part of the French government and parliament was the real problem. As we have seen, it was this ignorance that allowed the Colonial Party to formulate its own colonial policy and advance ever more conquests. What Martineau defined as utopia—connecting Senegal with Algeria and with Chad—would soon become a reality. The French government had little control over this process, and national sentiments helped to prevent public resistance.

As noted in Chapter 1, Jeandet was aware of the ignorance of the metropole about the colonies. He was full of contempt for most politicians of his time, and saw Paris as a sinful city full of people who lacked the values of the colonial man he turned into in Senegal. He often criticized decisions made in the metropole, which, according to him, were based on ignorance and misconceptions. What he perhaps did not realize was that, thanks to the metropolitan ignorance and lack of interest in Senegal and the military campaigns into West Africa, these conquests were to be materialized despite criticism regarding their immorality and futility. In any case, the affair that his murder had created was not enough to stop the French colonization of West Africa.

The end of the affair

There is a certain blur in official documents regarding what happened between Decori's failure in Paris in November 1891 and the formal end of the affair in early February 1892. A report on the legal debate in one of the newspapers assumed that Decori would appeal, but he did not.[47] Manchuelle expresses surprise that such an appeal did not take place as the court's decision was based on legal manipulations. It is difficult to know for certain what made a skilled attorney like Decori give up. He was certainly competent enough to continue the legal battle. We can only assume that the people who supported Ba's lawsuit, and especially Devès, decided to forsake the battlefield and stopped paying Decori.

There can be several reasons for Devès's retreat. He might have decided that the affair had lasted long enough and, while it certainly upset the colonial administration, it kept failing in court. Perhaps he did not want to spend more money on a case that seemed lost.

Another possibility is that, during the months following the failure in Paris, Devès was distracted by concerning political issues in the colony and had no time and energy to dedicate to Ba's lawsuit. Between late 1891 and 1894, the métis found themselves under attack from de Lamothe. The governor was concerned by the growing power of the General Council, which, since 1885, had been dominated by the métis. While during the affair de Lamothe succeeded in receiving support from the Descemet faction, the sworn enemies of Devès, towards the end of 1891 his policy of taking power from the General Council brought the two families closer together in an alliance against the administration and the French settlers. What worried Devès the most was de Lamothe's decision to deannex the territories outside the four communes and create new territories that eventually developed into an eight colonies' federation in 1895. De Lamothe made sure that the General Council would have no power over the protectorates' budget, thus weakening this institution considerably. De Lamothe's main ally in this battle against the power of the métis' was Jules Couchard. It is perhaps unsurprising that he was also the one who helped the governor put an end to the affair that had haunted him for almost 18 months.[48]

The only source that offers us a glimpse into the end of the affair is a legal document that Couchard formulated as Ba's new attorney. But before we examine what this document can teach us on the final manipulation that drove the widow back to her village, a few words are in order about the leader of the scheme against her. According to Manchuelle, and based on Couchard's correspondence with de Lamothe, the French attorney arrived at Senegal under a cloud. He wrote to the governor that he had come to Senegal 'to start anew, far from the theatre of unfortunate beginnings, a sort of political virginity.'[49] In response, de Lamothe insinuated a scandal in Dordogne in which Couchard had an important part. Dordogne being Bordeaux's 'backyard' seems to suggest that this scandal was related to the trading houses of this city. Couchard remained a shady character even when he moved to Senegal. He was able to gain no support among African voters and the métis rejected him as well. Like other '*petit colons*,' he saw the African electorate as an ignorant and easily corrupted mass.[50] In August 1890, just before Jeandet was assassinated, Couchard wrote in *Le Temps*, for which he had worked as an anonymous correspondent, a virulent attack against the voting rights of Algerian Muslims. He later continued his attempts to limit the rights of Africans in Saint Louis.

So how did such a character, who despised Africans and acted to limit their rights, became Ndiereby Ba's attorney? Ndiereby, of course, did not choose Couchard as her attorney. She had no reason to replace an empathetic man who offered her shelter, protected her from the administration and the police, and invested much effort in helping her try win her case. De Lamothe knew that Chadelle's protection prevented him from sending Ba back to Guédé. And by about March 1891, he was also worried that Chadelle was planning to appeal. He therefore tried then to get rid of him, as he did with the other judiciaries who insisted on pursuing Ba's lawsuit.

Pierre André Chadelle has not left much record in the colonial archives. Except for his letters to the governor and the colonial correspondence about his involvement in the affair, the only available information about him can be found in files containing professional observations about him while he served as a deputy judge in Pondicherry and later as an interim president of the Dakar tribunal. These observations, written before the Jeandet Affair, were mostly negative. He was described as restless, imprudent, capricious with the authorities (but good with the public), and negligent in style. The answer to the question about his readiness for promotion was—'not urgently.'

Somehow, despite these negative evaluations, Chadelle became in September 1889 the interim president of the Dakar tribunal. Shortly after his arrival in Dakar, Ursleur wrote a review on him. While admitting that he had known Chadelle for too short a time to form an opinion, he nonetheless stated: 'Since his arrival, this magistrate has been fulfilling the interim duties of presiding judge in Dakar, where he demonstrates a great deal of zeal and activity.'

Sometime between August 1889 and September 1890, Chadelle left the magistracy and returned to work as an attorney. According to de Lamothe, this change of career was a result of an incident upon which he did not elaborate. Chadelle's support of Ba's complaint, and his obvious compassion for her, were probably a result of those characteristics described by his superiors: capricious with authorities and good with the public.

As we have seen in Chapter 4, after failing to drive Ba away from Saint Louis, de Lamothe then aimed at Chadelle, whom he obviously detested. On 6 March 1891 he informed the colonial under-secretary that he had suspended Chadelle for a period of three months. He explained that this attorney maintained a position against the administration and had been working for a trading house whose specialization was fishing in troubled water to reinforce its clientele. The governor also suggested that it was Chadelle who had influenced the judges to support Ba's complaint and oppose the administration's attempts to put an end to it. He described him as Devès's straw man.

But Chadelle did not accept this measure without a fight. He soon found a legal clause that forbade the governor from suspending him without consulting the Saint Louis court. The governor was forced to cancel the suspension. Nevertheless, eventually Chadelle could not dodge the fate of his colleagues. Sometime after the case reached the court of the Seine, Chadelle was forced to leave Dakar and take a post in Vietnam. The road was now open for the exchange of lawyers, and Ba found herself at Couchard's mercy.

The first act Couchard performed as Ba's attorney was to prepare a document that put an end to all her hopes to attain justice for her slain husband. This very detailed legal document can only be described as a violent text. It was supposedly authorized by Ba but, given her determination up to that point to pursue her legal struggle, it is hard to believe that it was not either forced upon her or had been formulated without her consent.

The document begins with a statement according Couchard 'the power and authority, to act for her and in her name: to completely revoke, in its entirety, the power of attorney she had granted to Mr. Chadelle.' It then continues stating that Ba has authorized Couchard,

> to withdraw completely and simply all complaints and accusations that may have been filed in the name of the grantor, and all proceedings initiated also in her name, under the same power of attorney, notably against Messrs. Aubry-Lecomte, Tautain, Edouard Martin, administrators, Clément Thomas, former Governor of Senegal, and all other persons, for having contributed in one way or another to the execution of the said Sidir Sal [sic], with the grantor hereby renouncing all actions that may have been brought on this occasion.

Finally, the document accords Ba the sum she had deposited when filing her lawsuit in November 1890. No other payment is offered to her as recompense. The French thus saved themselves the 50,000 francs they were previously willing to offer Ba for withdrawing her lawsuit when they saw that pressure and harassment would not persuade her to quit.

The document was signed in the presence of,

> Messrs. Ernest Duffau, merchant, residing in Podor, and Georges Porquet, sales representative, residing in Podor. Their two instrumental witnesses, having the required qualifications and residing in Podor, as well as Messrs. Bacre Waly, merchant, and Maguèye N'dane, sales representative, both residing in Podor, having the required qualifications, and certifying the identity and individuality of the appearing party. Also present was Mr. Bou El Mogdad, requested as interpreter and additional witness, after taking an oath before us to faithfully translate the speeches exchanged between those speaking different languages, as the appearing woman and several witnesses could only express themselves in Toucouleur. After reading, the instrumental witnesses signed along with the interpreter and the administrator. As for Mrs. N'Diéribi Bâ [sic], she declared not being able to write or sign when asked to do so.

This refusal to sign the document was Ba's last act of defiance against those who denied her justice. With no support from Devès and his associates, and with her loyal attorney sent far away to Vietnam, this courageous grieving widow remained alone on the legal battlefield. Her new attorney had one purpose alone—to erase for good her lawsuit and its disturbing effects and allow the governor and the other implicated administrators to regain their peace of mind. Couchard probably also had in mind his own political interests. In the next couple of years, he would be embraced by the colonial administration who would help him in his political battles against the métis of Saint Louis. Being a shady character with a troubling past, helping de Lamothe to put an end to the Jeandet Affair must have helped Couchard to gain the governor's sympathy and trust.

As for Ndiereby, all she could do was return home without justice and with no recompense for her awful loss. She would later send her younger son, Mamadou, to his relatives in Saint Louis, those who helped her and gave her shelter during the affair. She would disappear from the French colonial mind. No longer a nuisance, she would soon be forgotten. Her descendants would be absorbed into the colonial administration and the military. As we shall see in the next and final chapter, in recent years some of them have invested efforts in reviving the memory of her inspiring legal struggle against colonial brutality and injustice.

Notes

1 *La Liberté*, 19 December 1888.
2 *La Cocadre*, 20 December 1888.
3 *La Liberté*, 19 December 1888.
4 *Le Petit Journal*, 10 January 1891.
5 *Le Temps*, 26 June 1891.
6 'Les Tribuneaux—Executions illégales au Sénégal,' *Le XIX siècle*, 21 November 1891.
7 Amédée Blondeau, 'À propos de l'exécution de Podor,' *Le Rappel*, 21 November 1891.
8 Bakshi, 'Continental System of Criminal Justice,' 420.
9 Thomas Ferenczi, L'invention *du journalisme en* France: *naissance de la presse moderne* à *la fin du xixe siècle* (Paris: Plon, 1996), 9–14.
10 Ivan Chupin, Nicolas Hubé, and Nicolas Kaciaf, '"L'âge d'or" de la presse (1870–1939),' in *Histoire politique et économique des médias en France* (Paris: La Découverte, 2012), 35–37.
11 Ferenczi, *L'invention du journalisme en France*, 15–16.
12 Chupin, Hubé, and Kaciaf, ' "L'âge d'or" de la presse (1870–1939),' 35; 43–45.
13 Ferenczi, *L'invention du journalisme en France*, 16.
14 *Le Monde*, which stopped appearing in 1896 and is unrelated to the current newspaper by the same name, was established in 1863 by Moïse Millaud and published mainly sensational articles *Le Figaro* published since 1854 became republican in its views during the 1880s.
15 In 1898, two French officers, Paul Voulet and Julian Chanoine, led an expedition into the Sahel, which resorted to extreme violence not only when it encountered armed resistance but also when the officers perceived the slightest sign of resentment. The officers massacred thousands of Africans on their way, including children, who they hanged from trees. See: Bertrand Taithe, *The Killer Trail: A Colonial Scandal in the Heart of Africa* (Oxford: Oxford University Press, 2009).
16 Augustin Gouffé was murdered in 1889 by Michel Eyraud and his young lover Gabrielle Bompard. Decori represented Bompard, who claimed she was hypnotized by Eyraud. The case drew much public

attention, and the press played a crucial role in it. See: Régine Plas, 'Hysteria, Hypnosis, and Moral Sense in French 19th-Century Forensic Psychiatry: The Eyraud-Bompard Case,' *International Journal of Law and Psychiatry* 21, no. 4 (1998).

17 Musée de Bretagne, letter from Decori Magdeleine Félix to Alfred Dreyfus, 3, July 1906, www.collections.musee-bretagne.fr/ark:/83011/FLMjo156816 (Accessed 10 April 2024).

18 Benjamin F. Martin, *The Hypocrisy of Justice in the Belle Epoque* (Baton Rouge: Louisiana State University Press, 1999), 6.

19 Martin, *The Hypocrisy of Justice in the Belle Epoque*, 13.

20 Martin, *The Hypocrisy of Justice in the Belle Epoque.*

21 Anatole France, *L'affaire Crainquebille* (Paris: Édouard Pelletan, 1901), 19. La justice est la sanction des injustices établies. La vit-on jamais opposée aux conquérants et contraire aux usurpateurs? Quand s'élève un pouvoir illégitime, elle n'a qu'à le reconnaître pour le rendre légitime. Tout est dans la forme, et il n'y a entre le crime et l'innocence que l'épaisseur d'une feuille de papier timbré.

22 Anatole France, *Crainquebille*, trans. Jacques Leclercq (New York: The Limited Editions Club, 1949), 38.

23 'Les Tribuneaux—Executions illégales au Sénégal,' *Le XIX siècle*, 21 November 1891.

24 Jean Frollo, 'Irresponsables!', *Le Petit Parisien*, 23 November 1891.

25 *Ibid.*

26 *La Loi*, 20 November 1891.

27 *Le Matin*, 20 November 1891.

28 'Les Tribuneaux—Executions illégales au Sénégal,' *Le XIX siècle*, 21 November 1891.

29 Christopher M. Andrew, 'The French Colonialist Movement During the Third Republic: The Unofficial Mind of Imperialism,' *Transactions of the Royal Historical Society* 26 (1976), 143–152.

30 When rumours on the atrocities performed by the two officers reached Paris, they were not believed. However, Klobb, the officer sent to investigate these rumours, saw, while entering the town of Birnin Konni in Niger through which the officers had passed on their way, over a thousand corpses, including young girls hanged on trees. Thaithe, *The Killer Trail*, 3.

31 Taithe, *The Killer Trail*, 41–42.

32 *Ibid*, 1–45.

33 *Ibid*, 46–47.

34 Martin Thomas, 'Mapping the French Colonial Mind,' in Martin Thomas, The French *Colonial Mind*: Mental *Maps* of *Empire* and

Colonial Encounters, vol. 1 (Lincoln: University of Nebraska Press, 2011), xi–xlvii.

35 Manchuelle, 'Métis et colons,' 485–502.

36 Emmanuelle Sibeud, 'Comment peut-on être créole? Les engagements impériaux d'Alexandre Isaac,' *Paris créole: son histoire, ses écrivains, ses artistes, XVIIIe-XXe siècles* (2020), 2.

37 Sibeud, 'Comment peut-on étre créole?,' 3–4.

38 *La Concarde*, 16 June 1891.

39 *Le Matin*, 20 November 1891; *Le Rappel*, 24 November 1891.

40 Henri Varennes, 'Les massacres du Senégal', *L'Intransigeant*, 21 November 1891.

41 *L'Événement*, 17 June 1891.

42 *Le Courrier de Saone-et-Loire*, 10 July 1891.

43 Martineau served as a member of parliament from 1889 to 1893. He later served as governor in various colonies. Martineau was an honorary professor in the Collège de France and an attorney in the appeal court. In 1912, he established the Société française d'histoire des outre-mers. www2.assemblee-nationale.fr/sycomore/fiche/(num_dept)/5051 (Accessed 6 April 2024).

44 In the late 1880s the minister of the navy and colonies conceived a plan to construct a railway from Dakar to Bamako in three stages: a line from Dakar to Saint Louis, another section from Saint Louis inland to Kayes (located in current day Mali), and finally a continuation of this line from Kayes on the upper Senegal River to Bamako on the Niger River. The French parliament approved the financing of the Dakar–Saint Louis segment, which was completed in 1885. In 1888 another segment was constructed between Kayes and Bafoulabé (a town in south-western Mali located at the confluence of the Bakoy and the Bafing rivers that join to become the Senegal), but the river still connected both segments. It took almost 20 years for the railway supporters to win this battle, when in 1904 the railway replaced the river as a transportation route. See: McLane, 'Railways or Waterways,' 100–108.

45 The affair to which Martineau refers is a petition supported by Isaac on the part of a Cadi in Algeria against the settlers and the unjust employment of the *indigénat*. See: Jean-Marc Ticchi, 'Le fonds Alexandre Isaac, Sénateur de La Guadeloupe (1845–1899), et son voyage en Algérie (1892) dans les archives du Sénat,' *Cahiers de la Méditerranée*, no. 101 (2020).

46 The debate, which took place on 1 December 1891, was quoted in full in *Le Monde*, 2 December 1891.

47 *Le XIX siècle*, 21 November 1891.
48 H. Oludare Idowu, 'Café au lait: Senegal's Mulatto Community in the Nineteenth Century,' *Journal of the Historical Society of Nigeria* (1972), 277–279.
49 Manchuelle, 'Métis et colons,' 486.
50 *Ibid*, 486–487.

7

The affair's afterlife

The Jeandet Affair troubled the colonial administration in Senegal deeply. It reached the colonial under-secretary, the court in Paris, the metropolitan press, and even the French parliament. Nevertheless, as important as it was at the time, the final failure of Ba's lawsuit, the completion of the French occupation, and the establishment of the federation of French West Africa in 1895 were enough to turn it into a disturbing yet forgettable episode for the French. As for the Africans involved in the affair, some remained or returned later to Saint Louis, while others accommodated themselves to life in Fouta Toro under colonial rule. Still, as in all African societies, certain individuals carried with them the duty to tell the story to the next generation rather than allow it to sink into the Senegal River along with the bodies of Sall, Yoro, and Kaccé. The French believed that, by preventing burial of the three executed men, they would prevent pilgrimage to their graves. But in most African societies, it is not graves or monuments that ensure remembrance, but rather the people who tell the story, the griots.

This final chapter aims to examine the vicissitudes of Jeandet Affair over the years since. This was a long process in which several factors played a part: the transmission of oral traditions into theatre plays, songs, and finally podcasts; the replacement of local griots with a celebrated singer; and the recent attempt to turn local traditions into a national Senegalese history. Following the fascinating itinerary of the Jeandet Affair, which is now often called the Baidy Kaccé Affair, and the transformations its remembrance went through, can teach us a great deal about much wider questions, such as the relations between the oral and the written, the 'nationalization' of history, and its relationship to current events and perspectives. It also teaches us about the selective way in which anti-colonial struggles are remembered today. I will first examine the mechanism of oral traditions in West Africa and their transmitters, the griots. Next, I will look at the various versions of oral traditions about the affair, one of which was written as a theatre play in the late 1960s. I will then discuss the 'nationalization' of the affair, meaning the process through which it ceased to be a very local story and became part of the Senegalese national heritage. As I will show, all these various forms of remembrance focused only on the first part of the affair: the assassination and the executions. Therefore, no attention was given to Ndiereby Ba's legal struggle. I will discuss the very recent attempts to insert her into the story and highlight her significant role in it. Finally, I will return to Verdun-sur-le-Doubs, Jeandet's small village in Burgundy, to examine the local remembrance of the affair from the French perspective.

The Jeandet Affair in oral traditions

Although oral sources now seem essential to the research of the African past, there is still some debate about the ways they should be used by historians. An important difference exists between two types of oral sources: oral traditions and oral history. Oral traditions can be defined as 'the body of information that has been preserved in a community or family and handed down from one generation to another by word of mouth.'[1] Such traditions usually refer to a distant past, so the people who tell them today did not witness the events described in them. The other type of oral source, verbal testimonies of more recent events, are not relevant to our discussion. Unlike these testimonies, which can be given by any person who has something to tell regarding a historical event or process, oral traditions are usually told only by certain selected individuals. In West Africa, they are called griots. Their role is to transmit to the next generation knowledge about major events, but also origins, migrations, relationships between communities, notable personalities, and even aspects of morality. Their aim is dual: to prevent oblivion and to glorify the past. This second aim often comes at the price of factual accuracy. Also, a mythical dimension is regularly added to the historical account. The griots transmit this information in various forms, such as folktales, songs, myths, legends, and popular stories. The griots are the only ones who are allowed to be the custodians of history.[2]

The lack of written sources available to historians of Africa made the use of oral traditions essential for the historian who wishes to write about pre-colonial or early colonial history. While it has taken some time for historians to get over their suspicion of this type of source, in time, and especially following the publication in 1965 of Jan Vansina's seminal work on oral traditions,[3] their problems, and the ways to overcome them, oral traditions have become a vital source of reconstructing the African past.[4]

In his discussion of oral traditions, Vansina distinguishes between the process of transmission and its products. In the introduction to the later version of his original work, published 20 years later, he pays special attention to this process. My own discussion will also highlight the process of transmission and what we can learn from it. Vansina describes various aspects of oral traditions that are highly relevant to the transmission of the Jeandet Affair. He first distinguishes between oral history, meaning recent accounts of people who lived at the time of the event they describe, and oral traditions that must be transmitted over more than one generation, and therefore are told by people who did not experience such events. The Jeandet Affair is over 130 years old and therefore matches this latter definition. Vansina argues that oral traditions include both facts and fiction and that those who listen to them know how to distinguish between the two. Fiction is usually told in certain artistic forms, such as tales, proverbs or sayings. As we shall see, in the case of the Jeandet Affair such a clear boundary between facts and fiction does not exist. Different informants regarded the same details as either fact or fiction.

Vansina also mentions that most oral traditions do not follow a clear and direct line from their origin to the present. Rather, after being told for the first time, many people continue to transmit them to many other people, and thus numerous different versions of the same tradition are created. We can see this happening during the transmission of this particular affair. The various versions that exist today are pretty similar to one another, but often include different and even contradictory details. Finally, an interesting point Vansina raises relates to the possibility that a historian can locate earlier recorded traditions of the same historical event and compare them to the one he or she collected years later. Vansina argues that such a comparison can teach us a great deal about the process of transmission itself, rather than the event recorded. Changes in the oral traditions along time can teach us about the values of the society in the period of transmission; what was important to this society; which values it wished to preserve; what they preferred to leave out of the tradition. As I will later recount, I had the good fortune of locating an older recorded tradition of the Jeandet Affair, which David Robinson had collected in 1968. It is indeed interesting to see how the affair was recounted in an earlier period and compare it to more recent versions.[5]

As we can see, Vansina sees the value of oral traditions not so much in the information they might offer on their own subject but rather on what they can tell us about the history and values of the transmitting society. Other historians support this view and do not believe there is much to be learned from oral traditions about the historical events they recount. Aworawo, for example, argues that the most difficult problem of oral traditions is the distortion of the past, as their purpose is political propaganda, which causes falsification. As we shall see, in the case of the Jeandet Affair the main problem is not falsification, although this happens as well, but rather the fact that an entire part of the story was never a part of the oral tradition about the affair.[6]

Unlike many of the past events historians of Africa attempt to reconstruct through oral traditions, there is no lack of documents regarding the Jeandet Affair. It can certainly be understood in general terms, but specific details and certain events related to it remain obscure, either because they are not mentioned clearly, or because there are several versions of them in written documents. In this respect, the use of oral traditions only complicates our attempt to understand what exactly happened, as these traditions add even more versions to events mentioned in written sources.

My aim, therefore, is different. This chapter seeks to follow the transmission of the Jeandet Affair through dozens of years, until today. The existence of so many written documents as well as various oral traditions regarding it, presents an excellent opportunity to analyse the process of transmission of a historical event over decades. We have here an unusual opportunity to see what versions were included in oral tradition and compare them to the version, or sometimes versions, that exist in colonial documentation. We can also see which aspects of the affair and which actors in it were included in these traditions and which were left out. One fascinating aspect of this process is the influence of music and social media on oral traditions, which accord them power to reach much wider audiences. Another is the transformation of these traditions into theatre plays and recorded podcasts and their impact on the remembrance of the affair.

As noted, most of this process of transmission over generations relates only to the first and shorter part of the affair—meaning, Jeandet's assassination and the French reaction to it. The second, longer and more complex part, Ba's legal struggle, remains mostly in the dark. While the first part of the affair was transmitted from generation to generation by the griots, the second part was not. There are several possible reasons for this. First, the second part of the affair took place far away from Guédé and there were no griots to witness it. Second, as we have seen, the legal struggle was very complex and perhaps more difficult to understand and transmit than the story of the murder and the executions, which was perhaps also more exciting as a heroic myth. The non-violent nature of Ba's struggle was possibly less attractive for an oral tradition than the killing of a powerful French administrator. And, finally, it might have been embarrassing for those responsible for the transmission of traditions to admit that the only person who continued resisting the French and fighting for justice after the executions was a woman, while some of the men in the family worked with the administration to return her home.

While I had no access to oral traditions of the affair before 1968, it is clear that it has been told over the years as, about 80 years after the affair, a man by the name of Ali Guèye Thiam mentioned it in an interview he gave David Robinson. Robinson's aim was not to study the Jeandet Affair. The interview was part of a much larger project of reconstructing the history of Fouta Toro. So, although not asked specifically about the affair, it seemed important enough for Thiam to mention it. The description of the affair in this interview is incoherent and confused. Thiam added a long list of suspects who were also supposed to be executed but were saved at the last moment by a telegram sent by Captain Mamadou Racine Sy, the African first officer in the French army who was probably the one who helped Boubakar Abdoul escape the other culprits' destiny. It is not clear though who were all the other people he mentioned. Thiam also mentions a horse that Jeandet asked Kaccé to give to a certain colonel whose name is not specified.[7] Both the telegram and the horse were mentioned in the colonial documents as well as in interviews conducted by me over 50 years later. But while the version offered in the 1968 interview is unclear, later versions become much more coherent. The telegram that can also be found in the colonial archives is probably the one sent by Fawtier on 15 September, the day of the second execution. It is not clear whether it arrived just before the execution and was ignored by the administrators on the ground, or if it simply arrived too late. The telegram ordered the suspects to be brought to trial in Saint Louis. As we shall see, in later oral traditions the telegram would become a tool of betrayal by a local post employee who falsified it to prevent the culprits from being sent to Saint Louis.

The horse was also mentioned in the colonial sources. To support the version of the conspiracy, the administration claimed that the Lam Toro promised Kaccé that he would receive Jeandet's horse as a present after he killed him. Another version of the horse story was offered by Saddick Sall. According to him, the French offered Ardo Mbantou, who caught Kaccé, the Lam Toro's horse, in recognition of his assistance. The horse's name was Bou Sba, which means 'lion' in Haasniya (the Arabic dialect spoken in Mauritania). It died a week later of colic, as Mbantou did not feed it properly.[8] These various incarnations of the horse and the telegram are wonderful examples of how oral traditions develop particular historical events in various directions.

Two years before Robinson interviewed Thiam, Elhadji Hamedine Kane, a school principal from Matam, a town on the Senegal River, 245 kilometres east of Podor, who was also a direct descendant of Lam Toro Sidick and his second wife, Faty Thiello, wrote a theatre play based on family traditions about the affair. This play could not have been read or seen by the person interviewed by Robinson, as at first it was only performed at Kane's school, with his pupils as actors.[9] In 1975 it was first presented in Podor and caused great commotion there because of the references in it to certain individuals who had betrayed the Lam Toro.

It was then only performed in Dakar, though the text of the play was distributed around Podor. When I visited the town in 2020, 45 years after the play was performed there, all the people I interviewed possessed a copy and knew it almost by heart. Its lingering impact is demonstrated by the fact that Kane's daughter warned the play had the potential to harm the descendants of the people who are mentioned in it.

The local knowledge about the play and its contents is important, as it explains how later versions of the traditions about the affair were much more coherent than that offered by Thiam, and are occasionally almost identical, quoting for example the same dialogue between Kaccé and Jeandet word for word. This is a rather rare occasion when a local tradition was written and thus became a kind of official version although, as we shall see, it is sometimes contested or added to.

Lamtoro (that is, Lam Toro) is a six-act theatre play. On its original self-printed cover, there is a lion, the animal Baidy Kaccé was associated with. According to Kane's daughter, Niasse Hamedine Kane, her late father did not write fiction, but rather what he saw as a historical account. It was important to him to write the family tradition of the affair, even though some people in the extended family preferred not to discuss it because of the associated issue of betrayal.[10] Other informants contested this claim. One informant referred to the play as pure fiction.[11] The play ends with the executions and does not mention Ndiereby Ba nor her legal struggle. When I asked Niasse about this she said she did not know much about the second part of the affair.

One informant said that the play enjoyed great success in Dakar.[12] Nevertheless, it did not seem to turn the affair into a historical chapter remembered outside the territory of Fouta Toro. What it did manage to do was influence the shape of the oral tradition, which partly became exact quotations from the play. Before we look into this interesting influence of a written source based on oral tradition shaping the oral tradition itself, let us briefly explore the main themes raised in the play.

The play's main aim is to present the Lam Toro and Baidy Kaccé as courageous men who did not bow before the colonizer The Lam Toro is also presented as a benevolent ruler, unlike his descriptions in the colonial documents. His only wish was to achieve peace with the French, but not at the price of surrender and shame. When an officer by the name of Bernard comes to Guédé to ask for porters on behalf of Jeandet, the Lam Toro first consults his warriors, who angrily say: 'Jeandet knows that we are warriors and not carrier donkeys.'[13] Finally, Sidick calms them down and agrees to give Bernard ten men, one of whom is Kaccé.[14]

The second scene describes the murder and its circumstances. It is in this scene that the dialogue between Jeandet and Kaccé, which was quoted word for word by some of my informants, appears. Unlike the descriptions in the colonial sources, in the play Kaccé was not brought before Jeandet by Boubakar Abdoul, who is nowhere to be found in the text. Jeandet encounters Kaccé on his way and calls him the Lam Toro's slave. Kaccé responds: 'the devil must have slapped you in the face if you confuse the Lam Toro's subjects with slaves.'[15] Jeandet then punishes Kaccé for his insolence, and sends him to carry twice as much as before; in the colonial version, Kaccé was not a porter before the murder, but a soldier. Baidy declares that he refused to serve an infidel and starts to leave, when Jeandet grabs his *boubou*, curses him, and asks who had taught him to speak like that to a Frenchman? Kaccé responds that the Lam Toro taught him how to fight French officers and reminds Jeandet of a recent French defeat in a battle Kaccé had taken part in. Jeandet's reaction is to slap Kaccé's face, to which the proud Kaccé can only respond by killing Jeandet. He then manages to escape as none of the present soldiers dare chase him. He is only caught because of betrayal by certain people who he knew and trusted. The accusation against the Lam Toro in the play does not come from Kaccé but from one of the traitors.[16]

The next scene describes the innocence of the Lam Toro. No one in Guédé knew anything about the murder and, when the Lam Toro is informed about it, he doubts if Kaccé had indeed killed Jeandet and goes to Aeré to try to help him. The fifth scene describes another betrayal, this time by two local post employees. Here we have another version of the telegram story. We have already seen two other versions, that it was sent by Fawtier to stop the executions, and that it was sent by Racine Sy who wanted to save at least some of the culprits. In the play, we have a third version. The content of the telegram as it appears in the play is very similar to that of Fawtier's telegram, but in the play it was sent by the governor,

Clément Thomas. The post employee is worried that, if Sidick were sent to Saint Louis, his relatives would help him and he would go free, thus exposing the employee's scheme to betray him. He therefore falsifies the telegram and writes one that allows the administrators on the ground to do whatever they pleased to the suspects. As we have seen, a similar telegram, which ordered the execution of the suspects in a most brutal manner, was sent by Tautin. The play thus takes the blame for the illegal executions away from the French and transmits it to local traitors.[17]

The last scene describes a trial that never took place. This is not a real trial, but rather a scheme to trap the Lam Toro by luring him into coming to the trial to attempt to help his loyal soldier, Kaccé. When Sidick realizes the scam, he strikes the French officer, who then orders his execution and that of Yoro and Kaccé within two hours. As we have seen, according to colonial sources there was a five-day delay between Kaccé's execution and those of Sidick and Yoro. Sidick again displays calmness and bravery. He exchanges a smile with Yoro and they both accept their fate with courage and serenity. The French do not guard them as they know they are too noble to escape.[18]

The play ends with Sidick's griot promising that he was witnessing the events with his eyes, his ears, his heart, and his brain. He promises the Lam Toro that he will ensure his immortality for centuries to come. He then tells the French officer that there was no comparison between Jeandet and the Lam Toro. In a speech before his execution, the Lam Toro then declares that he had never bowed before the colonizers, and curses those who had betrayed him, saying that they will pay for their bloody deaths before history.[19]

The version that the play conveys was repeated in two of the interviews I conducted. The other four informants did not accept this version, and had their own ideas about various issues related to the affair. They seemed to be more concerned with creating a historical narrative as close as possible to the truth than praising the glories of the past. All of them read colonial documents critically, much as professional historians do, and referred to oral traditions in the same suspicious manner. The different versions they offered to some of the main themes related to the affair point to the difficulty of understanding which of the many versions for almost every stage of the affair is the correct one. That is not to say that these informants, who are all direct descendants of Ndiereby Ba, do not have an agenda as well. They are all interested in giving her the importance they think she deserves and that has been marginalized in local traditions. Ndiereby is not mentioned at all in Kane's play, which, as we have seen, ends before her important role begins. The informants who accepted the play as the official tradition of the affair either knew nothing about her or did not accord much importance to her legal struggle in Saint Louis and Paris.

The best representative of the formal oral tradition that was written by Kane is, perhaps not surprisingly, the current griot of Guédé, Haruna Diop, who is the great grandson of Sidick's griot, Farba, mentioned in the play. He accurately recounted the play's plot—although probably it is the other way around and, in fact, it is Kane who was quoting the oral tradition he had heard from the griots. He spoke about Captain Bernard, whose name I could not find in colonial sources, and insisted that the Lam Toro was not involved in any conspiracy to murder Jeandet, and that he turned himself in to the French in the hope that his act would purchase peace for his people. When I asked him about Ndiereby, he doubted the importance of her actions as she was 'only a woman.' Nevertheless, he insisted on her agency, by explaining that she had a great deal of responsibility in her husband's court. She was in fact his personal advisor, the first and last to speak to him every day. She told him everything she heard in his court and, while her role was informal, it was still very important. Therefore, Diop thought it reasonable that she would decide to go to Saint Louis and file a lawsuit against the French administrators.

Diop insisted not only on the Lam Toro's courage, but also on that of Kaccé. He said Kaccé was very popular in all Fouta and is referred to as the 'lion of his village, Guiya.' Diop rejected the theory that Kaccé was deranged, violent or foolish, and said this was a theory backed by people with an interest in shaming him. Every branch of the Lam Toro's extended family had its own version of the affair because of the complicated relationships between them.[20]

Another informant who repeated the same tradition to me was the guard of the Podor fort, the late Ibrahima Sy. He too recited the text of the play. He told me he played the role of Baidy Kaccé, which explains how he could remember the text so well. He defined the play as history, but then added that history is never accurate, and that Kane was a descendant of the Lam Toro and had his own version. He also mentioned the problems the play had caused, as certain people preferred not to discuss the affair because of their ancestors' dubious part in it. Regarding Baidy Kaccé, Sy offered an interesting opinion about the apparent contradiction between the French version that saw him as crazy and the traditional view of him as a hero. He claimed that in fact this was no contradiction at all, as Kaccé was a man who feared nothing. Such a person is necessarily also insane.

Two contested issues were raised in the different interviews. One was the issue of the conspiracy, and the other was the question of Kaccé's character or, in other words, whether he was indeed a hero as the local traditions suggest or rather an unstable and easily manipulated man. Both issues concern the first part of the affair. So little was known about the second part that the many unclear issues related to it were not even raised as they were simply unknown. In one of the interviews, the informants I talked to began presenting questions to me about Ba's legal struggle. Some of them I could answer, but many remained a puzzle for me too.

One question that occupied the informants who contested the official traditions was that of the so-called conspiracy. Two of them were convinced that Baidy Kaccé had not acted on his own and that he had been manipulated by someone else. But while one suggested that this person was the interpreter who had brought Kaccé to Jeandet, the other raised another theory. He was convinced that the métis of Saint Louis were those who had conspired to kill Jeandet because of their opposition to French colonial policy. He also insisted that the person who organized this and later supported Ba's lawsuit was not Devès but, rather, Descemet.[21] While Descemet indeed had a close relationship with Sidick before the murder, he was never mentioned in the colonial documents as the one who backed Ba. The idea that the métis were those who planned Jeandet's murder seems improbable. But the existence of the theory shows how the most basic details of the affair remain unclear even today.

The other question raised in those interviews with the informants that related directly to Ba was the character of Baidy Kaccé and his negative description in the colonial sources. They tended to accept this description and agreed that he was either deranged or as one of them, Mamadou Sow, put it 'the village idiot.' What he meant by that was that Kaccé was ready to do any dirty assignment he was asked. He even went further to say he could not understand how such a man could be remembered as a hero: 'Even in our songs Kaccé is a hero. Why is he a hero? Did he do anything heroic? Nothing! He came and killed someone. There, I think we have distorted history a bit.' The real heroine, according to him, was none other than Ndiereby. What she did was courageous and remarkable: 'Can you imagine that, at the end of the nineteenth century, a woman rose up to defy France! This is a heroine [...] submitting a complaint against France!'[22]

Indeed, Ndiereby was not yet part of the local tradition of the affair when I carried out these interviews in 2020. At the time, even the first part of the affair was not remembered or discussed outside the boundaries of the region in which it had transpired. In recent years, though, this has changed, and it seems that the affair has slowly entered Senegal's national historical memory. As we shall see, the songs Sow mentioned were crucial in this process.

The 'nationalization' of the affair's remembrance

For many decades, the Jeandet, or Podor, Affair was known only in the surroundings of Fouta Toro through the oral traditions that had turned into a theatre play. People outside this area knew little about it. But towards the end of the twentieth century the two main heroes of the affair, at least according to tradition, Lam Toro Sidick and Baidy Kaccé, became the subjects of songs written and performed by a son of Fouta who was soon to become a worldwide celebrity—the musician Baaba Maal.

> He takes the stage like a cleric offering benediction: Baaba Maal, the pride of Senegal. His arms rise, lifting the folds of his shimmering green *boubou*, his head tilts back, and he opens his mouth. The nightclub falls suddenly silent, transfixed by the sonority of one long vowel, ululating, filling the air like a muezzin calling the village to prayer. Just when it feels like the moment will last forever, the tama and sabar drums come in slowly behind him. And his old friend, the blind griot Mansour Seck, begins to provide an eerie Sahelian harmony.[23]

Anyone who has ever seen Baaba Maal perform would certainly confirm the vivid description Charles Sugnet offers in an introduction to an interview he conducted in 1997 with this remarkable musician. Baaba Maal is indeed much more than a singer and a musician. Born in 1953 in Podor to a family of fishermen, Maal was not supposed to embark upon a musical career. Music and songs were kept for the griots. Nevertheless, he decided to follow his heart. In the interview with Sugnet, he offers this decision to breach the caste system rules of his community as an example of his ability to influence his society. Maal argues that Fula youth follow his lead, and the elders have been convinced to forsake this limiting system.[24]

Among the five most celebrated Senegalese musicians—the other four being Thione Seck, Youssou Ndour, Ismail Lô, and Omar Pène—Maal is unique. He is the only one whose language of origin is Peul, and the only one with academic training, which he gained in the Ecole des Beaux Arts in Paris, and which earned him the title of the 'intellectual of Senegalese music.'[25]

Maal sees his role as similar to that of the griots, and it is no coincidence that he includes a griot in his concerts. He appreciates the value of history and wishes to transmit it to younger generations through his music. Maal's land of origin, Fouta Toro, is very important to him. When asked why, he explains that it is culturally open to all of West Africa. The Fulani people travelled all over Africa and offered much to other ethnic groups. It is also important to him because of the language—they were the first people who understood what he was singing about. People who follow his music have established associations in every village in Fouta. But this loyalty to his community and the consequent emphasis on the history of Fouta Toro in his songs do not close Maal off to other cultures. He is, at the same time, a local, national, pan-African, and international musician. He sings in several languages: Peul, Wolof, French, English, and Bambara. Maal sees music as indifferent to international borders. People from Mauritania, Mali, Niger, and Gambia feel connected to his music. He accords great importance to Africans' oral culture. Information in his society, he argues, is not read but rather is transmitted orally by songs and by griots. Therefore, songs are not only important for their music, but also for their lyrics: 'you have to entertain, but you have to teach as well.'[26]

Maal's career began to soar in the late 1980s. In 1988 he performed with the English singer Peter Gabriel on the soundtrack of the film *The Last Temptation of Christ* and in 1994 his album *Firin' in Fouta* gained international fame. His success did not keep him away from Senegal nor from Fouta Toro. He continued performing in his country and in 2006 he launched an annual concert titled 'Le Blues du Fleuve' (the Blues of the River) on the banks of the Senegal River, near his hometown of Podor. Maal's biography demonstrates that he had become much more than a musician. Since the early 2000s, Maal has become a well-known international figure with great social impact. For example, in 2003 the United Nations appointed Maal as an 'emissary for youth' in the framework of the organization's development programme and, in 2009, he was invited to the Copenhagen Conference on Climate.[27]

One detail that is not mentioned in Maal's biographies and is important to the discussion was conveyed to me by Saddick Sall. In the mid-1970s, before Maal was known outside his land of origin, he watched Hamedine Kane's play in the Daniel Sorano National Theatre of Dakar. Although there is no concrete proof for this, watching the play might have led him, later in his career, to write several songs that relate specifically to the Jeandet Affair. The first album referring to the history of Lam Toro Sidick, *Lam Toro*, was released in 1992. Two years later Maal included the song 'Sidiki' in his successful album *Firin' in the Fouta*. In 2000 a song titled 'Baydi Kathie [sic]' was included in the album *Jombaajo*.[28] The song 'Baidy Kathie' offers homage to Kaccé and Sidick, saying that they defended their territories but were betrayed and killed for having refused foreign domination, and that Fouta would never forget them.[29]

The combination of Maal's interest in the history of Fouta Toro, his self-image as a modern griot, and his incredible influence and fame in Senegal managed to take the remembrance of the affair outside his home region to wider national audiences. The names of Sidick and Kaccé became known to every Senegalese who listened to Maal's music—and there were a great many of those. Nevertheless, songs alone are not enough to make people remember a forgotten historical episode as most people do not try to investigate the deeper meaning of songs and their lyrics. More than 20 years would pass until the historical meaning of these songs would also become known and discussed beyond the local oral traditions.

Maal's songs did help raise the familiarity of Sidick and Kaccé, so when the time came for them to enter the national historical narrative, in the course of 2022, they were no strangers to the Senegalese public. Two things happened that year that changed the scope of remembrance. One was the establishment of an organization called Galsi (Galle Lamtoro Salsabe Internationale). This organ unites all those who carry the name Sall in various countries, such as Senegal, Mauritania, the Gambia, Mali, Niger, and Guinea. The organization offered the then president of Senegal, Macky Sall, who originated from Fouta Toro (as do all those who carry the name Sall), an honorary membership. They even intended to offer him the position of the Lam Toro, but the family objected as Macky Sall did not belong to either of the two legitimate dynasties. Nevertheless, the involvement of Macky Sall in the organization's activities helped to draw wider attention to the history of the region in general and to the Jeandet Affair in particular, now no longer named after the murdered administrator but rather after his murderer, Baidy Kaccé. In November 2023, Galsi organized a festival in Guédé, to which several politicians were invited, including Macky Sall, and at which Baaba Maal gave a concert.[30]

Another contribution to the affair's wider remembrance was a project by Senegal's National Archives and the Goethe Institute of Dakar, which was launched in February 2021 and continued into 2022. This project, titled in Wolof 'Xam sa démb, xam sa tey' (Know your past, know your present), aimed at making Senegalese history more accessible to the Senegalese public. Imitating the griots' style of transmitting and glorifying the past, the project includes 50 bilingual podcasts, in French and in Wolof, accessible for free online, about important events in Senegalese history. Each 15-minute podcast begins in the same manner. The impressive voice of a famed storyteller, Massamba Guèye, recites the following text:

> Listen to me telling the marvellous history of our Senegal. Listen to me taking you on a voyage through the great acts of glory, make you relive the memory of its children. Daughters and sons whose image will speak for all the rest. Our history is beautiful and deserves to be known. I want you to listen with the ears of your heart. We are history. We have history. So, let's know our history. To know your history is to know your present. The greatness of a people is in the fertile memory of its children because the world is old, but the future comes out of the present.[31]

The scripts were written by Ibrahima Wane, a professor of African literature at Dakar's Cheikh Anta Diop University, and drawn from National Archive documents, which were then reworked and narrated by Guèye, the project's artistic director. The idea behind the project was to adjust the transferring of historical knowledge about Senegal to the Senegalese public, and especially to youth, in the traditional African mode of oral history, rather than a written one.

The project was released in two parts. In general, the podcasts represent various regions and ethnic groups in Senegal presenting all topics as part of one Senegalese history. The subject of the thirteenth podcast included in the first phase was Baidy Kaccé Pam. The story begins with a question: Who is the person about whom Baaba Maal sings? Who is Baidy Kaccé Pam? Guèye then presents Kaccé as an anti-colonial hero and begins to recount his life. He says that Kaccé objected to the division of Fouta Toro into cantons, and to the recruitment of Senegalese soldiers to fight in Madagascar, Indochina, and Dahomey. It is unclear where this information came from. While Lam Toro Sidick had indeed objected to the division of Fouta and the limitation of his power, and he might have objected to the recruitment of Africans to serve in the colonial army, there is no evidence that he or, even less likely, Baidy Kaccé, would have been interested in France's wars in other regions in Africa and beyond.

Guèye then goes on to describe Jeandet's assassination, also quite inaccurately. According to him, after Jeandet had punished Kaccé, the latter waited for nighttime and then went to kill Jeandet in his cabin. He then described how Baidy Kaccé was arrested, without mentioning who had caught him, adding that, along with him three other influential figures were arrested: Lam Toro Sidick, Mamadou Yoro, and Boubakar Abdoul. Abdoul's presence at the time of the murder is also not mentioned. He then mentions a trial (of which there is no evidence in the colonial documents) in which all the suspects, except Abdoul, were condemned to death. He describes the two brutal executions and the parading of the heads of the condemned. He explains the background of the lawsuit by saying that no judge had ordered the execution. He then dedicates one sentence to the second part of the affair—Lam Toro Sidick's widow, Ndiereby Ba, arrived at Saint Louis to fight against this parody of justice, but the administration removed the judges who were supposed to take charge of her lawsuit. He then returns to Baaba Maal's song 'Lam Toro,' which discusses the affair and denounces those who betrayed Baidy Kaccé. He concludes that in Senegalese culture death is preferable to shame. Baidy Kaccé is an emblematic figure of African resistance to colonial oppression. When the French threw his body into the river, they wanted to prevent a pilgrimage to his grave. They wanted to erase him from the memory of Fouta. But they failed to erase him from its people's hearts. The podcast ends with the following words: 'Here is the story of Baidy Kaccé Pam. Here is the story of a man of honour. Here is the story of the man who killed the colonial administrator Abel Jeandet. Baidy Kaccé Pam, a worthy son of Senegal.'

While this podcast, unlike Maal's songs, Kane's play, and the griots' oral traditions, does refer to the second part of the affair, and even mentions Ndiereby's name, she is certainly not presented as an anti-colonial heroine. Almost no details are offered about her legal struggle or the courage and perseverance it demanded. It is interesting to notice that the Lam Toro is also relatively marginalized in this version. The hero, who is presented at the end of the episode as a hero of Senegal, is Baidy Kaccé. The details given about him are misleading. One could think he was an important leader rather than a soldier of the Lam Toro. His so-called heroic act is wrongly described as his sneaking about in the middle of the night and shooting an administrator in his sleep. This description is strange, not only because of its inaccuracy but also because it makes Kaccé appear less bold than he actually was, as he shot Jeandet in broad daylight when the latter was wide awake. On the other hand, the courageous non-violent and persistent legal struggle of a woman who sought justice from a panicked administration is mentioned in a single sentence, with much less enthusiasm and pathos.

The same emphasis on Baidy Kaccé as an anti-colonial hero is evident in a Facebook discussion from the same period. A post dated 2 September 2022, sometime after the podcast's release, and marking the 132nd anniversary of Jeandet's murder, was published on the Facebook page of a society called La bibliothèque des érudits sénégalais. This society is responsible for similar discussions about offering different perspectives on historical, political, and social issues in Senegal. The post included a description of the Jeandet Affair, which they call the Baidy Kaccé Pam Affair. Unlike several other posts published around the same time about the affair, this one raised a lot of interest and attracted over 1000 likes and 443 replies. Some of the people responding to its contents were related to the Lam Toro's family, but most were not. The post was accompanied by a photo of an execution, supposedly the one the post discussed. This was, in fact, a photo of a later execution, in 1899, when a cook called Biram-Kandé was accused of poisoning his French patron. This case was not unrelated to the Jeandet Affair, as the administration referred to the latter scandal when it demanded a proper trial to avoid problems. It also brought a guillotine to Saint Louis so that the execution could be as 'civilized' as possible. Thierno Sall, Saddick's brother, corrected this error at an early stage of the discussion, but almost no one seemed to care.

In general, the responders can be divided into two main positions. One group, the much larger one, was horrified by the story, but especially by their ignorance of it, and insisted that it should be taught in Senegalese schools and universities. Some argued that Senegalese history is hidden on purpose for the benefit of the history of others. One commentator even went so far as to compare the affair to that of Dreyfus and demanded that it would replace the latter as a page in history. Suggestions were raised to name a street in Podor after Baidy Kaccé or build a memorial for him so that, when children saw it, their parents would be able to explain to them who he was. An especially interesting aspect of this position was its linking to the present and France's continued influence in Senegal. Some of the responders argued that this story showed that Senegal must free itself from its dependence on Europeans, Chinese, and Russians, as none of them sought Senegal's benefit. Another mentioned Ousmane Sonko, who was at the time the main opposition to Macky Sall's government, and who became prime minister in April 2024, saying that he wanted to eliminate French influence in Senegal. One other response suggested that historians helped politicians free Senegal from the colonial yoke, which still existed today, as the colonizers were still stealing Senegal's oil and gas. Finally, people who held these views were also appalled by the betrayal story. One of them said what he had understood from the affair was that every time the French wanted to kill, exile, or humiliate Africans, other Africans always stood behind them. The sad reality was that the enemies of the Africans were Africans.

While most of the replies to this post were in this same spirit, some other voices were occasionally raised. The narrative presented in the post was rejected by several responders. One claimed that Kaccé was no hero, but a marginal man manipulated by the Lam Toro. This person was soon attacked by another, who claimed that his family was involved in the betrayal. Another responder argued that Kaccé's action was not a sophisticated way of resisting colonization, as it was futile and motivated by pride. Another pointed to historical errors in this narrative, and for proof cited the article of Yamar's Samp, a Malian historian who published an article about the affair, focusing on its legal aspect. The response to that reference was a claim that historians often distort the past. None of the people who rejected the post's narrative, however, mentioned the second part of the affair and the role Ndiereby Ba had played in it. This includes the responder who had cited Samp's article, which is focused on this part.

Baaba Maal's music, the inclusion of the affair in Senegalese historical episodes through a project initiated by the Senegalese National Archives and the Goethe Institute, and the lively Facebook debate all demonstrate a process of a nationalization of the affair that has been, until recently, a very local one. Still, the emphasis on the supposed heroism of Baidy Kaccé and his presentation as an anti-colonial fighter with an elaborate agenda not only distorts the historical meaning of the affair but also hides its second part, which is a story of a sophisticated and lasting anti-colonial struggle that forced the French to debate the colonial idea and its validity. Even if this struggle failed at the time, it undermined, at least for a while, the colonial administration in Saint Louis and served those who objected to its policies both in Senegal and in France. As we shall see in the next section, some Ndiereby family members, and especially her great-grandson, Saddick Sall, are trying to include her legal struggle in the remembrance of the affair.

Including Ndiereby in the narrative

The marginalization of Ndiereby in the remembrance of the Jeandet Affair, even after it became a subject of songs and podcasts, cannot be discussed without referring to the more general theme of African women's place in the national remembrance of anti-colonial struggles. In recent decades ever more studies (tellingly written mostly by female scholars) have tried to incorporate African women into the history of anti-colonial resistance.[32] It seems that women are no longer ignored in studies on colonial history, yet they are not considered to be part of the story of anti-colonial resistance, unless the specific study is focused on gender or on a certain woman the author wishes to discuss in relation to this topic. In a 2021 volume about this subject, Yolande Bouka argues that the problem is not a lack of information about the roles women played in anti-colonial struggles, but rather the fact that the focus is always still on masculine spaces, such as combat or violent struggles. She gives, as an example, the scholarly fascination with the female warriors in Behanzin's army in Dahomey who were on the front lines in the war against the French in the early 1890s and the last to surrender. Bouka offers several problems in this kind of focus. First, while such female warriors inflamed Western imaginations, they still constituted a tiny percentage of all women who took part in anti-colonial struggles in Africa. Second, the emphasis on women in combat perpetuates the importance bestowed upon masculine militarism in anti-colonial struggles. Finally, focusing on female warriors suggests that only women who were able to adhere to male physical standards could assert their equality to men. Bouka suggests diverting attention away from these masculine spaces of resistance to other non-violent struggles in which women took part, such as economic struggles, literature, and even music. These spaces presented a different way of resisting colonialism that were often more compatible with women.[33] She quotes the South African singer Miriam Makeba, who used music as an anti-colonial weapon in her struggle against Apartheid explaining this point: 'In our struggle, songs are not simply entertainment for us. They are the way we communicate.'[34]

Ndiereby Ba did not use music, but her struggle was very different from that of the man who assassinated Jeandet. Her weapon was the colonizer's own law. The legal scene in nineteenth-century Saint Louis was certainly a masculine space, as only men operated within it and, without their guidance, Ba would never have been able to use the law against the French. Nevertheless, this was not a violent struggle, and violence is still the approach appreciated the most in local traditions. In this respect, Bouka raises another important point. She asserts that the greatest obstacle to the integration of women into the histories of anti-colonial struggles in Africa is African men who refuse to regard alternative spaces of resistance, in which women were more dominant, as being equal to those dominated by men.[35]

The glorification of Kaccé's violent action and the marginalization of Ba's courageous struggle certainly strengthen Bouka's argument.[36] Following Allman's encouragement, mentioned in Chapter 5, to investigate this marginalization rather than just trying to reconstruct women's voices, this part of the chapter looks deeper into the attempts to insert Ndiereby into the remembrance of the Jeandet Affair.

One day, back in the 1970s, when Saddick Sall was still a young college student, he received a parcel from his second cousin, Hamedine Kane. In it was a theatre play and a note. Kane entrusted Sall with a mission. He was to study history and write the family's story as recounted in the play. Sall read the play but preferred to study geography. Only later did he decide to study history as well and began investigating colonial documents to create a historical narrative about the affair described in the play. During his research, he realized that Kane's play only told half of the story, and not very accurately. The legal struggle of his great-grandmother had fascinated him. Before moving to construct the historical narrative of this story, he decided to follow his second cousin's path and write a play of his own.

Sall started his play exactly at the point that the play he had received as a young man ended. He did not deal in detail with the story of betrayal, which is at the centre of Hamedine Kane's narrative, but mentioned it just briefly. The emphasis was on the person he saw as the real heroine of this affair—his great-grandmother, Ndiereby Ba. The play relies in part on colonial documents, but the aim was not to write history but to tell a story. This story had not been told before and did not pass from generation to generation like the one told by Kane. While the events described in the play are all documented, Saddick took the liberty of changing their chronological order or combining some of them. Just like Kane's play, this one also aims to emphasize pride and courage before the French colonizer. Ndiereby's dialogues with administrative agents and male relatives are completely imaginary, but they have an important role in presenting the heroine as brave and proud.

The great difference between the two plays is the kind of resistance they highlight. Ndiereby's resistance is feminine, non-violent, and yet very determined and brave. Despite being 'a little uncultivated woman,'[37] she managed to resist pressure from the colonial administration and some of her male relatives to forsake her legal struggle. The motives for this insistence are revealed to us towards the end of the play when Saddick imagines the dialogue during the meeting between her and Ahmed N'Diack, Lam Toro Sidick's uncle.

N'Diack tells Ndiereby that, as a woman, she was incapable of leading a battalion. He urges her to think about her children and to invest in their education. She replies that all the men were paralyzed. Sidi Abdoul was afraid of French retribution, and Boubakar Abdoul was on the French administration's payroll. Therefore, she had no choice but to act: 'When the men are annihilated, it is for the women to defend their dignity.'[38] N'Diack then tries to scare Ndiereby by saying the French might kill her. When this does not work, he mentions the huge sum of money that was offered to her—five times the annual salary of a French officer. To that she responds that money will not return her husband to her, nor would it restore Guédé and Toro's dignity. The frustrated N'Diack then asks: 'So, what is it that you want?' And Ba answers: 'I want to see them punished for the crime that had been committed. I want them at my feet.'[39]

The character who opens and closes the play is interesting too. This is a woman by the name of Naama Seck who is a female griot. According to Sall, this was a real person he knew as a child, who was indeed a griot. It was no coincidence that he chose a female griot to tell the story of feminine heroism. At the end of the play, Seck tells the audience how Ndiereby should be remembered:

> Forgetting its glorious past, France found itself engaged in low political tasks, to the point of trembling before the direct attack of a native woman, helpless and unarmed. An empty-handed Amazon. Njerebi (Ndiereby) was not shaken by the terror that signalled the end of independence for her country [...] Her intervention provided African parties with the opportunity to emerge.[40]

Sall's play represents an alternative way to remember the Jeandet Affair, or perhaps the Ndiereby Ba Affair. In his play, the anticolonial struggle is a slow, non-violent one, that of an amazon; but, unlike those of Dahomey, she does not compete with men in the field of combat and violence, as her arms are empty of weapons.

Instead, she chooses another way to challenge the colonial administration. Her legal combat against a deceitful and unjust administration, which was aided by the judiciary of Saint Louis, was unsuccessful in the end, but, according to the play, it set the tone for similar subsequent struggles that eventually brought Senegal's independence, which indeed was won without violence. The emphasis on Ba's heroism and the use of a female griot to tell her story is, in some way, a call to remember not only acts of anti-colonial violence, but also non-violent struggles, which were more efficient even if they took many years to achieve their goal. In some sense, Sall here answered the call of Bouka, who criticized the African male intellectual elite for not telling the story of alternative anti-colonial struggles more typical to women than to men.

In November 2023, during a grand celebration of the history of Guédé organized by the Galsi organization, the play was performed on the Senegal River near Podor. Sall also discussed Ndiereby's part in the affair with the then president of Senegal, Macky Sall, as well as the possibility of establishing an annual award, financed by the Galsi organization, to be offered in Ndiereby's name for a Senegalese woman who has made outstanding contributions in her field. Hopefully, Ndiereby might be on the right track, leading her back to a place she deserves in Senegalese historical remembrance.

Back to Verdun-sur-le-Doubs

While it might take a bit longer for Ndiereby Ba to gain her deserved place in Senegalese historical memory, that of Baidy Kaccé seems to be already quite established. As we have seen, the affair is no longer referred to in Senegal as the Jeandet Affair but is named after his assassin. But what about the murdered administrator? It would have been quite difficult for someone like Jeandet to be remembered at the national level. After all, there were many more important colonial figures than he. One might expect, though, that after the efforts his parents made to commemorate him—his father by depositing his letters in the Mâcon archives, and his mother by selling her house to commission a known author to write a memorial book for him—he would at least be remembered in his local village.

Towards the end of my fieldwork for this book, in September 2022, I visited Verdun-sur-le-Doubs, where Jeandet's colonial journey had begun. At the Academy of Mâcon, where Jeandet's father had worked, I learned that some dispute exists regarding the family's grave. While the house and Jeandet's parents' grave belonged to the academy, the area surrounding the grave did not. That made it impossible for them to maintain the grave, as family members would not let them enter the area. Finally, a contract was signed with the heirs that gave the academy the right to take care of the grave. I was also told that everyone I encountered in the village would know Abel Jeandet, and would be able to point me to the family house and grave. I soon discovered that this was hardly the case.

The sleepy picturesque village of Verdun-sur-le-Doubs lies on the confluence of three rivers, the Saône, the Doubs, and the Dheune. One can easily understand how Jeandet might have loved this village, but also found it too boring for his energetic character. After a few attempts to ask locals about the location of Jeandet's house, I realized that no one had the slightest idea who he was. I then headed on to the tourist information office, thinking that I could get clear instructions there to this 'important' historical site. The kind young woman who greeted me was no more knowledgeable than the people on the street. She mentioned a local organization that studied the village's history, but their office was open only two hours a week. I continued to walk around the village and entered the only museum there—the Museum of Bread and Wheat (Musée du blé et du pain). Its enthusiastic manager (who was not a local) was also oblivious to the village's only celebrity and was surprised to hear of his existence. I could not locate the house and the graves and, eventually, had to give up.

Sometime later I contacted the local historical organization. The reply I received acknowledged and lamented the forgetting of Abel Jeandet in his native village. Agnes Tusseau, who belongs to the Association for the History of Verdun-sur-le-Doubs (Groupe d'études historiques de Verdun-sur-le-Doubs), kindly sent me an article from the association's bulletin, *Trois Rivières*, dated 2012 that clarifies the difficulties in commemorating Jeandet in the years following his assassination. It recounts in detail the *via dolorosa* Jeandet's mother, Flavie, had to endure to ensure that her son would not be forgotten. According to the article, commemorating her son became an obsession for Flavie, who outlived him for 31 long and painful years. As a devout woman, she first opened a shelter in the family home for poor old people. Soon, though, she began searching for a way to ensure public acknowledgement for her son. In 1905, six years after her husband had passed away, she commissioned Gausseron to write Abel's biography, giving the writer her memoirs and many other personal items. She paid Guausseron the lofty sum of 20,000 francs and had to close her shelter for lack of funds. It took eight years for the book to be published. After it was at last written, no publisher expressed any interest in it. All those Flavie approached explained that there were many similar accounts of colonial French heroes and Jeandet was not exceptional. Furthermore, they suggested that this literary genre did not attract many readers. Finally, Flavie had to pay more money to the Academy of Mâcon for the book's publication. When she tried to retrieve her emotionally precious documents from Guasseron, the latter rejected her pleas with all sorts of excuses. After long efforts with the help of lawyers, whom she obviously had to pay as well, Flavie managed to arrange for a floral wreath to be laid annually on Jeandet's grave and monument in Podor. This practice, though, did not continue after her death in 1921.[41]

It seems that Flavie did not manage to attract much sympathy by her efforts to commemorate her son. The village authorities did not help her much and initiated no commemoration projects of their own. When Jeandet's father offered the village municipality the artefacts his son had collected in Senegal so that a museum could be opened in the village, he was turned down. No interest was expressed in his son's letters, which he finally donated to the academy in Mâcon. The street in which Jeandet's uncle lived was named in 1900 after Jeandet's father but, in 1922, with no reason or explanation it was changed to *rue de la Liberté*. Probably, the timing was not a coincidence, as Flavie, the only person who cared about it, had died a year earlier.[42]

Considering Flavie's difficulties in commemorating her son so soon after his death, at a time when his actions were still considered heroic, it is quite understandable that Jeandet would be totally forgotten today, even in his own little village. Unlike Kaccé, sung about by a famous singer, known by taxi drivers, discussed on Facebook, and praised in the framework of a project aimed at transmitting major episodes in Senegalese history to youth, Jeandet has become completely anonymous even in his own community. While the Verdun-sur-le-Doubs history association has recently restored the grave of Jeandet's father, and its members are no doubt interested in the history of the Jeandet family, the son remains an unknown figure in his native village and certainly beyond its borders. It is tempting to assume that this forgetting was related to a more general wish to forget the period of French colonization but, as we have seen, Jeandet was never remembered by anyone but his own family. His letters, which his father deposited in the Academy of Mâcon, and the book his mother had commissioned for him did not manage to keep his memory alive, despite being written sources, supposed to endure forever.

In fact, while historians find it easier to reconstruct the past by relying on written sources, this is not always a reliable basis for historical memory. Jeandet and those who had cherished his memory left hundreds of written pages, but written material must be read to be meaningful. Apparently, it was not. As Jeandet had no descendants, there was no one to make sure it would be read. Kaccé, on the other hand, did not write a single word in his lifetime and, until very recently, nothing had been written about him. But Kaccé lived in a very oral society, in which the griots transmitted local traditions from generation to generation. His story, even if later reconstructed, was also much more meaningful for the society in which he had lived than that of his victim was to his own. As we have seen there are several versions of the affair, but the memory of Baidy Kaccé has remained even with those who refuse to see him as a hero. In the battle for memory, it was Kaccé who won. The question now is whether Ndiereby Ba may be allowed the same victory.

Notes

1 David Aworawo, 'Oral Sources and African History: The Historian's Task in the Twenty-First Century,' *Lagos Historical Review* 3 (2003), 20.

2 Aworawo, 'Oral Sources,' 22–24; Babacar Fall, 'Orality and Life Histories: Rethinking the Social and Political History of Senegal,' *Africa Today* (2003), 56.

3 Jan Vansina, *Oral Tradition: A Study in Historical Methodology* (Piscataway: Transaction Publishers, 1965).
4 Aworawo, 'Oral Sources,' 26.
5 Jan Vansina, *Oral Tradition as History* (Madison: University of Wisconsin Press, 1985), 3–31.
6 Aworawo, 'Oral Sources,' 26.
7 Michigan State University, Special Collections, David Robinson's Collections, Box 9, Folder 9.
8 Interview with Saddick Sall, Dakar, 14 March 2024.
9 Interview with Niasse Hamedine Kane, Dakar, 20 March 2024.
10 Interview with Niasse Hamedine Kane, Dakar, 20 March 2024.
11 Interview with Baba Sall, Rufisque, 14 February 2020.
12 Interview with Ibrahima Sy, Podor, 7 February 2020.
13 Elhadji Hamedine Kane, *Lamtoro*, 1966 (publicly performed in 1975), 2.
14 *Ibid*, 1–3.
15 *Ibid*, 4.
16 *Ibid*, 4.
17 *Ibid*, 7–12.
18 *Ibid*, 13–15.
19 *Ibid*, 16–18.
20 Interview with Haruna Diop, Dakar, 21 February 2020.
21 Interview with Baba Sall, 14 February 2020.
22 Interview with Mamadou Sow, Dakar, 14 February 2020.
23 Charles Sugnet and Baaba Maal, 'I Sing All the Space,' *Transition*, no. 74 (1997), 184.
24 Sugnet and Maal, 'I Sing All the Space,' 187.
25 Amadou Ndiaye, *Baaba Maal et le Fouta: message local et patrimoine universel* (Dakar: Harmattan-Sénégal, 2015), 19.
26 Sugnet and Maal, 'I Sing All the Space,' 191.
27 Ndiaye, *Baaba Maal et le Fouta*, 34–38.
28 Baaba Maal, 'Firin' in Fouta,' www.discogs.com/master/278345-Baaba-Maal-Firin-In-Fouta (Accessed 10 April 2024).
29 Translation of these lyrics was made by Saddick Sall. The song is accessible at: www.youtube.com/watch?v=-ee8OD5IBvM (Accessed 10 April 2024).
30 Interviews with Saddick Sall, Dakar, 14 March and 21 March 2024. Baaba Maal's concert at this event (November 2023) can be found at: www.youtube.com/watch?v=Y1KxjhBi0_8 (Accessed 10 April 2024). A link to a TV channel broadcast about the entire event (2STV) can be found at: www.youtube.com/watch?v=MWMWLeMV6uM (Accessed 10 April 2024).

31 Goethe Institute and the National Archives of Senegal, Podcast, soundcloud.com/goethe-dakar/xam-sa-demb-xam-sa-tey-alpha-molo-en-francais (Accessed 10 April 2024).

32 See, for example: Elisa Camiscioli, 'Women, Gender, Intimacy, and Empire,' *Journal of Women's History* 25, no. 4 (2013); Bradford, 'Women, Gender, and Colonialism'; Margaret Strobel, 'Women's History, Gender History, and European Colonialism,' in *Colonialism and the Modern World*, ed. Gregory Blue, Martin Bunton, and Ralph Criozier (London: Routledge, 2016);Susan Geiger, Jean Allman, and Nakanyike Musisi, *Women in African Colonial Histories* (Bloomington: Indiana University Press, 2002).

33 Yolande Bouka, 'Women, Colonial Resistance, and Decolonization: Challenging African Histories,' in *The Palgrave Handbook of African Women's Studies*, ed. Olajumoke Yacob-Haliso and Toyin Falola (London and Lausanne: Palgrave Macmillan, Springer Nature Switzerland, 2021), 1–12.

34 Bouka, 'Women, Colonial Resistance, and Decolonization,' 13.

35 *Ibid*, 10, 16.

36 Ba was of course not the only African woman to use the legal arena to challenge the colonial administration, but she did this at an especially early period of colonial rule. Another notable example, which is in several respects similar to Ba's struggle is the story of Abina, who in 1876 approached the British colonial court in the Cape colony in the Gold Coast to gain her release from slavery: Trevor R. Getz and Liz Clarke, *Abina and the Important Men: A Graphic History* (New York: Oxford University Press, USA, 2016).

37 Sidik Sall, *Njerebi, veuve du Lam Toro*, 2019: 21.

38 *Ibid*, 19.

39 *Ibid*, 19.

40 *Ibid*, 25.

41 Elisabeth Ducrot, 'Abel Jeandet et sa famille,' *Trois Rivières*, 79 (2012), 15–19.

42 Durcot, 'Abel Jeandet,' 22–23.

Conclusion

Writing micro-history is a challenge. On the one hand, unlike macro-histories, which simply cannot go into detail and do not need to, micro-histories tend to draw the author into the story, making each small twist in it look vital and worth the effort of analysing. On the other hand, the story, as fascinating and well-documented as it is, would not be enough. It must hold value for understanding wider phenomena and historical processes. The Jeandet Affair is a perfect story for writing micro-history. The plot is interesting, the characters are intriguing, the documentation is vast, although sometimes contradictory and confusing, and, perhaps most surprising of all, this affair, which took place so long ago and ended in failure, left its mark on Senegalese society. In some miraculous way, it withstood the test of time, even if in a somewhat partial way. In the previous chapters, I have connected each step of the affair to the main themes they shed light on—conquest, law, and resistance. In the Chapter 7, I also looked at what the transmission of the affair through time can teach us about the nature of oral traditions, the attempts to write a 'national' post-colonial history, and the impact of music and social media on remembrance and on forgetting. My conclusions here will focus on the contribution of the entire affair on the three major themes mentioned above, while emphasizing how micro-history can offer perspectives that often remain hidden or vague in macro-histories.

Conquest

The Jeandet Affair transpired at a time when the French colonial project was at a crossroads. The colonization of Algeria had ended 20 years before, and, only five years earlier, the Berlin conference, at which the European powers had divided the African 'cake' between them, set the rules of the colonial 'game'. The French government had no clear colonial policy but, on the ground, colonization was already taking place. The affair, and especially its final stage in Paris, demonstrates the ignorance and indifference in the metropole regarding colonial expansion in West Africa. Indeed, it shows that we cannot speak of a certain moment or political decision that opened a second phase of French colonial expansion. Although others had written about the chaotic nature of the French colonization in the nineteenth century, the affair offers a much deeper understanding of this chaos, as well as the measure of ignorance even at the highest colonial echelons regarding the conquest on the ground, its aims, its tactics and its violent nature. The parliamentary debate, in which the affair was raised as an example of a total lack of policy and control over the process of colonization, offers us an excellent understanding of this rupture between metropole and colony at the moment when the French empire was beginning to grow substantially.

The press reports on Ba's lawsuit in Paris also shed much light on the total lack of understanding of the nature of the new type of colonial rule in West Africa. Most newspapers could not even grasp Ba's status, which deprived her of any political or legal rights. She was a foreigner in the eyes of French law, even though French conquest had turned her life upside down and changed the entire reality of her society. The horror of the brutal and illegal executions raised in the press is also an indication of the ignorance regarding the degree of violence employed not only during military campaigns but also after a territory had come under French control. This is not to say, of course, that the metropole was not responsible for the crimes committed during colonial conquest. The role of the government, parliament, and the press was to know—and their ignorance stemmed, to a large extent, from indifference for unfamiliar and supposedly uncivilized parts of the globe that gradually became French territories.

As for the people on the ground who were performing the everyday tasks of conquest, Jeandet's letters offer a fresh perspective on them. Macro-histories on colonial administrators, of which William Cohen's seminal work is still the most illuminating, give us some idea regarding the 'typical' colonial administrator.[1] The detailed information the affair offers us about Jeandet both contradicts the image conveyed and reinforces it. Jeandet was certainly not the typical administrator Cohen describes. He was well-educated, talented, relatively knowledgeable about the territories he was sent to, and from a family of an elevated social background (albeit with some financial problems). Nevertheless, the attitude of his superiors towards him proves Cohen's point, as they treated him as an exception to the rule. His murder was therefore a severe blow for the administration, which can also explain the rushed and uncalculated response to it.

Jeandet's letters also shed light on the weakness of the colonial administration at the initial stages of colonial conquest. Despite his desperate attempts to brag about his power and successes, the letters also reflect his fears and dependence on African rulers, interpreters, and other intermediaries. While many studies have dealt with these weaknesses, the detailed stories about Jeandet's relationships with the Africans around him give shape to this balance of power, which was not always in favour of the administrators despite their obvious powers.

Another aspect that the affair reveals in detail is the myriad of actors who influenced the process of early colonization in West Africa and, more specifically, the involvement of the métis in this process. Hilary Jones's book on the métis serves as an excellent base to understand their involvement in the affair. Her work is vital to understand their delicate position between a colonial administration attempting to limit their influence and the African population of Saint Louis that tried to recruit their support.[2] The affair adds an important dimension to this analysis, as it allows us to examine a certain crucial crisis in métis relationships with the administration. The affair gave certain métis a wonderful opportunity to act against the administration's plans to colonize vast territories and thus harm the commercial and political interests of the métis. But the support they offered Ba in her legal struggle was also a way of reinforcing their image as protectors of Africans against colonial injustice. The legal training of so many of the métis enabled them to use the field of law as a battleground and, through it, try to strengthen their position in the colony. The affair thus sheds light on the modes of action of the métis, the administration's hostility towards them, and its fear of their power and influence on Africans, and especially on the *originaires* who, to the chagrin of the administration, had voting rights in the colony.

Law

It is no wonder that the métis chose the law as their means of challenging the administration. This was the arena they felt the most comfortable in. They were well acquainted with French law and knew how to use it to achieve their ends. They failed only due to foul play and deceit on the part of the colonial authorities, first in Saint Louis and then in Paris. Being first and foremost a legal scandal, the affair allows us a deeper understanding of the relationship between law and empire.

The brutal executions that took place on 10 and 15 September 1890 only became a scandal due to a seemingly insignificant detail—their location. This point was often raised by frustrated representatives of the colonial administration. But location meant so much because of the colonial system of protectorates. The idea that certain conquered territories would not be subject to French law created a situation in which these territories were not subject to any law. It allowed colonial administrators to act against the principles of French law, the same principles that were supposed to be the basis of the so-called 'civilizing mission.' The affair drew attention to the problematic situation of having a legal system that was not relevant to many of the newly conquered territories. While the French already established the *indigénat*, which allowed them to inflict immediate punishments on colonial subjects outside the French legal system, the existence of a singular legal system, the metropolitan one, in its West African colonies allowed colonial subjects to use it for their own ends. The idea that an African woman, who did not speak or read French could, with the help of the métis, sue French administrators based on the French legal system was something that the colonial administration did not see as possible before the Jeandet Affair. Therefore, one of this scandal's implications was an attempt to make sure this could never happen again.

To achieve this aim, the entire concept of law in the empire had to be revisited. If, until then, it was acceptable to employ the French system in the colonies, Ba's legal struggle demonstrated the undesired implications of this situation. The two debates in the Advisory Council, described in Chapter 5, expose the two main positions regarding the desired justice system in the colonies. While, in general, the divide was between French administrators and métis judicial personnel, there were some exceptions. A notable one is Paul Fawtier and his support of Ba's legal struggle. One position was that French principles of justice should be implemented in the colonies. The other was that these principles were not suitable for the expanding empire. The impossibility of implementing them derived from both ideology and practicability. The administration's position was that the people who were being colonized were not evolved enough for such advanced principles. It also argued that implementing French justice would put colonial administrators and other Europeans in the colony in danger and would prevent a successful colonization.

In the short term, the affair made the French administration in Senegal extremely cautious regarding the employment of capital punishment. During the 1890s there were only two more executions, and both were performed following a trial. In 1891, the murderers of Jeandet's cousin Amédée were condemned to death. The second execution took place in 1899 following the murder of Albert Palmade, the head of a trading post in Podor. His murderer was Biram-Kandé, a 20-year-old servant originating from Kankan in French Guinea. He shot Palmade dead on 31 May 1898. According to the report of his public execution in *le journal officiel de l'Afrique occidentale française* (the official journal of French West Africa, established in 1895), this was the first time after a long period that the assize court of Senegal had condemned a culprit to death. The report referred specifically to Jeandet's assassins without mentioning the scandal brought on by the illegal executions. Then it stated that 'indulgence has its limits' and, therefore, it was time to renew the use of capital punishment.[3]

Biram-Kandé's execution was, then, an attempt to return to the use of capital punishment in a way that would correct the mistakes made in the case of Jeandet's murder. Not only did a trial take place, but this was also the first time that a guillotine was used in the French African colonies. The guillotine, as noted in Chapter 3, was the means used extensively during the French Revolution, and was considered a 'civilized' tool for execution, because death was swift and supposedly painless. The French administration in Saint Louis made the efforts of bringing a guillotine from France, a complicated and pricy operation no doubt, just to demonstrate to the crowds that gathered to watch Biram-Kandé's execution that France knew how to punish in a civilized way. This ceremony of death was even celebrated on a series of postcards, the last one issued as late as 1912.[4] Unlike the problematic executions during the Jeandet Affair, the French now believed they could be proud of their use of capital punishment. But the affair served as a warning sign, and the decision to resort to capital punishment again was slow and demanded much effort and consideration.

The affair was also influential in the long term. Approximately a decade after Ba's legal struggle failed, a decree of 10 November 1903 established a parallel system of justice for colonial subjects that would apply to all territories beyond the four communes of Senegal in the federation of French West Africa, established eight years earlier. According to article 75 of the 1903 decree, the judgements rendered by the so-called *tribunaux indigènes* (native courts) were to be based on local customs, as long as they did not contradict the principles of French civilization. These principles were never defined, so some flexibility was left for the administration in case it wished to judge a case involving colonial subjects in a French court.

Although the new legal system for colonial subjects was supposed to be adapted to African traditions and cultures, the hierarchical structure of the metropolitan legal system was imported virtually intact to the African reality. The district (cercle) court was a criminal one but, unlike the French criminal court, it was presided over by the district commander who had no legal training and who served simultaneously as policeman, examining judge, and the authority responsible for executing the sentence. All district court sentences exceeding five years' imprisonment were automatically reviewed by the chambre homologation, a special department of the French appeals court, based in Dakar and presided over by the vice president of the appeals court.[5]

Unlike the carefully planned and orchestrated execution of Biram-Kandé, the establishment of a parallel legal system in the French African colonies in 1903 cannot be directly connected to the Jeandet Affair. Nevertheless, this system enabled colonial administrators much more freedom in condemning colonial subjects to prison or death easily and swiftly, without the need to follow the complicated rules and regulations of the French legal system. The new system also made lawsuits such as that of Ndiereby Ba impossible, as these could only be made through a legal system controlled by the administration. The Jeandet Affair demonstrated to the French colonial administration the dangers of expanding the French legal system into the newly conquered territories of West Africa. A parallel system, such as that established in 1903, was the perfect way to counter such dangers.

Finally, the Jeandet Affair linked the legal arena in the colony with that of the metropole. The debates it raised in the media regarding the legal implications of the decision to reject Ba's lawsuit in the Paris court of first instance demonstrated that the colonies and their legal problems had direct consequences for the already problematic French legal system. The manipulation of the law that took place during the affair in Saint Louis and later in Paris worried certain journalists, mainly because of the possible implication of such a miscarriage of justice on French citizens. The connection between justice in the colonies and in France turned the Jeandet Affair into a scandal—one of a series of scandals that shook France in the late nineteenth century. Ba's attorney, Félix Decori, who also took part in the Dreyfus trial, further personified this connection. The Jeandet Affair therefore reinforces the idea that the colonies should be considered an integral part of the history of metropolitan France, and certainly of its legal history.[6]

Resistance

The third major theme the Jeandet Affair sheds light on is that of resistance. This theme is related both to colonization and law. The penetration into the West African hinterland in the late nineteenth century was possible thanks to a number of simultaneous technological advances, such as steamboats, trains, and telegraph lines.

The first two allowed the colonizers access to the continent. The third allowed them to communicate with those sent to remote outposts to oversee military conquests and control the additional territories. Two of these three technological innovations and means of communication were paramount in the Jeandet Affair: steamboats and the telegraph. But while both served the colonial administration in their attempts to colonize vast areas in West Africa, the Jeandet Affair shows that they could also become tools of resistance to colonization.

While steamboats were the main means for the French to reach remote outposts and launch military campaigns, the Jeandet Affair demonstrates that these boats, which connected remote villages along the river to the capital Saint Louis, could also serve the interests of those who opposed the administration's expansionist agenda. Without the steamboat *Germaine*, which took Ndiereby Ba from Podor to Saint Louis, her legal struggle could not have materialized. Such a boat also brought Devès's allies to Podor, so that they could look for suitable candidates to submit the lawsuit.

The telegraph was also crucial to the affair, especially in its initial stages. As we have seen in Chapter 7, a specific telegram, which arrived in Podor just before, or perhaps just after, the second execution, still plays an important role in the local memory of the Jeandet Affair. Invented in 1837 by Samuel Morse, the telegraph played an important role in the establishment of colonial empires all over the globe. During the second half of the nineteenth century, colonial powers competed between themselves over concessions that would allow them to construct telegraph lines in areas they planned to take over. The entire telegraph network in the French possessions in West Africa was completed in 1903.[7]

The construction of the telegraph line from Saint Louis to posts along the Senegal River was a complicated process. The French had to overcome many obstacles to complete this mission. David Robinson describes in detail the French negotiations, between 1879 and 1885, with local leaders, especially with Abdoul Bokar, whose consent to the project was crucial.[8] The construction of the telegraph was in itself a sphere of resistance, in which a shrewd local ruler was able, at least for some time, to maintain his power in the face of the growing expansionist French forces. But as the affair demonstrates, even after its construction the line could still serve as a tool of resistance rather than just a tool of control. After the telegraph was installed, it could also serve the interests of those whom the colonial administration saw as its enemies.

Telegraphic communication played a crucial role in the affair's unfolding. News about the illegal executions reached Devès and, through him, Ursleur so quickly that the judge could announce the legal procedures against the administrators only 48 hours after the second execution. After Ursleur was removed from the colony, Devès used the telegraph to organize the search for a 'person of interest' to sue the administrators. His people on the ground were able to communicate quickly and easily and coordinate Ndiereby's voyage to Saint Louis. Without the telegraph, all this would not have been possible.

Another important tool of colonization that became a tool of resistance during the affair was guns and ammunition. One of the main uses of steamboats and trains during such military campaigns was to transfer weapons to the French forces. While the French relied heavily on guns in the process of colonization, they also feared that these sophisticated weapons could fall into the wrong hands and reinforce their opponents. African warriors wielding machetes before French guns was useful to French colonizers for two reasons. First, the Africans could be much more easily defeated. Second, it served French propaganda justifying colonization—the image of African weaponry reflected their so-called savagery and, therefore, justified more sophisticated French violence as a tool of civilization against 'barbaric' people. Africans using guns was, therefore, considered a grave danger.[9]

To prevent their enemies from acquiring guns around Saint Louis, the French issued a decree in 1834 prohibiting the sale of guns in the city. With the penetration into the West African hinterland, this decree was implemented in every area in which the French encountered local resistance. During the French conflict with al-Hajj Umar Tal and later his son Sheiku Amadou, the colonial authorities attempted to put a blockade on the sale of weapons, hoping to prevent their enemies from gaining an undesirable advantage. This prohibition was not easy to maintain for several reasons. African traders on whom the French relied for a wide range of other products found the sales of arms especially lucrative and protested vehemently against this decree. Additional opposition came from the French arms manufacturers lobby who, by 1881, were losing 500,000 francs annually due to the prohibition. Furthermore, rulers such as al-Hajj Umar Tall managed to buy arms in neighbouring colonies ruled by the British, Portuguese, and Germans. Al-Hajj Umar Tall accumulated a substantial quantity of rifles and gunpowder in Sierra Leone and the Gambia, while Samori Touré, who resisted the French colonization of Fouta Djallon (in current day Guinea-Conakry), traded in enslaved people, gold, and cattle for ammunition in Sierra Leone and the Gold Coast.[10]

Guns played a crucial role in the Jeandet Affair, being the weapon that put an end to Jeandet's life. The French efforts to prevent their African opponents from obtaining guns obviously could not have included Africans who served in their armed forces, and who were part of the colonization efforts. This was dangerous, as any of these recruited soldiers could have revolted at any time and use their guns against their French commanders. Nevertheless, the French could not rely only on French soldiers, as they were too expensive and too fragile. They were not used to the weather conditions in West Africa and often succumbed to local diseases before even firing a single shot. That was the reason why Faidherbe decided to establish the force of the *Tirailleurs Sénégalais* in 1857.[11] The French could not therefore have prevented someone like Kaccé from holding a rifle—and he did not even have to buy it.

But the affair also sheds light on the image of the gun. When Jeandet wanted to punish Kaccé, he ordered him to leave his gun at the entrance of his cabin and join the porters for the rest of the day. Taking the gun away from Kaccé was part of his punishment. The gun afforded those who carried them a special status. It was an advanced weapon, one could even say a 'civilized' weapon, unlike the 'barbaric' machete. It was this gun that Kaccé used to kill Jeandet. Ironically, though, when Kaccé was executed, the French did not use this 'civilized' weapon to end his life. Rather, at both executions, an African decapitated the culprits using the 'barbaric' machete.

The affair also connects the theme of resistance with that of law. The legal arena, first in Saint Louis and then in Paris, served also as a terrain of resistance. In a way, this was also a use of a tool of colonization used against the colonizers and, at least for some time, it proved more efficient than violent resistance, such as that used by Kaccé. The legal arena offered a young woman, such as Ba, the opportunity to challenge the French colonial administration and demand that it punish those who acted against French law. While the action eventually failed, it forced the French to re-examine their colonial policy in West Africa and question the colonization efforts in this region. Ba's legal struggle threatened the colonial administration in a way no assassination, even that of an efficient administrator like Jeandet, could have succeeded in doing. The story of this legal struggle reminds us that non-violent anti-colonial resistance could be much more sophisticated and subtle than a simple violent act, and should not be marginalized in historical narratives.

Notes

1 Cohen, *Rulers of Empire.*
2 Jones, *The Metis of Senegal.*
3 Jean Luc Le Bras, 'La peine de mort aux colonies, une exécution pour L'exemple à Saint-Louis du Sénégal en 1899,' *I & M Bulletin* 35 (2012), 37–38.
4 Le Bras, 'La peine de mort aux colonies, une exécution pour L'exemple à Saint-Louis du Sénégal en 1899,' 34–36.
5 Ruth Ginio, 'Negotiating Legal Authority in French West Africa: The Colonial Administration and the African Assessors, 1903–1918,' in *Intermediaries, Interpreters, and Clerks: African Employees in the Making of Colonial Africa*, ed. Benjamin Lawrance, Emily Osborn, and Richard Roberts (Madison: University of Wisconsin Press, 2006), 117–118.
6 Frederick Cooper and Ann Laura Stoler, *Tensions of empire: colonial cultures in a bourgeois world* (Berkeley: University of California Press, 1997), 1–58.
7 Javier Márquez Quevedo, 'Telecommunications and Colonial Rivalry: European Telegraph Cables to the Canary Islands and Northwest Africa, 1883–1914,' *Historical Social Research/Historische Sozialforschung* (2010), 112.
8 Robinson, *Chiefs and Clerics*, 124–138.
9 On the image of African weapons as representing savagery see: Dana S. Hale, *Races on Display: French Representations of Colonized Peoples, 1886–1940* (Bloomington: Indiana University Press, 2008), 26.

10 Sokhna Sané, 'Guerres de conquête et contrôle de la circulation des armes à feu et des munitions en afrique occidentale sous domination française (1834–1903),' *French Colonial History* 9, no. 1 (2008), 175–183.

11 Myron J. Echenberg, *Colonial Conscripts: The Tirailleurs Sénégalais in French West Africa, 1857–1960* (Portsmouth, NH: Heinemann, 1991), 7–8.

Bibliography

Archives and Special Collections

Archive Départementales de Saône-et-Loire, Mâcon
Archive Nationales, Paris (AN)
Archives de l'académie de Mâcon
Archives National du Sénégal, Dakar (ANS)
Centre de Recherche et de Documentation du Sénégal, Saint Louis
Centre des Archives d'Outre-mer, Aix-en-Provence (CAOM)
Special Collections, Michigan State University, David Robinson's Collections

Press

L'événement
L'Intransigeant
La Cocarde
La Justice
La Loi: journal judiciaire quotidien
La presse
Le Journal
Le Journal de Débats Politiques et Littéraires
Le Matin
Le Monde
Le Petit Journal
Le Petit Parisien
Le Radical
Le Rappel
Le Réveil
Le Temps
Le XIXe Siècle

Le Petit moniteur universel
Le Courrier de Saône-et-Loire

Secondary Sources

Agmon, Danna. *A Colonial Affair: Commerce, Conversion, and Scandal in French India*. Ithaca: Cornell University Press, 2017.

Aldrich, Robert. 'Colonial Man.' In *French Masculinities. History, Culture and Politics*, 123–140, 2007.

Allman, Jean. 'The Disappearing of Hannah Kudjoe: Nationalism, Feminism, and the Tyrannies of History.' *Journal of Women's History* 21, no. 3 (2009), 13–35.

Andrew, Christopher M. 'The French Colonialist Movement During the Third Republic: The Unofficial Mind of Imperialism.' *Transactions of the Royal Historical Society* 26 (1976), 143–166.

Andrew, C. M. and A. S. Kanya-Forstner. 'The Groupe Colonial in the French Chamber of Deputies, 1892–1932.' *The Historical Journal* 17, no. 4 (1974), 837–866.

Austen, Ralph A. 'Colonialism from the Middle: African Clerks as Historical Actors and Discursive Subjects.' *History in Africa* 38 (2011), 21–33.

Aworawo, David. 'Oral Sources and African History: The Historian's Task in the Twenty-First Century.' *Lagos Historical Review* 3 (2003), 19–34.

Ba, Daha Chérif. *Crimes et délits dans la vallée du fleuve Sénégal de 1810 à 1970*. Paris: Editions L'Harmattan, 2010.

Bakshi, PM. 'Continental System of Criminal Justice.' *Journal of the Indian Law Institute* 36, no. 4 (1994), 419–428.

Bée, Michel. 'Le spectacle de L'exécution dans la France d'Ancien Régime.' *Annales. Histoire, Sciences Sociales* 38, no. 4 (1983), 843–862.

Benton, Lauren. *A Search for Sovereignty: Law and Geography in European Empires, 1400–1900*. Cambridge: Cambridge University Press, 2009.

Bigon, Liora. 'Urban Planning, Colonial Doctrines and Street Naming in French Dakar and British Lagos, C. 1850–1930.' *Urban History* 36, no. 3 (2009), 426–448.

Bouka, Yolande. 'Women, Colonial Resistance, and Decolonization: Challenging African Histories.' In *The Palgrave Handbook of African Women's Studies*, edited by Olajumoke Yacob-Haliso and Toyin Falola, 1295–1313. London and Lausanne: Palgrave Macmillan, Springer Nature Switzerland, 2021.

Bradford, Helen. 'Women, Gender and Colonialism: Rethinking the History of the British Cape Colony and Its Frontier Zones, C. 1806–70.' *The Journal of African History* 37, no. 3 (1996), 351–370.

Burgh, Hélène de. *Sex, Sailors and Colonies*. New York: Peter Lang, 2005. www.peterlang.com/view/title/9707. Accessed 2 April 2025.

Camiscioli, Elisa. 'Women, Gender, Intimacy, and Empire.' *Journal of Women's History* 25, no. 4 (2013), 138–148.

Carteny, Andrea. 'Volunteers' Employment and Counterinsurgency in Italy: The Case the Hungarian Legion (1861–1862).' *Mediterranean Journal of Social Sciences* 3, no. 11 (2012), 397–403.

Chupin, Ivan, Nicolas Hubé, and Nicolas Kaciaf. ' "L'âge d'or" de la presse (1870–1939).' In *Histoire Politique Et économique Des Médias En France*, 35–52. Paris: La Découverte, 2012.

Cohen, William B. *Rulers of Empire: The French Colonial Service in Africa.* Stanford: Hoover Institution Press, 1971.

Cole, Joshua. *Lethal Provocation: The Constantine Murders and the Politics of French Algeria.* Ithaca: Cornell University Press, 2019.

Cooper, Frederick. 'Alternatives to Nationalism in French Africa, 1945–60.' In *Elites and Decolonization in the Twentieth Century*, edited by Jost Dülffer and Marc Frey, 110–137. London: Palgrave Macmillan, 2011.

Cooper, Frederick and Ann Laura Stoler. *Tensions of Empire: Colonial Cultures in a Bourgeois World.* Berkeley: University of California Press, 1997.

d'Andrurain, Julie. 'La correspondance privée des coloniaux.' In *Gouverner par les lettres: de L'antiquité à L'époque contemporaine*, edited by Agnès and Olivier Dard Bérenger, 95–113. Lorraine: Université de Lorraine, 2015.

Dahl's Law Dictionary—Dictionnaire juridique Dahl. Paris: Dalloz, 2007.

de Lamothe, Henri. 'Excursion au Canada et à la rivière Rouge du Nord.' *Le Tour du monde* 30, no. 5 (1875), 115–122.

Ducrot, Elisabeth. 'Abel Jeandet et sa famille.' *Trois rivières* 79 (2012).

Dupire, Marguerite. *Organisation sociale des Peul: étude d'ethnographie comparée.* Paris: Plon, 1970.

Echenberg, Myron J. *Colonial Conscripts: The Tirailleurs Sénégalais in French West Africa, 1857–1960.* Portsmouth: Heinemann, 1991.

Fabre, Martine. 'Le magistrat d'outre-mer: l'aventure de la justice.' In *Le juge et L'outre-mer: les roches bleues de l'empire colonial*, edited by Bernard Durand and Martine Fabre, 71–93. Lille: Centre d'histoire judiciaire, 2004.

Fall, Babacar. 'Orality and Life Histories: Rethinking the Social and Political History of Senegal.' *Africa Today* (2003), 55–65.

Ferenczi, Thomas. *L'invention du journalisme en France: naissance de la presse moderne à la fin du xixe siècle.* Paris: Plon, 1996.

Fertiault, F. *François-Abel Jeandet—Sonnets.* Lyon: Imprimerie A Waltener et Cie, 1891.

Foster, Elizabeth. *Faith in Empire: Religion Politics, and Colonial Rule in French Senegal.* Stanford: Stanford University Press, 2013.

France, Anatole. *Crainquebille.* Translated by Jacques Leclercq. New York: The Limited Editions Club, 1949 [1901].

Gallet, Jean-Louis. 'La procédure d'élévation de conflit le conflit positif.' 1–19. www.tribunal-conflits.fr/documents/Actualites/La_procedure_de_conflit.pdf. Accessed 23 January 2024.
Gausseron, Henri Bernard. *Un français au Sénégal*. Paris: Librarie Ancienne Honore Champion Editeur Edouard Champion, 1913.
Gauthier, Julien. 'La société de géographie commerciale de Bordeaux: sur les traces des explorateurs entre 1874 Et 1911.' *Dynamiques environnementales. Journal international de géosciences et de l'environnement*, no. 39–40 (2017), 36–53.
Geiger, Susan, Jean Allman, and Nakanyike Musisi. *Women in African Colonial Histories*. Bloomington: Indiana University Press, 2002.
Gendry, Thaïs. 'Le droit de tuer: la peine de mort au service de l'ordre colonial en Afrique occidentale française, 1900–1950' (PhD dissertation, EHESS UNIGE, 2020).
Getz, Trevor R. and Liz Clarke. *Abina and the Important Men: A Graphic History*. New York: Oxford University Press, USA, 2016.
Ginio, Ruth. *The French Army and Its African Soldiers: The Years of Decolonization*. Lincoln: University of Nebraska Press, 2017.
——— 'Negotiating Legal Authority in French West Africa: The Colonial Administration and the African Assessors, 1903–1918.' In *Intermediaries, Interpreters, and Clerks: African Employees in the Making of Colonial Africa*, edited by Benjamin Lawrance, Emily Osborn, and Richard Roberts, 115–135. Madison: University of Wisconsin Press, 2006.
Grimal, Pierre. *The Dictionary of Classical Mythology*. Oxford: Blackwell, 1996.
Hale, Dana S. *Races on Display: French Representations of Colonized Peoples, 1886–1940*. Bloomington: Indiana University Press, 2008.
Harris, Ruth. *Dreyfus: Politics, Emotion, and the Scandal of the Century*. New York: Metropolitan Books, 2010.
Harrison, Christopher. *France and Islam in West Africa, 1860–1960*. Cambridge: Cambridge University Press, 2003.
Hélénon, Véronique. *French Caribbeans in Africa: Diasporic Connections and Colonial Administration, 1880–1939*. New York: Palgrave Macmillan US, 2011. https://doi.org/10.1057/9780230118751
Hynd, Stacey. 'Killing the Condemned: The Practice and Process of Capital Punishment in British Africa, 1900–1950s.' *The Journal of African History* 49, no. 3 (2008), 403–418.
Hynd, Stacey and Thaïs Gendry. 'African Women, Colonial Justice and White Man's Mercy.' *Histoire & Sociétés / Crime, History & Societies* 27, no. 1 (2023), 107–132.
Idowu, H. Oludare. 'Café au Lait: Senegal's Mulatto Community in the Nineteenth Century.' *Journal of the Historical Society of Nigeria* (1972), 271–288.
Irvine, William D. *The Boulanger Affair Reconsidered: Royalism, Boulangism, and the Origins of the Radical Right in France*. Oxford: Oxford University Press, 1988.

Johnson, G. W. *The Emergence of Black Politics in Senegal: The Struggle for Power in the Four Communes, 1900–1920*. Stanford: Stanford University Press, for the Hoover Institution on War, Revolution and Peace, 1971.

Jones, Hilary. 'Fugitive Slaves and Christian Evangelism in French West Africa: A Protestant Mission in Late Nineteenth-Century Senegal.' *Slavery & Abolition* 38, no. 1 (2017), 76–94.

———.*The Metis of Senegal: Urban Life and Politics in French West Africa*. Bloomington: Indiana University Press, 2013.

———. 'Rethinking Politics in the Colony: The Métis of Senegal and Urban Politics in the Late Nineteenth and Early Twentieth Century.' *The Journal of African History* 53, no. 3 (2012), 325–344.

Kubicek, Robert V. 'The Colonial Steamer and the Occupation of West Africa by the Victorian State, 1840–1900.' *The Journal of Imperial and Commonwealth History* 18, no. 1 (1990), 9–32.

Lawrance, Benjamin N., Emily Lynn Osborn, and Richard L. Roberts. *Intermediaries, Interpreters, and Clerks: African Employees in the Making of Colonial Africa*. Madison: University of Wisconsin Press, 2006.

Le Béguec, Gilles. *La république des avocats*. Paris: Armand Colin, 2003.

Le Bras, Jean Luc. 'La peine de mort aux colonies, une exécution pour L'exemple à Saint-Louis du Sénégal en 1899.' *I & M Bulletin* 35 (2012), 29–39.

Le Cour Grandmaison, Olivier. 'The Exception and the Rule: On French Colonial Law.' *Diogenes* 53, no. 4 (2006), 34–53.

Loti, Pierre. *Le roman d'un spahi*. Paris: Calman-Lévi, 1881.

M'bayo, Tamba. *Muslim Interpreters in Colonial Senegal, 1850–1920: Mediations of Knowledge and Power in the Lower and Middle Senegal River Valley*. Lanham: Lexington Books, 2016.

Manchuelle, François. 'Le rôle des antillais dans L'apparition du nationalisme culturel en Afrique noire francophone [The Role of West Indians in the Emergence of Cultural Nationalism in French-Speaking Africa].' *Cahiers d'études africaines* (1992), 375–408.

———. 'Métis Et colons: la famille Devès et L'émergence politique des africains au Sénégal, 1881–1897.' *Cahiers d'études africaines* (1984), 477–504.

Mann, Gregory. 'What Was the Indigénat? The 'Empire of Law' in French West Africa.' *The Journal of African History* 50, no. 3 (2009), 331–353.

Mann, Kristin and Richard Roberts. *Law in Colonial Africa*. Portsmouth: Heinemann, 1991.

Martin, Benjamin F. *The Hypocrisy of Justice in the Belle Epoque*. Baton Rouge: Louisiana State University Press, 1999.

Martschukat, Jürgen. 'Nineteenth-Century Executions as Performances of Law, Death, and Civilization.' In *Cultural Lives of Capital Punishment: Comparative Perspectives*, 49–68, 2005.

McLane, Margaret O. 'Railways or Waterways: The Dakar Railway Network and the Senegal River in the "Mise en valeur" of French West Africa.' Paper presented at the Proceedings of the Meeting of the French Colonial Historical Society, 1992.

Ndiaye, Amadou. *Baaba Maal et le Fouta: message local et patrimoine universel*. Dakar: Harmattan-Sénégal, 2015.

Osborn, Emily Lynn. 'Interpreting Colonial Power in French Guinea: The Boubou Penda-Ernest Noirot Affair of 1905.' In *Intermediaries, Interpreters, and Clerks: African Employees in the Making of Colonial Africa*, 56–76. Madison: University of Wisconsin Press, 2006.

Pacteau, Bernard. 'Les conflits entre l'ordre administratif et l'ordre judiciaire, avant et donc sans le tribunal des conflits.' In *Les désunions de la magistrature*, edited by Jacques Krynen and Jean-Christophe Gaven, 355–375. Toulouse: Press de l'université Toulouse Capitol, 2012.

Plas, Régine. 'Hysteria, Hypnosis, and Moral Sense in French 19th-Century Forensic Psychiatry: The Eyraud-Bompard Case.' *International Journal of Law and Psychiatry* 21, no. 4 (1998), 397–407.

Quevedo, Javier Márquez. 'Telecommunications and Colonial Rivalry: European Telegraph Cables to the Canary Islands and Northwest Africa, 1883–1914.' *Historical Social Research/Historische Sozialforschung* (2010), 108–124.

Roberts, Richard. *Litigants and Households: African Disputes and Colonial Courts in the French Soudan, 1895–1912*. Portsmouth: Heinemann, 2005.

Robinson, David. *Chiefs and Clerics: Abdul Bokar Kan and Futa Toro, 1853–1891*. Oxford: Clarendon Press, 1975.

———. 'French "Islamic" Policy and Practice in Late Nineteenth-Century Senegal.' *The Journal of African History* 29, no. 3 (1988), 415–435.

———. *Paths of Accommodation: Muslim Societies and French Colonial Authorities in Senegal and Mauritania, 1880–1920*. Athens: Ohio University Press, 2000.

Roshwald, Aviel. 'Colonial Dreams of the French Right Wing, 1881–1914.' *The Historian* 57 (1994). www.tandfonline.com/doi/abs/10.1111/j.1540-6563.1994.tb01334.x. Accessed 2 April 2025.

Samp, Yamar. 'Affaire Albert [sic] Jeandet: La peine de mort sans procès.' *Revue malienne des sciences juridiques, politique et economiques de Bamako* 5 (2018).

Sané, Sokhna. 'Guerres de conquête et contrôle de la circulation des armes à feu et des munitions en Afrique occidentale sous domination française (1834–1903).' *French Colonial History* 9, no. 1 (2008), 175–190.

Sarr, Dominique and Richard Roberts. 'The Jurisdiction of Muslim Tribunals in Colonial Senegal, 1857–1932.' *Law in Colonial Africa* (1991), 131–145.

Seesemann, Rüdiger and Benjamin F. Soares. '"Being as Good Muslims as Frenchmen": On Islam and Colonial Modernity in West Africa.' *Journal of Religion in Africa* (2009), 91–120.

Sibeud, Emmanuelle. 'Comment peut-on être créole? Les engagements impériaux d'Alexandre Isaac.' *Paris créole: son histoire, ses écrivains, ses artistes, XVIIIe-XXe siècles* (2020), 58–64.

Sinou, Alain. *Comptoirs et villes coloniales du Sénégal: Saint-Louis. Gorée, Dakar*. Paris: Editions Karthala, 1993.

Soupé, Philibert A. *Bio-Bibliographie François-Abel Jeandet.* Lyon: Imprimerie Waltener et Cie, 1891.

Sow, Abdoul. *Mamadou Racine Sy: premier capitaine noir des tirailleurs sénégalais (1838–1902)*. Paris: Éditions L'Harmattan, 2010.

Strobel, Margaret. 'Women's History, Gender History, and European Colonialism.' In *Colonialism and the Modern World*, edited by Gregory Blue, Martin Bunton, and Ralph Criozier, 51–68. London: Routledge, 2016.

Sugnet, Charles and Baaba Maal. 'I Sing All the Space.' *Transition*, no. 74 (1997), 184–198.

Sy, Seydou Madani. *Le Capitaine Mamadou Racine Sy, 1838–1902: une figure sénégalaise au temps des tirailleurs*. Paris: Editions Karthala, 2014.

Taithe, Bertrand. *The Killer Trail: A Colonial Scandal in the Heart of Africa*. Oxford: Oxford University Press, 2009.

Thomas, Martin. *The French Colonial Mind: Mental Maps of Empire and Colonial Encounters*. Vol. 1, Lincoln: University of Nebraska Press, 2011.

Ticchi, Jean-Marc. 'Le Fonds Alexandre Isaac, Sénateur de la Guadeloupe (1845–1899), Et Son Voyage En Algérie (1892) Dans Les Archives Du Sénat.' *Cahiers de la Méditerranée*, no. 101 (2020), 185–197.

Tran, Van Troi. 'How "Natives" Ate at Colonial Exhibitions in 1889, 1900 and 1931.' *French Cultural Studies* 26, no. 2 (2015), 163–175.

Unknown. *François-Abel Jeandet: un héro de nos colonies africaines*. Dijon: Imprimerie Darantiere, 1892.

———. *Quelques documents relatifs à la mort Fr F--J.-E. -Abel Jeandet*. Mâcon: Protat Frères, 1892.

Vandermeere, Auguste Louis Nicolas. *Mémoires du Général Comte Van Der Meere*. Bruxelles: C. Muquardt, 1880.

Vann, Michael G. 'Of Pirates, Postcards, and Public Beheadings: The Pedagogic Execution in French Colonial Indochina.' *Historical Reflections/Réflexions Historiques* 36, no. 2 (2010), 39–58.

Vansina, Jan. *Oral Tradition: A Study in Historical Methodology*. Piscataway: Transaction Publishers, 1965.

———. *Oral Tradition as History*. Madison: University of Wisconsin Press, 1985.

Zalc, Claire and Tal Bruttmann. *Microhistories of the Holocaust*. New York & Oxford: Berghahn Books, 2022.

Interviews

Haruna Diop
Mamadou Goudiaby
Niasse Hamedine Kane
Abdourahmane Niang
Xavier Ricou
Aliou Sall
Cheick Baba Sall
Saddick Sall
Mamadou Sow
Ibrahima Sy

Index

EU authorised representative for GPSR:
Easy Access System Europe, Mustamäe tee 50,
10621 Tallinn, Estonia
gpsr.requests@easproject.com

www.ingramcontent.com/pod-product-compliance
Ingram Content Group UK Ltd.
Pitfield, Milton Keynes, MK11 3LW, UK
UKHW021834100926
8556IPUK00004B/327
9781526187376